The Success Principles™

for teens

How to Get From Where You Are to Where You Want to Be

Jack Canfield and Kent Healy

Health Communications, Inc.
Deerfield Beach, Florida

www.hcibooks.com

Library of Congress Cataloging-in-Publication Data

Canfield, Jack, 1944-
The success principles for teens : how to get from where you are to where you want
  to be / Jack Canfield and Kent Healy.
       p. cm.
    ISBN-13: 978-0-7573-0727-0 (trade paper)
    ISBN-10: 0-7573-0727-2 (trade paper)
    1. Teenagers—United States. 2. Self-esteem in adolescence—United States.
    3. Self-perception in adolescence—United States. 4. Self-confidence in
    adolescence—United States. I. Healy, Kent. II. Title.
HQ796.C332 2008
155.5'182—dc22
                                                                    2008008854

Publisher: Health Communications, Inc.
            3201 S.W. 15th Street
            Deerfield Beach, FL 33442-8190

R-10-08

Art Director Kent Healy
Cover design by Sharon McPeake
Interior design by Brian Bengelsdorf
Illustrations by Paul Combs, for more information about Paul & his artwork visit www.artstudio7.com
Inside book formatting by Dawn Von Strolley Grove

CONTENTS

If we **did** all the **things** we are **capable of doing**,
we would literally **astound ourselves**.

—*Thomas A. Edison*
American inventor and businessman

Dedication & Acknowledgments

You're holding this book today because of the many people who have helped us enjoy success in our own lives. This book has been created as a result of a remarkable team effort. We'd like to give our heartfelt thanks and gratitude to:

Our families, who have shared their love, enthusiasm, insight, and support.

Jack's Family: Inga, Travis, Riley, Christopher, Oran, and Kyle.

Kent's Family: Doug, Nina, and Kyle.

Our publisher and friend, Peter Vegso, for his continuous support and vision to make this book a reality.

Patty Aubery and Russ Kamalski, for sharing their valuable time, guidance, and creative ideas.

D'ette Corona, our coauthor liaison, who impeccably managed countless details with care and diligence that has made this book possible.

Michele Matrisciani, Carol Rosenberg, Andrea Gold, Allison Janse, and Katheline St. Fort, our editors at Health Communications, Inc., for their devotion to excellence. Lori Golden, Kelly Maragni, Sean Geary, Patricia McConnell, Kim Weiss, Paola Fernandez-Rana, Christine Zambrano, and Jaron Hunter for doing such an incredible job supporting our books.

Tom Sand, Claude Choquette, and Luc Jutras, who manage year after year to get our books transferred into thirty-six languages around the world.

Thank you Liz George and Jan Thompson in the "Cool Stuff" Media office for their continual support and willingness to work hard and persist until the job is done.

Paul Combs, for your incredible artistic ability. Your creative and humorous illustrations have made this book more appealing and engaging.

Brian Bengelsdorf, for your creative layout design ideas that have helped us develop a unique book that is visually stimulating and enjoyable.

Sharon McPeake, for your keen eye and edgy design style used to create a cover for this book that makes it stand out from the crowd.

Tiffany George, for being open and supportive of the information in this book and allowing us to work closely with her students, who all provided such valuable feedback.

Our incredible panel of readers who helped make this book the best it could be by offering their feedback, personal experiences, and insight: Monia Akter, Alex Aponte, Victoria Baker, Kara Bluntach, Brittany Bogard, Cadience Buchanan, Carla Byrne, Kaylie Clendenon, Alice Clifford, Josh Davis, Audrey Egan, Rob Engel, Brianna Gibbons, Joanne Hein, Mary Hernandez, Teresa Huggins, Hailley Hukill, Nancy Hurtado, Kimia Kalbasi, Bita Khaleghi, Rachel Kramer, Crystal Kreisel, Alexandra Langford, Dana Law, Armando Lopez, Claire McLauchlan, Krystal Medellin, Jacob Miller, Jaime Nunez, Janelle O'Mara, Ashley Ortiz, Kelsey Remmes, Mandy Richardson, Kylee Sims, Nicole Vandever, and Lisa Wada

To everyone who submitted a story, we deeply appreciate your letting us into your lives and sharing your experiences with us. For those whose stories were not chosen for publication, we hope the stories you are about to enjoy convey what was in your heart.

From Kent to Jack: Thank you for being a continuing source of inspiration, support, and compassion. It has been an absolute pleasure and a unique privilege to work with you in creating this book. Your depth of knowledge and love for people is something I respect and admire. I am grateful to be part of your life as we work together to help others improve their lives.

introduction

I f you've had that thought before, then we already have something in common. But before you put this book down, let us tell you one thing:

This is **not a book** of **"good ideas."**

This book doesn't tell you how to live your life. Far from it. This book includes what we call the timeless "ingredients of success." Just like there's a recipe for your favorite dish, there's a recipe for achievement, too. We don't know about you, but we wouldn't get comfortable in our favorite chair to read an entire cookbook . . . but a recipe for success? We'll devour that!

So, how could there be a recipe for success? Well, there are very specific trends, patterns, and similarities in the way successful people live their lives. They have developed very similar skills and habits that we can all learn from (the "success ingredients").

Have you ever wondered why some individuals have so much happiness, energy, money, respect, and great friendships? Were they born with extra talent and abilities? Some people believe this, but we didn't buy it. Instead, we discovered:

Successes are not born; **they're made**.

It's true. We don't start out with the finely tuned skills we need to create the life we want. We must learn them as we go through life. However, we can fast-track our journey by applying the "recipe of achievement" from those who have already accomplished outstanding results.

What you're **saying is great**, but this **isn't for me**.
I'm different . . . I'm in a very unique situation.

If only we were given a dime for every time we heard that! The truth is, we used to think the same thing. "How could *somebody else's life* be similar to mine?" And, "How would *somebody* else know about my challenges and what I need to do to turn my life around?" You're right, we're all faced with unique situations, and we all have our own definitions of success, but the tools we need to get from *where we are* to *where we want to be* are universal.

It doesn't matter what your unique goals are. Maybe you want to ace an upcoming test, get straight A's in school, become a famous rock star, a world-class athlete, a multimillionaire, a successful entrepreneur, or even become the president. If you learn the principles of success—especially as a teenager—and practice them every day, they *will* transform your life.

Remember, the challenges you are facing right now do not impact your future nearly as much as the way you react to them and what you do to change things. And, by the way, who doesn't want to improve their life and make it more interesting? *We all do!* We'd all like more happiness, money, freedom, confidence, friendships, and so on. The question is, "How?" Don't worry, we have you covered. You'll learn from some incredible individuals who have used the principles in this book. Their stories explain how:

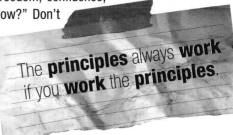

The **principles** always **work** if you **work** the **principles**.

- ❈ **A sixty-three-year-old woman lifted a 2,000-pound car to save her grandson.**
- ❈ **Entrepreneur Colonel Harlan Sanders overcame rejection to start KFC, the international restaurant phenomenon.**
- ❈ **Tim Ferris achieved a San Shou kickboxing national title just six weeks after being introduced to the sport.**
- ❈ **Actor Jim Carrey wrote a check to himself that changed his life.**
- ❈ **World-renowned painter Robert Wyland went from starving artist to multimillionaire.**
- ❈ **Chad Pegracke used the "power of asking" to raise $2.5 million to clean the Mississippi River.**

- ❋ Gymnast Peter Vidmar used one of the Success Principles to win a gold medal at the Olympics.
- ❋ John Assaraf began life as a street kid but now operates a franchise company that has topped $3 billion in revenue.

These stories and many others like them will inspire you to follow the principles in this book so that you will discover how to:

- ❋ Change the outcome of any event.
- ❋ Break through fear and build your confidence.
- ❋ Ask for and get everything you want.
- ❋ Set empowering goals that will energize your life.
- ❋ Surround yourself with friends and mentors who will boost your success.
- ❋ Reject rejection and persevere until you succeed.
- ❋ Use feedback to excel faster and further.
- ❋ Exceed expectations and achieve outstanding results.
- ❋ And this is just the beginning . . .

> Only those **who will risk going too far** can possibly **find out how far they can go.**
>
> Writer, poet, and Nobel Prize winner —*T. S. Eliot*

You might be thinking, "Yeah, easier said than done." And you're right, but that's why we created this book. We wanted to give *you* an excuse to spend some time designing *your* life and strengthening your most important asset: **YOU**.

We know how crazy life is today. You have to deal with many demands, expectations, distractions, and pressures, such as standardized testing, SATs, billions of Internet web pages, sports practice, work, video games, walking the dog, extracurricular activities, volunteering, and the list goes on. But on that note, it's also a really exciting time to be a teenager because you have more opportunity than any previous generation in history! If you can get your hands on the right tools and start right now, who knows what you'll be able to accomplish in the next year, five years, ten years, or twenty years? The possibilities are endless!

The "YOU" Factor

Each person who has experienced the rewards that these principles can offer had to first understand this concept:

We couldn't have said it any better. In life, there are certain things we must do to enjoy the rewards. In order to get the most value out of this book, *you* must use the principles yourself. No one else can do these things for you. Whether it's exercising, stretching, reading, studying, setting goals, visualizing your success, or practicing a new skill, you are going to have to do it.

> You **can't hire someone** else to **do your push-ups for you**.
>
> —*Jim Rohn*
> *Self-made millionaire, success coach, and philosopher*

We'll give you the recipe, but you will have to cook the meal. We will teach you the principles, but you will have to apply them. If you choose to put in the effort, we promise you the rewards will be well worth it. That's our promise to you. Now it's your turn to make an agreement with yourself and commit to following through and acting on the information you will learn in this book. We look forward to taking this journey together.

Your pals in success,

It's time to **start living** the **life you've imagined**.

—*Henry James*
American writer and author

Who is Kent Healy?

As told by Kent . . .

I've attended four high schools, lived in twelve houses, and resided in eight cities and on two continents. (Yeah, we moved around a lot.) As a teen, I struggled in school. Let's just say I was one of those students who made the top 50% possible. Because I was a below-average student, I thought that I would be below average at everything else I did. I accepted what many of my teachers told me: "Kent, you're doing just fine for your abilities."

One teacher, however, proved me wrong. "Kent, what are you doing?" he said. "You're capable of so much more than this." My jaw dropped to the floor. What? Who? *Me?*

And so I met the first teacher who saw more potential in me than I could see in myself. He shared various strategies and techniques with me—but, most importantly, he just held me accountable. If I didn't do my homework, he was on my case the next day. Sure enough, I started to see A's on my report card for the first time.

My confidence began to grow. At about this time, my brother and I teamed up to start a business called Reactor. We made skimboards, skateboards, hats, shirts, and so on. Business was going very well for a while . . . until the company rapidly grew out of our control. There's no happy ending here . . . eventually Reactor was shut down.

"How could this happen to me?" I said to myself. "I finally improved my grades in school, so why did my business fail?"

It was then, at age seventeen, when I realized there were some key fundamentals of life that were not taught in school. But where could I get this information? I asked myself questions such as, "What separates those people who live an ordinary life from those who live an extraordinary life? What makes someone successful?"

In doing my research, I came across a couple of Jack Canfield's books. And when I discovered that he was also one of the cocreators of the massively successful Chicken Soup for the Soul book series, I was even more impressed. I set a goal: "I will meet this amazing Jack Canfield."

I continued to search for answers on how to succeed in the real world and applied everything I learned. Again, my performance improved in all areas of my life. I couldn't believe it! In fact, it was such a dramatic change that my brother and I soon recognized a new opportunity: We should write our own book with our own perspectives, experiences, and life lessons.

Now, believe me, writing a book was something neither of us had ever dreamed of, but we wanted to share what we had learned so other people could benefit as well. We had no idea what we were about to get ourselves into . . .

We were terrified at first. "Could we really do it?" "What if no one likes it?" "What if we fail?" "What if, what if, what if?" But almost on cue, my brother and I had the opportunity to meet Jack Canfield at a local entrepreneur conference in our area. We shared our idea with him—and he didn't laugh at us! Instead, he offered us the support, encouragement, and insight we needed to realize our goal. As a result of his support, we wrote our first book while we were still teenagers: *"Cool Stuff" They Should Teach in School.* Since its publication, we have enjoyed seeing its impact on readers around the world.

Now, at the ripe old age of twenty-three, I've been able to do things I never even dreamed of: traveling around the country to appear on TV and radio shows; speaking to audiences of all ages and backgrounds; writing columns for newspapers; composing articles for magazines; training teachers; and teaming up with some of the most respected people in the world.

> In life, lots of **people know what to do,** but **few** people actually **do what they know.** **Knowing** is **not enough!** You must **take action.**
>
> —*Anthony Robbins*
> Bestselling author and inspirational speaker

But I'm no extraordinary human being. As I just told you, I wasn't born with any exceptional abilities. I'm just a normal person. I'm just like you. All I want is to make my dreams a reality and have fun in the process—and I'm sure you do, too.

The only advantage I have is that I've found the tools for success and put them to use. Now I've worked with Jack to pass these tools on to you so you can get that same "life advantage" and do incredible things. It is absolutely amazing what can happen in just a couple of years if you have the right information, then take action and use it.

Who is Jack Canfield?

As told by Jack . . .

hen my friend Mark Victor Hansen and I came up the idea to create a new series of books, people thought we were nuts. They told us things like "You're dreaming!" "It will never work." "You're not serious, are you?!"

In spite of all of the negativity, we persevered. When the first manuscript was done, more than 140 publishers turned it down. We thought, "Maybe everybody is right." When there seemed to be little hope, we tried one more time. It worked.

A publisher decided to take the book. This marked the beginning of the Chicken Soup for the Soul series. To date, we've sold over 110 million copies in forty-seven different languages around the world, and we hold a *Guinness Book* world record for having seven books on the *New York Times* bestseller list.

> When **ordinary** people decide to do
> **extraordinary things**,
> they **transform their lives** and the **lives** of
> **others** around them.
>
> *—Oprah Winfrey*
> Emmy Award–winning host of *The Oprah Winfrey Show*,
> the highest-rated talk show in television history

I've also had the opportunity to appear on every major talk show in America (from *Oprah* to *Good Morning America*), earn a multimillion-dollar net income each year, give speeches around the world, write a newspaper column read by millions each week, travel to exotic places for vacation, have outrageous relationships, and enjoy personal happiness.

I don't say this to brag; I'm telling you this because I want you to know that anything is possible. I'm speaking from personal experience because I sure didn't enter this world with any special privileges. I grew up in Wheeling, West Virginia, where my dad worked long, hard days making only $8,000 a year. My mother was an alcoholic, and my father was a workaholic.

I faced many other challenges right through college, where I worked as a lifeguard at the local pool to pay for books, clothes, and dates. When I ran out of money, I ate what became known as my "twenty-one-cent dinners," which consisted of tomato paste, a sprinkle of garlic salt, and an eleven-cent bag of spaghetti noodles.

As you can see, my life back then was definitely not what you'd call a picture of success. I was more concerned about surviving through the day than chasing my dreams!

However, a few years after graduate school, things started to change. I worked for a man by the name of W. Clement Stone, who soon became my mentor. He shared with me the fundamentals of success that I still operate from today—many of the same principles that have allowed me to enjoy the lifestyle I now have.

I've worked with more than a million people from over thirty countries around the world, and I've witnessed some amazing transformations . . . people who overcame lifelong phobias, who were broke and became multimillionaires, who were lost and depressed but discovered their passion and positively impacted thousands of lives. It's been an amazing journey, but one of my strongest passions is helping teens. I've seen firsthand what young people, like you, are capable of doing. All you need is the right information and support so you can reach your full potential.

When I wrote my original *Success Principles* book, I wanted to offer other people these same principles that changed my life. The only catch was that I had designed the book for my peers, not for teenagers. I needed someone who spoke "teen" and could relate to this group as their peers. This is why I've asked Kent to work with me on this project. He knows your generation well, and he knows even more about what it takes to be successful.

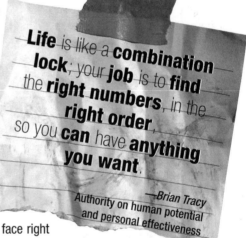

Life is like a combination lock; your job is to find the **right numbers**, in the **right order**, so you **can** have **anything you want**.

—*Brian Tracy*
Authority on human potential and personal effectiveness

No matter what challenges you face right now or how far away your dreams appear, there are certain principles that, if you use them, will forever change your life. Kent and I have a goal to provide these basic instructions for success in this book. We hope you enjoy reading it as much as we have enjoyed creating it.

PRINCIPLE 1

TAKE 100% RESPONSIBILT FOR YOUR LIFE

You must take personal responsibility. **You cannot change the circumstances, the seasons, or the wind,** but you can change yourself.

— *Jim Rohn*
Self-made millionaire, success coach, and philosopher

It's going around like a bad flu. It's infecting innocent people and restricting their potential. What is it? The shocking myth that we are simply *entitled* to a great life.

How could this happen? Well, many of us today believe that somehow, somewhere, someone (certainly not us) is responsible for filling our lives with continual happiness, exciting career options, entertainment, money, amazing friendships, and relationships because . . . well . . . we exist. Isn't that enough? We wish!

If you're reading this book, we're sure you are aware that the answer is "no." Unfortunately, life doesn't work that way. There is one major defining factor that separates those who hope for a better life and those who have a better life. This determining factor is also the one lesson that this entire book is based on. Here it is:

The only person responsible for the quality of your life is . . . **YOU**.

1.1 The Straight Facts

If you want to be successful, retire early, gain the respect of others, and just have more fun, then you need to take 100% responsibility for everything that you do and experience in life. This includes the level of your achievements, the quality of your relationships, your emotions, the results you produce in and out of school, and the state of your health—yes, everything!

But let's get one thing straight: *This is not always easy.*

In fact, most of us have been conditioned to blame something outside ourselves for the parts of our life that we don't like. We blame our parents, teachers, friends, MTV, the weather, or even the star-sign forecasts! It's crazy! Most of the time we don't even know we're doing it. The truth is, the real problems or challenges we face usually have little to do with our "outside world." We're often scared to look at the source of it all . . . ourselves.

Sure, we will all experience our own unique challenges that happen out of our control, but taking responsibility means that we don't dwell on the problem, ignore it, complain about it, or blame someone or something else for what we're experiencing. Instead, it means that we take control of our thoughts and our actions, and do whatever we can to improve the situation.

Sure, life's challenges come in all shapes and sizes, but there is always *something* that we can do differently to change what we are currently experiencing. And we must first believe this before we will find any new solutions.

Whether someone is super-successful or struggling to survive, the quality of their life depends on their thoughts, actions, and beliefs. Do you notice a trend here? These three things all have to do with the individual—not the teacher, the weather, or outside circumstances. The truth is, success starts with one person . . .

That person is you.

1.2 When I First Met Jack

 athan, 18 (Indianapolis, IN): I didn't meet Jack Canfield under the best circumstances, but looking back, I'm glad we crossed paths.

Jack was at my school working with a group of teachers when he heard me arguing with one of my teachers outside the staff room. He left his meeting, walked over to me, and asked me to explain the situation. I told him (in a loud voice) that I had just been suspended from the baseball team and that this wasn't fair. They couldn't do this to me. Not now!

"What's not fair? And why not now?" asked Jack.

I said, "We're about to go to the state championships next week, and there will be all kinds of scouts for college teams there, and if they see me pitch, I can get a scholarship to college. I can't afford to go to college without a baseball scholarship. This is my only chance. It's not fair!"

I expected some sympathy, but instead, Jack said, "Let me ask you a question."

"Okay."

"When did you first learn that school was not fair? Really . . . tell me the truth."

"When I was in grade school," I told him.

"Okay, so why are you standing there pretending to act like you don't know that school is not fair? Every teacher has a different set of rules. Some teachers enforce some rules and not others. Sometimes good kids get bad breaks, and kids who don't play by the rules get away with breaking them. Isn't that true?" asked Jack.

"Yes."

"So it's not about whether school is fair or not. The real question is 'What did you do to get yourself suspended?' I doubt they just randomly picked your name out of a hat. So how did you create this situation—getting yourself suspended?"

"I was late to school."

"Just once?"

"No, several times."

"How many times?"

"I'm not sure. Maybe six or seven times."

Jack then turned to my principal who was now watching our conversation and asked, "What's the rule here? How many times do you have to be late without a legitimate reason before you get suspended from an athletic team?"

"Three times," my principal said.

Jack turned back to me and asked, "Were you aware of this rule?"

"Yes."

"Then why did you break it so many times?"

"Well, after the third time nothing happened, so I didn't think they were serious."

Jack turned back to the principal and said, "So this is where the school participated in creating this situation. By not consistently enforcing the rules, you helped him believe there were no rules. This is why he claims it's unfair."

Jack turned back to me and said, "But that doesn't let you off the hook. You did know the rule, and you chose to ignore it. So, what did you make more important than playing baseball and getting a scholarship to college?"

I looked Jack straight in the eyes and said, "Nothing's more important than playing baseball. It's the most important thing in my life."

Jack responded by saying, "Not true."

As you can imagine, this made me angry. He continued, "You made something else more important than getting to school on time so you could play baseball. What was it?"

I could feel the pressure, and there was no way to back out. I thought about his question for a moment and then said, "You mean sleeping in?"

"I don't know. You tell me," Jack responded.

"I guess that would be it."

"Is sleeping in really more important to you than playing baseball?"

"No. No way!"

"Then why didn't you get up?"

"Well, when the alarm goes off, I hit the snooze button—sometimes more than once—and then I end up being late."

We talked for a little longer, and then Jack convinced my principal to give me one more shot now that I was more aware the situation and was accepting full responsibility. But, we all agreed, if I was late one more time, I would be suspended with no rights to complain or fight about it.

There was one last problem to solve. I needed a new strategy to make sure I would get up on time. Hitting the snooze couldn't be an option. We brainstormed and came up with several strategies. First, I had to put my clock on the other side of the room so I would have to get out of bed to turn it off. And, second, if I wasn't up by a certain time, I had to pay my mom a dollar to pour ice water on me. I knew my mom would be very happy to do that!

I was not late anymore. Jack helped me realize what it really meant to take 100% responsibility. The rest of my baseball season went well—even my coach commented on my change of attitude. Now, I'm attending college on a baseball scholarship. It's a good feeling to know that I was able to take control and make it happen.

1.3 Inside Out

ight has fallen, and the city has become dark. A man is on his hands and knees searching for something under a streetlamp when a young woman passing by asks the man what he is doing. He explains that he lost a key and is desperately looking for it. The young woman offers to help him search for the key.

An hour later, the woman says in a confused tone, "We've looked everywhere for it, and we haven't found it. Are you sure you lost the key here?" The man replies, "No, I lost it in my house, but there is more light out here under the streetlamp."

This is a great example of how we look outside of ourselves for the solution to our problems because it's easier than searching for the real cause, which is inside us. We are the source of our problems, and we need to face that fact because until we do, we can't change anything. We need to look life straight in the eyes and face the facts—no matter how uncomfortable it may be.

Of course, we all want things to get "better," but it simply won't happen if we refuse to see things as they are right now. Change can only begin once we acknowledge that there is something we need to change. You might be happy with the way things are in your life—and that's fantastic—but every successful person knows there is always room for improvement.

The very first step to achieving major success and enjoying the things that are most important to you is to take 100% responsibility for your life. Anything short of that won't get you what you really want.

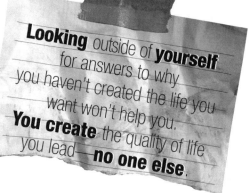

Looking outside of yourself for answers to why you haven't created the life you want won't help you. You create the quality of life you lead—no one else.

1.4 EXCUSES or EXCELLENCE? YOU choose

Ninety-nine percent of **all failures** come from **people** who have a habit of **making excuses**.

—*George Washington Carver*
American agricultural researcher and educator

Taking responsibility means more than just taking initiative and owning up to mistakes. It also requires that we stop making excuses.

As long as there are excuses, there will be no positive results. Think about it: Every excuse is like pushing the ejection button on an airplane. The minute you push it, you've committed to exit the plane. In that instant you're heading in a completely new direction, leaving the opportunity for success behind. Excuses allow us to give up mentally and justify why something can't be done or why we're not good enough—and once that happens . . . game over.

Kent: Truly successful people know that even the best excuses don't help anything. It doesn't even matter if the excuses are truthful and accurate. A few years ago, my brother and I learned this lesson the hard way while we were writing our first book.

Like **opposite forces** of a magnet, success and excuses just refuse to work together. They simply cannot co-exist. It's **either one** or **the other**.

When we started the project, we were in school, playing sports, working, and trying to write the book as well. There were many times we barely had enough energy or time to finish our homework, let alone work on our book.

"How's the book coming along?" people would ask us. We'd tell them the truth, "Well, we just haven't had the time lately. By the time we finally get home from morning practice, school, and afternoon practice, we are exhausted. Then we have homework. So we haven't been able to work on the book."

It was almost as though people expected to hear this response. They listened to our explanation (which was really an excuse) and responded with a simple, "Huh, okay." That was it. Nothing more.

The truth was, we really *were* tired, and we were short on time, but believing that we couldn't do anything to change the circumstances meant we weren't really taking full responsibility. Taking 100% responsibility means that we are committed to finding a solution to the challenges we face.

Here's what we learned: No matter how truthful your excuses are, people don't want to hear them. All excuses do is slow us down, and nobody benefits from them. The only way my brother and I were able to finish our book was when we stopped making excuses, stopped complaining, and just got to work.

So, what's step number one? Believing that we have the power to make things better and produce the results we really want. We all make excuses for different reasons, but it really doesn't matter what those reasons are. All that matters is that from this point forward we choose— that's right, it's a choice—to act as if we are 100% responsible for everything that does or doesn't happen to us. In short, YOU must decide to be in control.

A lot of people roll their eyes when they hear the word "responsibility." They say, "Yeah, yeah, yeah . . . I've heard all of that before!" (And, yes, we were two of "those people.") But there is a big difference between "knowing" about something and "acting" on something.

Jack: When I wrote the original *The Success Principles* book, taking responsibility was also the very first principle—and that book was designed for *adults*! Sometimes we just need to be reminded of what we already know so we can put the ideas into practice.

1.5 The Blame and complain Game

All **blame is a waste of time**.
No matter how much fault you find with another,
and regardless of how much you blame him,
it will not change you.

—*Wayne Dyer*
Bestselling author and inspirational speaker

Question: What are the two easiest things to do when we don't get the results we want?

Answers:

1) Place the blame on someone or something else

2) Complain about it

How do we know this? Because we've been guilty of both these things. Believe us, we know how easy this is. Anyone bold enough to admit it would also say that they, too, have fallen into this trap. But just because it's easy doesn't mean it's right.

Let's take a look at the first trap: *blaming*.

Taking responsibility means that you don't blame other people or things outside of yourself. If you think about it, blaming is really just another form of excuse-making. It's a way for us to come up with a reason why we didn't perform. And, you guessed it, all it does is slow us down.

Blair, age 22 (Salt Lake City, UT): I wanted good grades; I wanted to be MVP on my volleyball team; and I wanted to be fit and healthy . . . but I guess that wasn't enough.

My intentions were good, but achieving all of this was a much bigger commitment than I thought. When I didn't get the grade I hoped for or I didn't make a good serve on the volleyball court, I immediately looked for things that other people weren't doing right. I refused to admit that I was probably the cause.

I blamed my teachers for not teaching well enough. I blamed my teammates for not trying hard enough. And I blamed my piles of homework for the reason I couldn't exercise enough. This made me feel good in the moment because, after all, "It wasn't my fault." Nothing was my fault . . . and that's where I ran into trouble.

Blaming became a habit that I wasn't even aware of. I didn't see it at the time, but my blaming made me a "good" complainer as well. Finally, someone challenged me. He said, "What are you going to do to change things?" I quickly responded by saying, "I can't do anything. It's out of my control." My friend then said, "So, are you saying that other people control your life, your results, and your happiness?"

Wow! I was taken by surprise. I never looked at the situation like that before. I noticed that the reason I never achieved my goals was because I was letting the world walk all over me. I realized that I do have the power to change things. I'm now twenty-two, and I have accomplished more of my goals in the last year than in the previous twenty-one years of my life. For me, the power of responsibility was life-changing.

TIP: Instead of pointing the finger at other people, use it to identify a new solution.

Now let's look at trap number two: *complaining*.

The **man who complains** about the way the ball bounces is likely the **one who dropped it**.

—*Lou Holtz*
Former football coach at Notre Dame

Blaming and complaining work really well together . . . too well. Sure, we can blame our problems on someone else or something else and complain all we want. We certainly aren't going to stop you—and it's likely that no one else will either. But if you do this, realize you're only hurting yourself because life will move on . . . with or without you.

There's another way to look at complaining that most people don't think about. Consider this: In order to complain about something or someone, you have to believe that something better exists. Hmmm . . .

In order to complain, part of you must believe that something *can* change for the better. You need to have a reference point of something you prefer, something that you don't yet have.

Look at it this way: People usually complain about things they can actually do something about. We don't complain about the things we have no power over. Have you ever heard anyone complain about gravity? No way!

Here's the raw truth: The circumstances we do complain about are, in actuality, situations that we have the power to change—but have chosen not to. We can always study more, eat healthier, change classes, work out harder, practice longer, choose better friends, and feed our minds different information. Yes, we do have that control.

Now, you might be thinking, "Well, Kent and Jack, if it's that simple, then why don't more people have what they really want?" Good question! The answer is that these actions require change, and they also involve risk. For most people, the risk of losing friends, being alone, or being critically judged by other people is much scarier than sitting back and just "letting life happen" to them.

By taking responsibility and changing things, we run the risk of failure, confrontation, or being wrong—and these fears hold a lot of us back. So, to avoid any of those uncomfortable feelings and experiences, it's easier to stay put, blame others, and just complain about it. However, every successful person we've had the opportunity to meet believed that we all have two choices in life:

1) **Accept that you are making the choice to stay where you are and stop complaining.**

2) **Step up to the challenge and take the risk of creating your life exactly the way you want it.**

To get from where you are to where you want to be, you're going to have to take some risks. That's just part of life.

*If you **risk nothing**, you **risk getting** nothing.*

1.6 The Power of You

ost people dance around the truth and deny that *they* are the reason for the quality of their life. If you want to be a winner, you have to acknowledge the truth—it's *you* who took the actions, thought the thoughts, created the feelings, and made the choices that got you where you are now. But here's the good news:

If it's **you** who got you to where you are **now**,
it's also **you** who can get you to where **you want to be**.

You can change anything and everything simply by doing or thinking something different. Einstein once said that insanity was "doing the same thing over and over again and expecting a different result." Amen! If we continue to eat junk food, we won't become healthier. If we continue to ignore our homework, our grades won't get better. If we continue our current behaviors, our life will not get any better. It's that simple. Fill in the blank: "In order to change my life, I must first change _____."

1.7 The Law of Life

f you truly understand this law of life, you will have complete control of your destiny.

$$E + R = O$$

No need to worry; this isn't algebra. It's much simpler than that! It stands for:

Event + Response = Outcome

The basic idea is this: Every outcome we experience in life (whether it's success or failure, health or illness, happiness or frustration) is the result of how we have responded to an earlier event (or events) in our lives.

If you don't like the outcomes you are currently getting, there are two choices you can make:

1) **You can blame the event (E) for your lack of results (O).** In other words, you can blame your parents, your teachers, your friends, your teammates, your childhood, the weather, racism, your lack of support, and so on. But how useful is the "blame game"? Sure, these factors do exist, but if they were the *deciding* factors, nobody would ever succeed.

Michael Jordan would have never made it to the NBA. Helen Keller wouldn't have been able to inspire millions of people. Martin Luther King Jr. would never have influenced our entire nation. Oprah Winfrey wouldn't have had the country's top daily talk show, Bill Gates would never have founded Microsoft. Need more? The list goes on . . .

Lots of people have overcome these so-called "limiting factors"—so it can't be these factors that limit you. It's not the external conditions or other people that stops us—*it's us*! We stop ourselves. We think limiting thoughts, defend our self-destructive behavior, ignore useful feedback, waste time on gossiping, eat unhealthy food, fail to exercise, spend more money than we make, don't plan for the future, avoid risk, and fail to tell the truth—and then wonder why our lives don't work. As you know, this option is not beneficial.

2) **You can instead simply change your responses (R) to the events (E)—the way things are—until you get the outcomes (O) you want.** This is the option that creates wealth, opportunity, freedom, and so much more. At any given moment, we can change our thoughts, change the way we look at ourselves, and change our behavior—that's the power of YOU. And that's all we need to control anyway.

Unfortunately, for many people these factors are controlled by old habits. We tend to react without thinking things through. However, the moment we take responsibility and commit to making a change, we can take back that control. It's not something that happens over-night, but catching ourselves in the middle of a negative thought

*If you **don't like** your outcomes, **change** your **responses**.*

and changing our behavior just a couple of times each day can make all the difference.

It's like poker; you **can't** determine the **cards** you're **dealt**. But you **can** determine how **you play** them.

In the end, it's not what happens to us; it's how we respond that matters. And how we respond is completely up to us.

⑱ Response in Action

Kent: It was Tuesday, and the school day had just started. The principal announced over the intercom, "Today, during first period, the junior class will be taking a surprise examination. Please meet in front of the gym."

Immediately following the announcement, I heard an uproar from the students—moaning, groaning, and complaining. I'll admit it . . . I wasn't very happy to hear about an exam either. As I made my way to the gym and waited in line, I could hear students complaining and see them bickering with each other.

"I can't believe we have do this!"

"What a waste of time!"

"I'm probably going to fail it."

"Me, too."

Then I noticed a different group of three or four people who appeared to be unaffected by this surprise exam. They were smiling at each other and laughing, and I wondered why. I walked over to them and listened to what they were saying.

"What do you think is going to be on the test?" one girl asked. Her friend replied, "If it's multiple choice, I can do it with no sweat." "Yeah, I'm not worried about it either. I've been doing all my classwork. Besides, since I don't know what the test is on, there is nothing I can do right now to prepare for it, so there is no point in stressing about it. Right?" She laughed.

Then I saw someone else who was listening to his iPod as he read a book. I remember thinking to myself, "Hmmm, if the test was really the determining factor to the way people felt, then everyone should be upset." But not everyone was. It depended on one thing: their response.

It was each individual's *response* (R) to the exam that gave each person his or her own unique *outcome* (O). It was a combination of attitude and behavior that created their completely different experiences.

1.9 creating Today . . . yesterday

Pop Quiz! What was the main point of the previous section?

Answer: Everything you experience in life—both internally and externally—is the result of how you have responded to a previous event.

When we explain this idea, it's interesting to see how people respond. Some people are very quick to say, "What!? Yeah, right . . . that's not true!" The fascinating thing is the same people who react this way are often the same people who:

* Don't have what they want in life
* Get frustrated constantly
* Have a lot of anger toward other people
* Feel that they are doomed to fail no matter what they do because life is out of their control

The cause for all this stems from one thing: *denial.* Seems like an oversimplification, but take a moment to think about this. You'll often hear these same people use phrases like this:

* "It's not my fault."
* "Well, what do you expect? I'm just not that talented."
* "If only other people had done their job, I would have succeeded."
* "My grades would be a lot better if I had better teachers."

They've heard their own excuses for so long that they have created an "alternative reality"—a reality that tells them there is nothing they can do to change the way things are. And with that perspective, no wonder each day is a struggle.

1.10 Pay Attention . . . Results Don't Lie

The easiest and fastest way to find out if something isn't working is to pay attention to the outcomes (O) we're currently getting. We're either getting good grades or we're not. We're either healthy or we're not. We're either happy or we're not. We either have what we want or we don't.

Kent: I hope we don't come across as being rude here. That's not our intention. I remember when one of my teachers told me, "Results don't lie," after I tried to explain my poor performance on a test. I felt offended. This concept took a while for me to digest, but the more I thought about it, the more I realized how true it is.

The fact is, *nobody* likes looking at results they're not proud of—it's not a good feeling. But the moment we gather our courage to face the truth, we're able to see what we need to see in order to make the necessary changes because . . . *the facts speak for themselves.*

You either **create** or **allow** everything that **happens to you.**

You might want to read that last quote again. Once we realize how true this is, we open our eyes to see the warning flags before disaster strikes. You will almost always receive an advance warning in the form of telltale "signs," comments from others, gut instinct, or intuition. These warnings give us time to prevent an unwanted outcome. The better we become at recognizing these signs and responding quickly, the more control we have and the less pain we have to experience.

Some *external* warning signs may be:

❉ Your parents warned you.
❉ Your friends told you.
❉ You continue to get results you don't want.

Some *internal* alerts may be:

❉ That butterfly feeling in your stomach.
❉ Your inner voice saying, "Something isn't right about this." (Also known as *intuition.* Yes, it's there if you listen.)

These alerts give us time to change our response (R) in the E + R = O equation. However, too many people ignore the alerts because paying attention to them would mean they would have to do something uncomfortable to change things. Just remember, pretending not to see these warnings only encourages a disaster later on. Sooner or later, you will have to face the consequences of your actions—or lack of action—so you may as well confront things before they get worse.

On the other hand, you may also get alerts that tell you you're on the right track. Those are important to listen to as well. We'll talk more about that later.

1.11 Life Should Be Fun, Right?

Do you know someone who always seems to be facing a dilemma? We sure do. And some of these people we know well enough to recognize that many—or most—of their "problems" could have been completely avoided. But life should be fun, right? Why spend time dealing with problems that could have been prevented?

Successful people don't wait for disasters to occur. Instead, they respond quickly and decisively to the signals and events as they occur. As a result, life becomes so much easier and much more fun. Old self-talk such as, "I'm a failure," or "Nothing ever seems to work out for me," will slowly turn into "I feel great," "I'm in control," and "I can make things happen."

Once our internal conversations change, our confidence and self-esteem grow. And once that happens . . . watch out! A whole new world of possibilities will appear. To be more successful, all we have to do is act in ways that produce more of what we want. That's it. It's that simple.

QUESTION: *What are five things you repeatedly tell yourself on a daily basis?*

Initially, you might say, "What are you guys talking about? I don't have conversations with myself!" We don't mean the conversations you would have at an imaginary tea party. We're talking about phrases that you silently repeat to yourself during the day. They can be positive or negative. Here are some examples:

POSitive:
※ "I can do this."
※ "I am good enough."
※ "I can make it happen."
※ "I'm in control."

Negative:
※ "I'm not good enough."
※ "Oh, well, that's all I'm capable of anyway."
※ "Why me?"
※ "I just don't have enough skill."

So what do you say to yourself throughout the day? You might need to think hard about this because we're often not even consciously aware of what we repeatedly say to ourselves. But taking full responsibility for our lives means that we must take control of our thoughts because our thoughts affect *everything* we do! In a journal or on a piece of paper, list five phrases you say yourself on a regular basis.

So, what did you find? Were your internal conversations positive or negative? Or both? How do you think these phrases affect your performance?

Now, take another look at the five things you wrote and put a line through the things you no longer want to say to yourself. This will help your brain start to erase this negative self-talk.

The negative things you say over and over again just sit in your head and eat away at your potential. But just imagine what can happen if you reverse the process by feeding your mind with positive information. Even if we don't believe what we say initially, eventually our mind will accept it as the truth, which is why it's so important to say *constructive* things to yourself.

On the same piece of paper, list five empowering phrases you can repeat to yourself each day. (You may include any *positive* phrases from your previous list.)

TIP: If you want to change what you already say to yourself, you will have to constantly remind yourself of what you'd like to say. Put the list next to your bed or tape to your bathroom mirror. This will remind you each day of your new empowering self-statements.

(1.12) Simple Isn't Necessarily Easy

 alking with your friend is easy, right? Well, what about when you're put on a stage and told to talk to the audience and give a speech? It's a simple concept, but simple doesn't mean it's easy.

Although this first Success Principle is simple, it isn't necessarily easy to implement. Taking full responsibility requires awareness, dedication, and a willingness to experiment and take risks. You have to be willing to pay attention to what you are doing and to the results you are already producing.

TIP: Ask yourself, your family, your friends, your teachers, and your coaches for feedback. It might be awkward at first, but they can really help you out by pointing out some of your habits and behaviors you may not be aware of.

Some questions to ask might be:

* ❋ *Is what I'm doing working?*
* ❋ *Could I be doing it better?*
* ❋ *Is there something that I should stop doing?*
* ❋ *How do you see me limiting myself?*

Don't be afraid to ask. Many people avoid this opportunity because they're afraid of what they might hear. There is nothing to be afraid of. The truth is the truth. You are better off knowing the truth than avoiding it. And once you know what's missing, it won't be missing for long because you will know what needs to be done to improve things. You cannot improve your life, grades, sports performance, or friendships without feedback.

Life will always give you feedback about the effects of your behavior *if* you take the time to pay attention. Slow down every once in a while and look at your life and the people in it. Are you happy? Are they happy? Is there balance, organization, happiness, and excitement? Are your grades as good as they could be? Are you healthy and fit? Are you getting the results you want?

Remember, the only way to change your results is to change your behavior. And you must start by facing reality—and that reality comes from the truth. If you face the truth squarely and make changes quickly, success will come to you in more ways than you ever thought possible.

1.13 The Challenge

This book is full of proven Success Principles and techniques you can immediately put into practice.

You will never know if these principles work . . . unless you give them a try. And here's the thing: No one else can do this for you. It's all up to you. If you want all the great things life can offer, it all starts with taking responsibility. Will *you* step up to the challenge? We sure hope you do!

MY "TO-DO" LIST

☑ Realize that the person in charge of my life is ME. I am accountable for the quality of my life.

☑ Search for the facts and look at things as they are, so I can improve them. Then create a new vision by seeing things as I'd like them to *be*.

☑ Eliminate my excuses because (a) no one wants to hear them and (b) all they do is slow me down.

☑ Acknowledge that blaming stems from denial and doesn't accomplish anything because no matter how much I blame things outside of myself, blaming won't change me or my circumstances.

☑ Realize that I can change anything and everything simply by doing or thinking something different. Understand that it's not what happens to me; it's how I respond that matters. And how I *respond* is completely up to me.

☑ When I ask myself a different question, I will trigger a different response, which will, in turn, create a different outcome.

☑ Remember that results don't lie. The easiest and fastest way to find out if something isn't working is to pay attention to the outcomes (O) I'm currently getting.

☑ Pay attention to alerts or signals that I get from other people or my intuition. These are often signs that can help me prevent unwanted consequences later on.

☑ Keep in mind that I have everything I need to get the results I want.

PRINCIPLE 2

Believe IT'S POSSIBLE

Believe in yourself!
Have faith in your abilities!
Without a humble but reasonable
confidence in your own powers, you
cannot be successful or **happy.**

—*Norman Vincent Peale*
Bestselling author and speaker

Anybody who has accomplished anything had to first believe in himself or herself—otherwise, why on Earth bother taking on a challenge, chasing a dream, or working to achieve a goal? If you truthfully didn't believe you were capable of reading a book, would you go to the library and check one out? Would you have picked up this book? Probably not. What does this tell us?

It tells us that our beliefs precede our actions—and, more specifically, it's the beliefs about ourselves and our abilities that have the greatest impact. If you're going to create the life of your dreams, you have to believe that you are capable of making it happen.

Napoleon Hill was hired by Andrew Carnegie (once the richest man in the world) to make a long study of success. Hill's study resulted in the book *Think and Grow Rich*, which has now become an all-time bestseller. One of the most powerful things Hill discovered was— you guessed it—the power of belief.

Whatever the **mind can conceive** and believe, **it can achieve**.

Napolean Hill

2.1 Believing Is a Choice

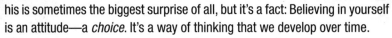

Sooner or later, **those who win** are those **who think they can**.

—*Richard Bach*
Bestselling author and motivational speaker

This is sometimes the biggest surprise of all, but it's a fact: Believing in yourself is an attitude—a *choice*. It's a way of thinking that we develop over time.

Although it helps if you've had positive and supportive parents, teachers, coaches, and friends, this is *not* the long-term determining factor of your level of confidence. Remember, there is no payoff in blaming other people for who you are today. It's now *your* responsibility to take charge of yourself and your beliefs.

Of the hundreds of super-successful people we've interviewed for this book and others, almost every one of them told us, "I was not the most gifted or talented person, but I did choose to believe that anything was possible. I studied, practiced, and worked harder than the others, and that's how I got to where I am."

Stephen J. Cannell failed first, fourth, and tenth grades. He couldn't read and comprehend like the other kids in his class. He would spend five hours with his mother studying for a test and then fail it. Stephen finally came to the conclusion that he just wasn't intelligent.

"But I simply decided, as an act of will, to put it out of my mind," he told us. "I simply refused to think about it. Instead, I focused my energies on what I was good at, and that was football. If it hadn't been for football, which I excelled at, I don't know what would have happened to me. I got my self-esteem from playing sports."

Athletics taught him that if he tried hard enough at something, he could achieve excellence. Later, he used this belief to excel in other areas of his life. Oddly enough, he ended up writing scripts for television. Eventually, he formed his own production studio where he created, produced, and wrote more than 350 scripts for thirty-eight different shows. Soon he had over 2,000 people working for him! And after he sold his studio, he went on to write eleven bestselling novels! Not bad for someone who was considered unintelligent. His story shows:

Stephen is a great example of the fact that it is not what life hands you, but how you respond to it that matters most. He chose to live by beliefs that built confidence within him.

> The **choice** of what to **believe** is purely **up to you**.

(2.2) YOU GET WHAT YOU EXPECT

To accomplish **great things**, we must not only **act**, but also **dream**; not only plan, but also **believe**.

—*Anatole France*
French author

cientists used to believe that the human brain was designed to respond to information it received from the outside world. But today, they're learning the brain *reacts to* what it *expects to happen next*.

Here's an example: A few years ago, doctors in Texas studied the effects of knee surgery. Specifically, they compared three procedures: (1) scraping out the knee joint, (2) washing out the knee joint, and (3) doing nothing to the knee joint.

During the "nothing" operation, doctors anesthetized the patient, made three incisions in the knee as if they were inserting surgical instruments, and then pretended to operate. Two years after surgery, patients who underwent the "pretend surgery" reported the same amount of relief from pain and swelling as those who had received the actual treatments. Their brains *expected* the "surgery" to improve the knee, and it did—even though nothing was actually done. Amazing!

Why does the brain work this way? (Warning: big word ahead!) Neuro-psychologists who study this "expectancy theory" say it's because we've been conditioned to expect certain things to happen our entire lives. Think about this. Throughout life, our brain actually learns what to expect next—whether it eventually happens that way or not. And because our brain expects something will happen in a certain way, we often experience exactly what we anticipate. (You may want to reread that . . .)

Brianna, 17, (Jackson Hole, WY): Since I was twelve years old, I've always struggled with mathematics. Things just became worse and worse. I hated going to class, and I hated doing the homework. Eventually, I just believed that I was no good with numbers.

Every time I went to class, I would expect to get stressed out and struggle—and, not surprisingly, I did. My mind was searching for things that backed up my expectations. if I tried hard on a specific equation and got it wrong, my first response was, "See! I knew I'd get it wrong. It doesn't matter how hard I try because I still can't get it right."

This year, I have a different math teacher who opened my eyes to some new techniques that really helped. For the first time, I feel some confidence in math. This made me realize that, for the last five years, I was actually creating expectations that were hurting my performance because I really believed I was no good. I'm glad I learned this now because I know what to look for in the future. It's true: we usually experience what we *expect* to happen.

This is why it's so important that we hold positive expectations in our minds. When you replace your old negative expectations with more positive ones, your brain will help you accomplish those expectations. And, even better than that, your brain will actually expect to achieve the positive outcomes. How cool is that?!

2.3 I can!

 can't do that!"

Is that a fact, or is it just a belief? Hmmm, consider this: What we believe becomes a fact. Far too often we just react and say (or think) "I can't" without really thinking things through. We are capable of doing so much more than we think we can do.

If you are going to be successful, you need to give up the phrase "I can't" and all of its relatives, such as:

* **"I wish I were able to . . ."**
* **"If only I were . . ."**
* **"I would try, *but* . . ."**

These phrases instantly disempower us. As a result, we miss other opportunities to try new things, challenge ourselves, and grow as individuals.

Tony Robbins, the bestselling author and speaker, conducts seminars around the world. (Tony is also the guy who appeared in the elevator scene of the movie *Shallow Hal*.) At one of his events—which included us (Kent and Jack)—the entire audience of 3,000 people was told that we would all have to walk on red-hot coals by the end of the evening as an exercise to break through our fear. The moment this was announced, most people responded by saying, "Are you kidding me? I can't do that!" At first, we were afraid that we might not be able to do it—that we would burn and blister the soles of our feet.

As part of the seminar, Tony asked us to write down everything we thought we couldn't do: "I can't get straight A's," "I can't ever be good enough to get my dream job," "I can't be a millionaire," "I can't be league MVP," "I can't ask that person out on a date," etc. Once we wrote these beliefs down on paper, we threw them into the burning coals and watched them go up in flames. Two hours later, more than 3,000 people walked on those same red-hot coals without getting burned. Can't walk on hot coals? A lie! (Trust us . . . we did it!) That night we learned that the limiting beliefs we held about ourselves and our abilities were just lies.

We're not telling you to light a bonfire and walk across its hot coals. This requires professional guidance and the right state of mind. But don't miss the real lesson:

*The only **real limits** to our potential are those **we give ourselves**.*

In 1977, in Tallahassee, Florida, Laura Schultz, who was sixty-three at the time, picked up the back end of a 2,000-pound car to get it off her grandson's arm. Before that day, she jokingly said she hadn't lifted anything heavier than a Pepto-Bismal bottle. Laura was a petite woman who looked unable to hoist anything heavier than a 25-pound bagOf catfood.

Dr. Charles Garfield tried to interview her after reading about her in the newspaper. At first, Laura would not talk about what she called "the event." But with enough persistence, Charlie finally got his interview. She said she didn't like talking about "the event" because it challenged her beliefs about what she could and couldn't do. She said, "If I was able to do this when I didn't think I could, what does that say about the rest of my life? Have I wasted it?"

Charlie convinced her that her life was not yet over and that she could still do whatever she wanted. He discovered that her passion was geology. She had always wanted to go to school and study geology, but since her parents didn't have enough money to send both of their children to college, her brother won out. At sixty-three, with a little bit of coaching from Charlie, she decided to go back to school and study geology. She eventually got her degree and went on to teach at a local community college.

Want to wait until you're sixty-three to decide that you can do anything you want—or would you rather start *now*? **Don't waste your life believing you can't.** Go for it!

(24) "YOU GOTTA BELIEVE"

If you **believe** you can, you probably can.
If you believe you **won't**, **you** most assuredly **won't**.
Belief is the ignition switch that gets you **off the launching pad**.

—*Denis Waitley*
Bestselling author and consultant to NASA

Tim Ferris is only twenty-nine years old, and what he has already accomplished is mind-boggling. He says the reason he's been able to accomplish so much is his strong belief in what's possible. In fact, Tim believed so strongly in his abilities that he won the national San Shou kickboxing title just six weeks after being introduced to the sport. (Yes, we said "weeks," not "years.")

An all-American and a judo team captain at Princeton, Tim had always dreamed of winning a national title. He had worked hard, and he was good at his sport. But repeated injuries over several seasons had continually denied him his dream. So when a friend called one day to invite Tim to watch him in the national Chinese kickboxing championship six weeks away, Tim instantly decided to join him in the competition. "*Join*," not "watch."

Because he had never been in any kind of striking competition before, he called USA Boxing and asked where the best trainers could be found. He traveled to a tough neighborhood in Trenton, New Jersey, to learn from boxing coaches who had trained gold medalists. After four grueling hours a day in the ring, he put in more time conditioning in the weight room. To make up for his lack of experience in the sport, Tim's trainers focused on his strengths instead of making up for his weaknesses. Tim didn't want to merely compete. He wanted to win.

When competition day arrived, Tim defeated three highly acclaimed opponents before making it to the finals. As he anticipated winning the final match, he closed his eyes and visualized defeating his opponent in the very first round (another powerful principle we'll explore later in this book). Tim believed. And he won.

Later, he told us that most people fail not because they lack skills or ability, but rather because they simply don't believe in themselves. Never underestimate yourself by doubting your capabilities. Success all begins with a belief. Start believing that you can achieve the smaller goals in your life, and you will eventually build the confidence to believe that you can achieve your wildest dreams as well.

25 Find a support crew

You only have to **believe** that you can succeed;
that you **can be whatever** your heart desires.
Be willing to **work** for it, and you **can have it**.

—*Oprah Winfrey*
Emmy Award-winning host of *The Oprah Winfrey Show*,
the highest-rated talk show in television history

WANTED

SUPPORT GROUP

POSITIVE ATTITUDES ONLY.

Y ou now know that believing in yourself is a key part of success. But how about support from *others*? This is a perfect way to get the extra confidence we need to go for it and make things happen!

When twenty-year-old Ruben Gonzalez showed up at the U.S. Olympic Training Center in Lake Placid, New York, he had in his pocket the business card of a Houston businessman who believed in Ruben's Olympic dream. Ruben was there to learn the sport of luge, a sport that nine out of ten people give up after the first season. Almost everyone breaks more than one bone before mastering this ninety-mile-per-hour race against time in an enclosed mile-long downhill track of concrete and ice. But Ruben had a dream, passion, and a commitment not to quit, and the support of his friend Craig back home in Houston.

When Ruben returned to his room after the first day of training, he called Craig.

"Craig, this is nuts! My side hurts. I think I broke my foot. That's it. I am going back to soccer."

Craig interrupted him. "Ruben, get in front of a mirror!"

"What?"

"I said, 'Get in front of a mirror!'"

Ruben got up, stretched the phone cord, and stood in front of a full-length mirror.

"Now repeat after me: No matter how bad it is, and no matter how bad it gets, I'm going to make it!"

Ruben felt like an idiot staring at himself in the mirror, and his voice betrayed his wimpy, wishy-washy attitude as he said, "No matter how bad it is, and how bad it gets, I'm going to make it."

"C'mon! Say it *right*. You're Mr. Olympic Man! That's all you ever talk about! Are you going to do it or not?"

Ruben started getting serious. "No matter how bad it is, and no matter how bad it gets, I'm going to make it!"

"Again!"

With each word, his strong belief returned: "No matter how bad it is, and no matter how bad it gets, I'M GOING TO MAKE IT!"

And again and again and again and . . .

After five or so repetitions, Ruben thought, "Hey, this feels kind of good. I'm standing a little bit straighter." By the tenth time he said it, he jumped up in the air and shouted, **"I don't care what happens. I'm going to make it. I can break both legs. Bones heal. I'll come back, and I *will* make it. I *will* be an Olympian!"**

It's amazing what happens to your self-confidence when you get eyeball to eyeball with yourself, then tell yourself what you're going to do. Being honest with yourself and believing in yourself can win the support of others. To get the most out of ourselves, sometimes we need a friend or a coach to give us some extra encouragement. (We'll talk more about how to do this in later chapters).

Whatever your dream is, try Ruben's technique for success—it really does work. Look at yourself in the mirror and promise yourself that you are indeed going to achieve it—no matter what the price. Ruben Gonzalez made that promise to himself, and it changed his life. He went on to compete in three separate Olympic Winter Games.

> Believe big. The **size** of your **success** is determined
> by the size of your belief. Think **little goals**, and you
> can expect **little achievements**.
> Think **big** goals and **win big** success.

—David J. Schwartz
Bestselling author and motivational speaker

㉖ If YOU Believe It, YOU Can Achieve It

Recently, we interviewed a really interesting person named Chris Barrett. Chris is only twenty-five today, but his success began as a teenager. He has accomplished many incredible things. He has produced many successful independent films, appeared in the award-winning documentary, *The Corporation*, been a guest on several major TV shows, become close friends with many big Hollywood actors, and even managed to get a big corporation to pay for his college education! But that's not all: He also made $100,000 writing a book that he says, "Nobody wanted." How did he do it? He believed he could. We'll let Chris tell the story.

In high school, I noticed one of my friends getting into concerts for free. I wanted to know how he was doing this, so I asked him. He explained that he had the idea to become a self-made "journalist."

He'd write a quick story for a newspaper or e-zine about a concert he wanted to see, and sure enough, he got free tickets from the concert promoters in hopes that he would give the band some exposure by writing an article about them. So, instead of saying, "I don't know how to be a music journalist, so I think I'll just keep saving up my allowance for those pricey concert tickets," I said, "I want to get into concerts for free, and this guy has just shown me that there's no reason I can't do that very thing."

Right then, I decided I'd be a music journalist. Soon, I was banging on tour managers' doors backstage, interviewing groups like G. Love and Special Sauce, Weezer, and even Green Day. Until that time, I'd never interviewed a rock star before, or even written about one for the school newspaper. But I found something I wanted to do, built up the courage, and took action. Along the way, I'd discovered that I really had a passion for it. Besides, I was now getting into any show I wanted for free!

After doing this for awhile, I decided to share my secrets by writing a guidebook about how to get into concerts for free. But the minute I told someone about it, the first thing they said was, "You can't do that. Who would want to read that—let alone spend good money on it? You're wasting your time."

I felt bummed and began to doubt myself, but part of me knew what I could achieve if I were prepared to give it my best shot. Little did I know, this was just the beginning. More and more people told me the same exact thing:

✳ **"You can't do that."**

✳ **"Who would want to read that—let alone spend good money on it?"**

✳ **"You're wasting your time."**

But from that point on, every time I heard discouragement, I would tell myself, "Of course, I can do that. Kids my age *will* want to read that. I'd spend my money on it!" Soon, this negativity only made me more determined to write my guidebook and make it a success. Eventually, I finished it, published it, printed it, and made a website. I was even selling copies of my book on eBay!

In a short amount of time, a lot of people were buying it. Actually, there were thousands of people from all over the country placing orders. I couldn't wait to get home from school and check my e-mails to see all my new orders. In time, I made over $100,000 on a book that many people told me "nobody would ever want."

The only reason I was able to do it was because I believed in myself and chose to hear "yes" every time someone said "no."

Chris Barrett cofounded Powerhouse Pictures Entertainment with actor Efren Ramirez. Chris is currently directing the documentary, *After School*. Chris and Efren are coauthors of the book *Direct Your Own Life: How to Be a Star in Any Field You Choose* (2008). For more information, visit www.DirectYourOwnLife.com.

You have to **believe in yourself** when no one else does. That's what **makes you a winner**.

—*Venus Williams*
Olympic gold medalist and professional tennis champion

I f having others believe in you and your dream was a requirement for success, most of us would never accomplish anything. You need to base your decisions on what you want to do and write goals that inspire you. Don't worry about what other people think about your dreams. It's important to follow your heart. We like Dr. Daniel Amen's 18/40/60 rule:

When you're **eighteen**, you **worry** about what **everybody** is **thinking** of **you**; when you're **forty**, you **don't** give a darn what anybody thinks of you; when you're **sixty**, you realize **nobody's** been **thinking** about **you** at all.

Surprise, surprise! Most of the time, nobody is thinking about you at all. They're too busy worrying about their own lives—and if they are thinking about you, they're probably just wondering what you're thinking about them. Most people do not live their lives just to see you miserable. Think about all the time you are wasting thinking about what other people think about your ideas, your goals, your clothes, your hair, your body. Couldn't all of that time be better spent thinking about and doing the things that *will* achieve *your* goals? Absolutely.

Don't wait for someone to tell you, "You have what it takes." And certainly don't stop when someone tells you, "You can't." Believe in yourself, and start living the life you deserve. Don't make the fatal mistake of thinking you're alone. Use the power of belief to transform your life. Confidence is contagious. The more you believe in yourself and your abilities, the more faith and support other people will have in you.

If your friends or family don't offer the support you need, look to your teachers, coaches, church leaders, community leaders—and don't stop until you get it. There is always someone who will support you . . . sometimes we just need to look a little harder. We know you can do incredible things, but now it's your turn to believe it. Just remember, plenty of support is available—but it may not come to you . . . you may need to seek it out. Want to learn more about gaining the support of others? Then keep reading. (We've devoted an entire principle to this topic.)

If a twenty-year-old Texan can take up the luge and become an Olympic athlete . . . if a college dropout can become a billionaire . . . if a dyslexic student who failed three grades can become a bestselling author and television producer, then you, too, can accomplish anything if you simply believe it's possible. You have nothing to lose. Believe in yourself and go for it.

MY "TO-DO" LIST

☑ Remember that believing in myself is an attitude and a choice.

☑ Focus on my expectations, remembering always that they often create my experiences.

☑ Expect the best from myself and from my life.

☑ Realize that belief is more powerful than natural ability or skill. Often it's not so much skill that makes people the best at what they do, but rather the solid belief that they can do something—and, of course, putting that belief in action when they give their best each day.

☑ Remember Napoleon Hill's words: "Whatever the mind can conceive and believe, it can achieve."

☑ Repeat to myself, "No matter how bad it is, and no matter how bad it gets, I'm going to make it!"

☑ Remember that the only real limits to my potential are those I give myself.

CHP 03

PRINCIPLE 3

DeCide What YOU WANT

The indispensable **first step**
to getting the things
you **want** out of **life** is this:
decide what **you want**.

—Ben Stein
Actor

question: What is the number-one reason people *don't* get what they really want in life?

Answer: They don't know what they really want in the first place! No mystery here. The challenge we face is that we're just not trained how to discover what we want from life. Besides making a Christmas wish list, we rarely—if ever—clarify what we really want.

hat do you want to accomplish? What do you want to experience? Who do you want to meet? What things would you like to have? Who do you want to become? What does success really mean to you?

For most of us, these are really tough questions . . . especially if we're not used to thinking about them. Ready for the good news? There are some great techniques to finding *your unique answers* to these questions—and, yes, we'll share them with you!

Look at it this way: Imagine that your new car has a killer GPS navigational system. It can guide you exactly where you want to go—no problem! But what good is all that sophisticated technology if you cannot enter a destination? If you don't know where to go, it's useless, right? Well, you have your own inner GPS in your brain, similar to a car's system, and your inner GPS works the same way. *You must give it a destination!* Your life's journey (like your car's journey) depends on your deciding *what you want* and *where you want to go*.

Your inner GPS regularly displays your next steps on your designated route as you continue to move forward to your destination. Similarly, once you clarify and stay focused on your vision *(what you want)*, the exact steps you need to take will also keep appearing along the way. Once you're clear about what you want and remain focused on it, the *how* (the process) will become clear, too.

"**S**top it! What the heck are you thinking! C'mon, get real . . . you can't do that!"

Kent: Have you ever heard that before? Jack and I definitely have—*many times!* I remember a few years ago, after my seventeenth birthday, I told my friends that I was going to write a book. I'll never forget their reactions. The words were very clear: "You? Yeah, right! And then you're gonna be president, right?"

Inside every one of us is that tiny seed of "you" that you were meant to become. Unfortunately, the seed may be buried in response to your parents, teachers, friends, coaches, and other role models as you were growing up.

Think about this: When you were a baby, you knew exactly what you wanted, right? You ate when you were hungry and spit out the foods you didn't like. You had no trouble expressing your needs and wants. You simply let the whole world know by crying loudly until you finally got what you wanted.

We're not saying that tantrums are still the best way to get you what you want, but this example shows that infants instinctively know what they want and are very passionate about getting it. When you were younger, you had everything that you needed to get fed, changed, held, and rocked. You crawled around and moved toward whatever held the most interest for you. You were clear about what you wanted, so you headed straight for it with no fear. Your inner GPS wasn't sophisticated, but it worked just fine!

But then what happened? As you got older, different people gave you "feedback" about your actions that quickly put a stop to your adventurous spirit and shut down your inner GPS system. Somewhere along the way, someone said . . .

※ **Don't touch that!**

※ **Stay away from there.**

※ **Keep your hands off that!**

※ **Eat everything on your plate whether you like it or not!**

※ **You should be ashamed of yourself!**

✻ **Stop crying. Don't be such a baby.**

✻ **You don't _really_ want that.**

✻ **You don't _really_ believe that, do you?**

How many more can you add to this list? As you got older, you heard additional roadblocks:

✻ **You can't have everything you want simply because you want it.**

✻ **Money doesn't grow on trees, you know.**

✻ **Can't you think of anybody but yourself?**

✻ **Stop doing what you are doing and come do what I need you to do!**

No wonder our inner GPS systems stop working! But yours wasn't disabled . . . it was only on pause! You still have everything you need inside you to create the life you really want.

**Sergio, 18 (Los Angeles, CA):** Every time I talked about a new goal or something I wanted to accomplish in my life, my parents would say things like, "It's okay to have dreams, but remember, you don't want to chase them your whole life only to find you can't have it in real life." I think they said this because things didn't work out in my parents' life like they had hoped, and they eventually got bitter and stopped trying. But soon it started to rub off on me—I started to expect things not to work out in my _own_ life. Every time I began to think big and set challenging goals, my mind would be filled with doubt. "Am I wasting my time?" "Am I being ridiculous?" "Am I really capable of this?" Many times I still decided to try to achieve my goals, but I never gave my full commitment because I was too afraid of being let down.

Fortunately, there was something inside of me that didn't want to listen to the negativity. I wanted more from my life. My friend and I started a computer repair business when I was sixteen, and it taught me a lot. I got a taste of what was really possible and made a decision to just go for it in life—no holding back!

I look at things very differently now. Last year, I found a quote that I put on my wall: "When you reach for the stars, you may not quite get one, but you won't come up with a handful of mud either." I love that. It reminds me that you're better off thinking big and giving your best than settling for less than you deserve. And there's nothing to be afraid of. So what if I don't accomplish everything! At least I will know I tried. And I also know that bigger goals force me to step out of my comfort zone and grow more. Life is too short to be negative. Just go for it!

32 DON'T LIVE SOMEONE ELSE'S DREAMS

We have to **dare to be ourselves**, however **frightening** or **strange** that self may prove to be.

—*May Sarton*
American poet and novelist

"**B**ut you will be such a great doctor. Don't stop now."

"You have a natural ability to communicate. You ought to be a lawyer."

"Your dad and I have always known you'd grow up to take over the family business and become a successful dentist."

If you allow others to make *your* decisions (choose your career, find your life mate, select your car, apply to colleges for you, etc.), then it's likely you will end up fulfilling their dreams and not yours. It doesn't matter how passionate other people are about the life they envision for you. What matters is that you are passionate about *your own* dreams and desires.

We recently saw an interview with Donald Trump, and he made a really good point. He said that nothing extraordinary has been accomplished without the presence of an immense personal passion. He's right! Rarely do individuals accomplish amazing things without being genuinely curious, enthusiastic, and passionate about what they're doing. His message is clear: Spend time on things that interest you—something that you choose to do. Ultimately, you need to be excited about what you do . . . after all, it is your life.

Danger: *Your brain will believe whatever it hears over and over again.*

Classic brainwashing relies on simple repetition. If you repeatedly hear, "You're not good enough," or "You don't deserve that," or "That's just unrealistic," eventually you will start to believe it. (This is also why it's so important to spend time with the right groups of people.) If you hear the negativity often enough, you will eventually lose touch with what you really want from life and get stuck trying to figure out what *other people* want you to do. As a result, you now do a lot of things you don't want to in order to please a lot of other people.

Time out! Let's clarify something: We are not suggesting you go on a selfish and self-serving rampage! We cannot *only* do the things we *want* to do. Yes, we're still going to have to take out the trash, do our chores, finish our homework, and treat others with respect. Sorry, these are simply *musts*. But we *are* talking about things like:

- Striving to get into medical school (or law school) simply because Dad has decided that career was for you.
- Feeling the pressure to get married at a certain age just to please your mother.
- Shelving your passion for film, art, or writing because you're told you need to get a "real job" because film, art, and writing are not "practical."
- Taking a specific job for the big salary rather than getting involved in the career that you love.
- Majoring in finance because that is what your career counselor thought was best for you.

When we try to be "sensible" or "practical" (by other people's standards), we become numb to *our* desires. No wonder that people who are asked what they want to do or what they want to be often honestly say, "I don't know." They live with too many layers of "shoulds," "ought to's," and "you'd betters" piled on top of them, suffocating them, separating them from what they really want. *But it can change!*

Bottom line: Listening to other people and getting advice *is* very important, but never abandon your true passions to live the dreams other people have for you. If you ignore what your heart is telling you, then you may miss out on some great things life has to offer.

33 Discover Your Drive

When you know exactly what you want and you're excited about getting it, then you will feel a new sense of motivation, drive, and energy. Some individuals believe there are only two kinds of people in the world: 1) motivated people and 2) lazy people. We don't buy that. We believe those people who are considered "lazy" just don't have a goal that really inspires them.

Consider this: We've never met anyone with an outrageous goal or personal dream who didn't have a dynamic passion and zest for life. There is definitely a trend here! All successful people we have met are clear about what they want. They know why they want it, and they are excited to make it happen. In their own unique way, these high achievers always say that discipline and drive come as a result of having a goal or outcome that inspires them to take action, work hard, and persevere.

The key to unleashing this hidden drive within you is to discover what *you* want. Vague ideas and other people's dreams will rarely give you the motivation to work hard. But when it's *your* vision and *your* goal, it's a different story—there is a deeper sense of satisfaction and incentive to wake up early each morning, push through challenges, and give your best effort when you know that *you* are steering the boat and calling the shots.

Tyler, 26 (Houston, TX): Since I was a little kid, it was expected that I would become the owner and manager of our family restaurant. It felt as though I didn't really have any other choice. Through school, I took classes such as organizational leadership that would prepare me to run the restaurant, but I noticed that I started losing interest in school and didn't really get excited about life.

When I graduated, I began working full-time with my parents. As time progressed, I became more and more frustrated. Eventually, I had to break the news to my parents. "I can't do this anymore." It was a difficult decision, but I had to do it. During the next few days, I wrote down all the things I wanted to do in my life. It was definitely needed. I felt a new rush of energy that I hadn't had in a very long time.

I spent the next two years doing the things on my list while trying new jobs and traveling the world. At the end of it all, I found myself back where I started: with my family in Texas. This time, it was *my* decision to start working at our restaurant, and I was surprised to find that I really enjoyed it. I realized that the reason I was resisting it before was because I felt I "had to" do it—it wasn't my choice. But after taking some time to discover what I wanted from life and see my options, I found a new drive to do what I did, in fact, enjoy. Who knows, I could have ended up doing something entirely different—and that would have been okay, too—but at least now I know for sure that I am doing what *I want* to be doing.

(34) settle for more

Ah, that's good enough. It doesn't really matter anyway."

That is a "poison phrase." It can seem harmless, but over time that attitude will literally destroy the quality of your life. If you want to claim your personal power and get what you really want from life, you will have to stop saying:

❋ "I don't know."   ❋ "It doesn't matter to me."
❋ "I don't care!"   ❋ And our all-time favorite, "What*ever!*"

When you're confronted with a choice, no matter how small it seems, remind yourself that *everything counts*. If you care about the little things (the *details* in life), then the bigger parts of life will take care of themselves and come together nicely. Next time you're in a situation where you would normally let things slide, ask yourself:

❋ "If it did matter, what would I do differently?"
❋ "If I did care, what would I prefer?"
❋ "If I did know what I wanted, what would it be?"

Jack: Many years ago, I attended a seminar that greatly impacted my life. As all of the attendees, including myself, entered the room, I noticed that somebody had put a spiral notebook on everyone's chair. Some were blue, some were yellow, and others were red. The one on my chair was yellow. I remember thinking, "I hate yellow. I wish I had a blue one."

Then the speaker said something that changed my life forever: "If you don't like the color of the notebook on your chair, trade with someone else and get the one you want. You deserve to have everything in your life exactly the way you want it."

Wow! What a concept! For twenty-some years, I had not lived with that frame of mind. I had settled, thinking I couldn't have everything I wanted. So I turned to the person to my right and said, "Would you mind trading your blue notebook for my yellow one?"

Losers let it happen.
Winners make it happen.

She responded, "Not at all. I prefer yellow. I like the brightness of the color. It fits my mood." I now had my blue note-book—not a huge success in the greater scheme of things, but it marked the beginning of my taking complete control of my life and designing my life the way I wanted it.

From that day forward, I made a commitment to myself never to settle for less than I could do, be, and have.

Why settle for a color you do *not* want—or anything else for that matter? Remember, you always have a choice. You can let things slide or you can take control, give your best, and not settle for anything less than what you deserve.

35 NO LIMITS!

Think back a few years. As a young child, it wasn't hard to answer the question, "What do you want?" Heck, the problem was finding a chance to breathe between all the possible answers that flowed through our brains. That's why there's a time limit when sitting on Santa's lap—otherwise, kids would go on forever!

But like we already discussed, as we get older we're programmed to think more "realistically." But what is "realistic" anyway? It wasn't realistic for John F. Kennedy to think of putting a man on the moon. But we did it. It wasn't realistic for the Founding Fathers to write the Declaration of Independence, making the United States an independent country. But they did it. It wasn't realistic for Martin Luther King Jr. to lead a nationwide movement for equal rights. But he did it.

When you're thinking about what you want and who you want to be, don't limit yourself by being "practical" or "realistic." We encourage you not to limit your dreams because, if you do, you instantly limit your potential.

When Monty Roberts was in high school, his teacher gave the class an assignment to write about what they wanted to do when they grew up. Monty wrote that he wanted to own his own 200-acre ranch and raise thoroughbred racehorses. To his surprise, he received an F for the project. The teacher explained that his grade reflected the fact that his dream was unrealistic.

> If you **only pursue** what **other people think** is realistic, you will **never** discover what **you** really want or experience what you **really deserve.**

His teacher said, "No boy whose parents don't own property and who live out in the back of rodeo grounds would be able to earn enough money to buy a ranch, purchase horses, and pay the necessary salaries for the ranch's employees." When he offered Monty the chance of rewriting his paper for a higher grade, Monty told him, "You keep the F; I'm keeping my dream."

Today Monty owns his own 154-acre ranch in Solvang, California, raises thoroughbred horses, and trains hundreds of horse trainers.

High achievers see the world from a different perspective—as a place where amazing things can happen. They believe that anything is possible, and they also believe that they can be part of the solution. They see no limits. (That's why they're willing to say, "You keep the F; I'll keep the dream.")

36 Attract What You Want

When we give speeches, we often approach someone in the audience and ask one simple question: "What do you want in life?" The responses never cease to amaze us. Some people look at us with a blank face, and other people mumble a brief thought, but many people will say something such as:

* ❋ **"I don't want to be broke."**
* ❋ **"I don't want to fail my class."**
* ❋ **"I don't want to be lonely."**
* ❋ **"I don't want a car that constantly breaks down."**
* ❋ **"I don't want to be like Matthew, who ended up in jail."**

Do you notice the pattern? Every sentence begins with the three words "I don't want." How did that happen? Sometimes eliminating what you *don't* want from your life can help you discover what you *do* want. But be sure you place more attention on the positive than the negative. Why? Because in life . . .

*You **will get more** of what you **focus on**.*

Have you ever noticed that those who are constantly thinking and talking about what they don't want are also often battling those exact or very similar challenges in their lives? Well, it's not a coincidence. Our mind is the most powerful instrument we have. It can work with us or against us. It largely depends on what we *choose* to focus on. This universal principle is called The Law of Attraction and it's always in effect. It operates on the idea that *energy flows where attention goes*. You are always attracting more of *whatever* you are focusing on. When you focus on what you want in your life, you will get more of it—and what you don't want will gradually disappear.

TIP: Wear a bracelet or a rubber band on your wrist to remind you to think about what you appreciate in your life and what you would like more of. Every time you catch yourself in the midst of a negative thought, take the bracelet off and put it on the other wrist. This will help you become aware of your daily thoughts, develop positive thoughts, and begin attracting what you want into your life.

3.7 The Big 101

We're going to offer you a challenge that might seem a little crazy at first. We call this exercise *The Big 101*. Since focusing on the positive is so important, this exercise will give you plenty of things to keep your mind on the *right* track.

So what's involved? Just write a list of 101 things you want to do, be, or have in your life. Yes, we said, one hundred and one! It may seem like a lot at first, and it can be a challenge, but we guarantee it is both fun and extremely rewarding.

We often hear people say, "I don't know what I want." And, of course, we're always compelled to ask, "Have you ever seriously thought about what you might want?" The typical answer is, "No, not really." Don't go through life without a treasure map. This exercise gives you the chance to discover what you really want from your life and can supply an additional boost of energy and drive to help you get the most out of yourself.

Lou Holtz, the legendary football coach of Notre Dame, knows how powerful this little exercise can be. When he was only twenty-eight years old, he had just been hired as assistant coach at the University of South Carolina. He wife was eight months pregnant, and he had spent every dollar he had on a down payment for a house. One month later, the head coach who had hired Lou resigned, and Lou found himself without a job. He was devastated.

His wife was desperate to lift his spirits so she gave him a book—*The Magic of Thinking Big*, by David Schwartz. The book said that you should write down a giant list of things you want to achieve in life. Lou sat down at the dining-room table and turned his imagination loose. Before he knew it, he had listed 107 things he wanted to achieve before he died. He wrote down everything he could think of, including having dinner at the White House, appearing on *The Tonight Show* with Johnny Carson, meeting the pope, and shooting a hole-in-one in golf. So far, Lou has achieved eighty-one of those goals, including shooting a hole-in-one—not once, but twice!

The Big 101 ensures that life becomes an exciting adventure worth living to the fullest. Take the time to make a list of 101 things you would like to do, be, or have in your life. Write everything down in detail. You might want to write them on 3" x 5" cards, on a goals page, or in a goals book. (We'll talk more about this in Chapter 7.) Every time you achieve one thing on your list, check it off and write *victory* next to it. See for yourself how this simple exercise can transform your life.

Excerpted from *The Success Principles*. Reprinted by permission of HarperCollins.

3.8 Ink It, Don't Just Think It

Okay, enough talk. Let's get down to business. We've discussed how important it is to know what you want, but how do you go about discovering what you desire? The first step involves getting a pen and a piece of paper and going to a place where there are no distractions. Set aside at least twenty to thirty minutes. This is *your* time.

We've created a unique list of questions below. If you want to get the most out of this, then you'll have to ignore all of the negative thoughts and voices inside your head that say, "I can't do that!" or "Me? Yeah, right!" It's natural to have these thoughts, and it might be uncomfortable at times to write down some of the ideas that come to your mind, but that's okay. It's not unusual to have doubts, but successful people *choose*—yes, it's a *choice*—to boldly move ahead.

We encourage you to write down your thoughts regardless of how ridiculous you or anyone else thinks the ideas are. Don't be too serious about this—have fun with it. After all, you're creating a preview of life's coming attractions.

The trick to answering these questions is to keep your pen constantly moving. Don't let yourself stop. Write down everything—no matter how small or big the idea is. Keep the thoughts flowing and challenge yourself to dedicate at least five minutes to each step. The more detail, the better.

Step 1: Emotional: The way you feel is crucial for success. Think about it: It's nearly impossible to do well if you don't feel good about yourself. It's also difficult to have fun and enjoy life if you're not in the right mood. What type of emotions or feelings would you like to experience every day? How would you like other people to describe your personality? Examples: happy, vivacious, cheerful, humorous, creative, passionate, helpful, outgoing, courageous.

Step 2: Material Things: These things should never be our sole focus, but they can help us get excited and encourage us to work hard. So what "things" would you like to have in your life? Maybe a new car, great wardrobe, killer stereo, incredible boat, lots of shoes, a nice house? While listing the items in this category, be very specific when you describe each thing. For example, if you said you'd like a nice house, describe the style, size, location, colors, landscaping, etc. Ready . . . *go!*

Step 3: Dreams and Fantasies:
In your perfect world, what would you be doing? Where would you like to travel? What would you like to do there? What type of lifestyle would you like to have? Who is part of that lifestyle? Who would you like to meet?

Step 4: Personal:
This is perhaps the most important step because who you are is the greatest determining factor of the quality of life you live. What kind of person do you want to be in two to five years? How will people treat you? What will they say about you? What will you think about yourself? How will you dress? How will you stand? What will you stand *for*? You might want to start this step with these words: "In two years, I will be the type of person who . . ."

Step 5: School and Education:
Education means paving your future for success. Your experience at school may be frustrating and unproductive or enjoyable and successful; it all depends on you. What do you really want to get from your schooling experiences? What kind of friends will you have? What kind of relationships will you have with your teachers? What would you like to learn? What sports do you want to participate in? What school programs do you want to be involved in?

Step 6: Money and Finance:
Money is always an emotionally charged subject, but financially successful individuals make important decisions about their spending and earning habits because they are clear about what they want. So, on that note, how much money would you like to save for your education? How much spending money would you like to have each week? How much money do you think you're going to need to support the lifestyle you want?

Step 7: Contribution and Service:
The greatest satisfaction in life comes from knowing that your life matters to other people. Giving back and sharing your time, talents, and resources with others is an immensely rewarding experience. Truly successful and happy individuals think about ways they can serve others. What do you see yourself contributing to your family, school, community, country? How can you use your talents and abilities to help others?

The things you list should get you excited and give you something to look forward to. In life, we always need a dream or a vision or an exciting future that shows us the rewards are worth the sacrifices.

The purpose of this exercise is to consciously show your mind exactly what you want in your life. The clearer you are about what you want, the more you empower your brain to make it part of your reality. Your mind will automatically help you find ways to get it. We will revisit this exercise in later chapters. We hope you enjoyed it!

MY "TO-DO" LIST

☑ Be clear about what I want! Realize that the #1 reason people don't get what they want is because they are not clear about what they want in the first place.

☑ Remember that my mind is my inner GPS system and that in order to use this natural inner resource, I must enter the destination. I must be clear about what I want.

☑ Focus on my passion. If I'm passionate enough about what I want, then I will discover how to make it happen.

☑ Never abandon my true passions and swap them to live out the dreams that other people have for me.

☑ Prepare myself for those who will try to talk me out of my goals and dreams. Stand strong and surround myself with people who will support me and my aspirations.

☑ Make my life an ongoing adventure by completing my list of 101 things I want to accomplish in my life.

☑ Write down what I want (don't just *think about* what I want) by completing the exercises in this chapter.

Be clear Why You're Here

Outstanding people have one thing in common: an absolute **sense of mission.**

—Zig Ziglar
Author and motivational speaker

Life can get crazy! At times it seems as though things are moving at the speed of light! It's easy to get swallowed up by all the day-to-day things we must do. Usually by the time we come to the end of our daily tasks (school, practice, work, cleaning our room, club meetings, homework, time for recreation, listening to music, etc.), we're exhausted. Have you ever been there? Both of us have.

It's a dangerous cycle to get caught up in. Why? Because you can wake up one day and find that you've been working hard only to end up somewhere you *don't* want to be. Not such a good feeling. It's like the old adage of climbing the ladder of success and working hard to get to the top only to find that the ladder was leaning against the wrong wall!

Based on our experience, we believe that every person is born with a life purpose. In fact, discovering and honoring this purpose is perhaps the most important action successful people take. Some of you might be thinking:

But that's **other people**. Their lives might have purpose, but **I'm not like them**.

Well, you're right about one thing: You're not like them. You are unique . . . and your purpose is, too. This is not a time to think, "Blah, blah, blah." Don't miss the main point! Many people overlook this fact: The path to finding your own purpose is also unique. People discover their purpose in life at different times and in different ways, but the key factor is the same: It comes down to your desire to seek it out and find it.

Remember this: If you have a heartbeat, you have purpose. If you're alive, you're here for a reason. One of the biggest mistakes people make is not taking a break in their busy lives to think about why they are here. They get caught up in the day-to-day tasks of life and fail to stop and think about what they want most from life, only to wake up one day feeling dissatisfied about their lives. Now that is ultimate failure—definitely not a place you want to be.

People tell us all the time that they don't know what they want from life. "Well, when was the last time you set aside at least an hour to think about what you really want, plan it, and map it out?" we ask them. Their response? "Uhhhhhhhh . . . I don't know." The truth is, living without discovering your purpose is like building a house on a foundation of sand. Long term, it won't work out. We're not going to tell you it's an easy process, but if you have faith and are willing to search for answers, you will find a purposeful meaning for your life.

Success without satisfaction is **senseless**.

4.1 What were you put on the Earth to do?

There are **two great days** in a person's life:
the **day we are born** and the **day we discover why**.

—*William Barclay*
Author, radio and television presenter, professor, and minister

So what were you put on the Earth to do? If discovering your life purpose seems overwhelming, you're not alone. The good news is, it doesn't have to be. It should be fun and exhilarating. But, sometimes, the best starting point is simply *deciding* on a purpose that inspires you right now.

You can always change your purpose statement as you go along, but having an idea of what your purpose might be is much better than having no idea at all.

Jack: My purpose is simple: *To inspire and empower people to live their highest vision in a context of love and joy.*

Kent: My purpose is: *To help others recognize their true abilities and potential by offering them the insights they need to fulfill their own destinies.*

Your purpose should be unique to you. It doesn't need to be complex. It just needs to inspire you to work hard to become the best "you" you can be.

* Look at the Walt Disney dynasty, for example. Their purpose is extremely simple: *To make people happy.* Do you think this mission will affect the way Disney designs rides and interacts with their customers? Absolutely.

* Thomas Edison, the inventor of the light bulb, said his mission was: *To create inventions that people needed. Inventions that people would pay for and would become profitable.*

* Andrew Carnegie, the famous American steel industrialist and founder of the American library system, was once the richest man in the whole world. Carnegie's mission? Simple: *Spend the first half of my life making as much money as I can and the second half giving it all away.*

Do you see how simple, yet very powerful, these mission statements are? For many professional athletes, their mission might be *to be the best in the world at what I*

do and inspire other athletes to push their own boundaries to become better and better.

We have both created mission statements that have led us to write books like this one and travel around the world to speak in front of thousands of people. The interesting thing is, neither of us was born with these exact missions in mind. We simply clarified what we wanted our lives to be about and then decided to live by it. Now, it's easy to see how our simple one-line missions have completely shaped our lives.

> Where **your talents** and the **needs** of the world cross, your **calling** can be **found**.
>
> —*Aristotle*
> Greek philosopher, fourth century BC

"What do I want my life to be about?" You don't need to have an answer in this instant, but now is the time to start asking yourself that question.

It's our purpose that directs our lives. You see, without a purpose in life, it's easy to get sidetracked on your life journey. Having a purpose—no matter how simple it may be—helps you make decisions because you will know if each decision you make is aligned with your personal mission or not.

Monique, 16 (Ventura, CA): I wrote down my purpose not really knowing how it would help me . . . until I found myself in a tough situation. In the past, I would have spent a long time deciding what to do, but one look at my purpose statement and I knew what I had to do. Since I had something to compare my options with, I could better tell what decision would take me closer to where I really wanted to go. Now, it's so much easier for me to make decisions and not feel confused and guilty about it.

4.2 What's the Point?

f we think about our entire life, it can sure seem like a long journey. However, if we look a little closer we'll notice that even the longest lifetime is still made up of single days—and it's what we do with those days that ultimately shapes our lives.

So what do many of those days consist of? School, sports, work, band practice, hanging out with friends, traveling, celebrating holidays, spending time with the family, talking on the phone, surfing the Internet, etc. Many people get used to going through these motions without thinking twice about what they're doing or why they're doing it. Of course, most of these people survive and make it through their lives, but we don't want to simply "survive"; we want to thrive! If we get into the habit of taking a moment to stop and think about what we're doing and why, we can boost our performance, effectiveness, and satisfaction.

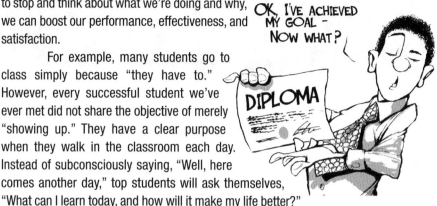

OK, I'VE ACHIEVED MY GOAL – NOW WHAT?

DIPLOMA

For example, many students go to class simply because "they have to." However, every successful student we've ever met did not share the objective of merely "showing up." They have a clear purpose when they walk in the classroom each day. Instead of subconsciously saying, "Well, here comes another day," top students will ask themselves, "What can I learn today, and how will it make my life better?" It seems like such a small change, but it makes a *big* difference long term because their brain is engaged and searching for new information instead of just passively "existing."

The same is true in sports. There are people who just show up, and there are those who arrive with a purpose: "I know everything I do will matter, so I will give my best during this practice so I can be at my best every game this season." Do you think this would make a difference in an athlete's performance? Definitely!

Even if you're just hanging out with your friends, going to a social event, or about to talk on the phone, ask yourself, "Why am I doing this? What do I want to accomplish? What do I want these people to know?" Maybe for one of these last three examples, your purpose is as simple as, "I want to have fun and make a new friend." Or "I just want to let my friends to know that I value our friendship." As simple as it may be, it's still better than just mentally showing up.

Martie, 16 (Flagstaff, AZ): Class time was social time. Show up, talk, exchange notes, do it again the next day. I never thought much more about it. But when I read about the importance of always having a specific purpose, something clicked for me. Before I walk into class, I now ask myself questions like, "What do I want to accomplish?" Today, I look at things very differently than I used to. If I'm going to be somewhere, then I may as well get the most out of it. Just by thinking ahead and knowing the outcome I want, I feel like I have discipline I never had before.

Whenever you can direct your focus and engage your mind, you will be much, much better off. Whether it's plotting your life course or just a daily task, knowing the exact result you want and acting with a clear purpose will instantly increase your chances of getting the outcome you want. As a result, you will be happier as well as more effective with your time and energy.

Fortunately, Julie Laipply made a "course correction" in her life before it was too late. When Julie was a child, she loved animals. All she ever heard was, "Julie, you should be a veterinarian. You're going to be a great vet." So when she got to Ohio State University, her path seemed obvious: Take biology, anatomy, and chemistry. She was on the road to becoming a vet.

A Rotary Ambassadorial Scholarship allowed her to spend a year studying abroad in Manchester, England. Away from the pressures from home, she had time to think. One dreary day, she was sitting at her desk surrounded by biology books and staring out the window. Suddenly it hit her: "I'm totally miserable. Why am I so miserable? What am I doing? I don't want to be a vet!"

Then Julie asked herself, "What job would I *really* love? What job would I love enough to do it for free?" She reflected on all the things she'd done. "Which ones made me happiest?" At the top of her list were the youth leadership conferences that she had volunteered for and the communications and leadership courses she had taken.

"How could I have been so ignorant? Here I am in my fourth year at school, just finally realizing I'm on the wrong path and not doing the right thing. But it's been here in front of me the whole time. I just never took the time to acknowledge it until now."

Excited that she had found her real purpose, Julie spent the rest of her year in England taking courses in communications and media performance. When she returned to Ohio State, she was eventually able to convince the administration to let her create her own leadership studies program. Even though it took her two years longer to graduate, she went on to become a senior management consultant in leadership training and development *at the Pentagon*!

Along the way, she also won the Miss Virginia USA contest and became the host of a TV show in New York that allowed her to further her impact as a positive leader and role model. Experiencing the success of being focused on her purpose, Julie now travels across the country as a professional speaker for teens on the power of leading your own life through successful choices. Recently, she also started her own girls' mentoring program, "Be-YOU-tiful," which teaches young women how to be leaders by focusing on their own unique strengths. Oh, by the way, Julie has been able to accomplish all of this while in her twenties—a true example of how finding your purpose can transform your own life and the lives of those around you.

But hold on! Here's the good news: You don't need to buy that ticket to England for a year abroad to get away from your daily pressures to discover *your* purpose! But you do need some time to think. Remember, *now* is the time to lay the foundation for the rest of your life—not tomorrow, not next week, and certainly not ten years from now. The sooner you do this, the sooner you will have the life you really want.

(4.4) Passion and Purpose

"**H**ow do I know when I'm doing what I'm meant to do with my life? How do I know when I've found my purpose?"

No need for a calculator here. The answer isn't that complicated. It's actually quite simple. You will know when you're on or off purpose by the amount of happiness you are experiencing. The things that bring you the most happiness in life are big clues when you're searching for your purpose.

TIP: To zero in on your purpose, start with a list of the times you felt most happy, passionate, and alive. What do these experiences have in common? Can you figure out a way to make a living doing these things?

Well, Pat Williams did. Pat is the senior vice-president of the Orlando Magic basketball team. He has also written fifty books and is a professional speaker. When we asked him what he thought the greatest secret to success was, he replied:

Jonathan Wendell grew up playing sports competitively. He also had a passion for playing video games. He excelled at both, and when he heard about a professional video tournament, he excitedly signed up. After performing well in the competition, he decided to take it more seriously. People thought he was nuts, but he followed his passion and his dream anyway. Since his first tournament, seven years have passed. He is now twenty-six years old and recently won a $150,000 first-place prize in a video-game tournament in New York. Over the past seven years, he has won ten world titles!

> Figure out what you **love to do** as young as you can, and then organize your life around figuring out how to **make a living at it**.

As a result of his passion to play video games, he has discovered his purpose. He's started a company titled Fatal1ty, where he produces new products to help other people perform better while enhancing their gaming experience. He has made a living doing something most people said could never be done. He followed his passion, discovered his purpose, and has helped thousands of gamers enjoy their passion as well. You just never know where your passion will take you. Jonathan would be the first to tell you that following your passion helps you find your purpose.

4.5 What's My Purpose?

The **purpose** of **life** is a **life of purpose**.

—*Robert Byrne*
Champion chess player, author, and newspaper columnist

ow, let's start designing *your* life purpose. No need to get analytical here. Just be creative, let your ideas flow, and have some fun.

Step 1: What specific words provoke emotion in you? What words appeal to you? List them on a blank piece of paper or in a journal.

Examples: Courage, Creativity, Destiny, Empower, Energy, Enthusiasm, Freedom, Gratitude, Happiness, Help, Inspire, Journey, Lead, Love, Passion, Playfulness, Powerful, Serve, Sincerity, Succeed, Support, Uplift, etc.

Note: Chances are that the words you wrote above appeal to you for a reason. Why do you think you wrote these specific words? When you start piecing your mission together, refer to this list. You may want to include some of these words.

Step 2: What are some famous quotes or phrases that you like? (They don't need to be exact; just write down the basic idea.) What do you like about these quotes or phrases? What are the key words or ideas? (These will show you what you already stand for and what already inspires you.)

Step 3: In the space provided, summarize each quote or phrase in just two words. What is the real message?

Step 4: List some of your unique personal qualities.

Examples: Attention to Detail, Compassion, Creativity, Communication Skills, Decisiveness, Enthusiasm, Happiness, Listening Skills, Leadership Skills, Organization, Optimism, Persistence, Witty Sense of Humor, etc.

Step 5: List a few different ways you most enjoy expressing the qualities you listed above. What do you normally do that brings out these qualities?

Examples: I support others. I inspire people to try hard. I make decisions with confidence and assume a leadership role. I take the time to listen to and understand other people. I don't give up. I focus on the positive things in life and strive to make other people happy by being a genuinely cheerful person. I tutor other students with patience and consideration.

Step 6: Look at what you wrote in Steps 1–5 and begin to combine the words, phrases, and ideas into several different sentences. Don't worry about making the ideas flow—just write down sentences and ideas.

Here are some examples other students had:

* *I use my creativity and sense of humor to show others how life can be fun. When other people are happy, I feel better as well.*—Sean
* *My focus and determination are best when I lead a group discussion or activity. I like to make decisions and take control.*—Ciera
* *I'm most happy when I'm painting and when I'm outdoors. Nature is important to me. I want to express that in my art.*—Jocelyn

Step 7: The home stretch! Refine what you wrote in Step 6 and piece the sentences or ideas together. The result will be your first draft of your life purpose. It can be a few sentences or just one. Remember, the intention is to develop and write something that inspires you and represents the type of person you want to become.

Here is what the students mentioned in Step 6 came up with:

* *My purpose is to make people laugh and feel good so they can enjoy life and find their own purpose.*—Sean
* *My purpose is to be a leader. I will achieve my goals by helping others reach their goals. I will be an example of a good leader by living with compassion and integrity.*—Ciera
* *My purpose is to preserve the environment by using my paintings to appreciate nature.*—Jocelyn

Keep in mind, this purpose will not be tattooed to your soul. You can rework your purpose statement as you go through life and grow as a person. Your purpose statement will help you make important decisions that will shape your character and the quality of your life.

4.6 Your Purpose in Action

Decide upon your major definite **purpose in life** and then **organize all** your activities **around it**.

—*Brian Tracy*
Author and motivational speaker

aving a purpose is extremely important. Now you have an internal GPS system that will help guide you throughout your life. But perhaps the most important part of having a purpose statement is putting it into action and living by it.

Question: What can you do to make sure you remind yourself of your personal purpose statement?

Answer: No single answer works for everyone, but here are some ideas:

※ **Write it on a sheet of paper. If you prefer, type it or print it from your computer.**

*Everything you **do** should be an **expression** of **your purpose**.*

※ **Put the sheet on the wall in your room, on your desk, in your diary—somewhere you're sure to see it regularly. If you'd like, work on the presentation of your statement and then frame it.**

※ **Program your computer screensaver to flash your purpose statement on the screen or make it into your desktop wallpaper.**

※ **What else can you come up with?**

NOTE: You may need more time to think about your mission statement. That's fine. But we recommend that you draft something—*anything!*—before you move on to the next chapter. A draft is fine. It does not need to be final.

Make your **work** in **keeping** with your **purpose**.

—*Leonardo da Vinci*
Sixteenth-century scientist, mathematician, inventor, and artist

If you are truly living your purpose, things seem to fall into place. If a certain activity doesn't fit the formula and won't help you grow, then don't do it. When you find yourself at a fork in the road and you're not sure what to do, look at your purpose statement and see what option best agrees with it. Decisions that were once difficult will become clearer.

(4.7) Staying on Purpose

taying on purpose is easier when you have help. For example, when you read your life purpose every morning, you help yourself to stay focused and do things aligned with your purpose throughout the day.

Discovering and **honoring** their **life purpose** is perhaps the most important action **successful people** take.

Jocelyn, 17 (Albany, NY): I'm an artist, so I don't think in words. I wanted to remind myself of my purpose, but in a different way. I grabbed some paper and drew some sketches until I came up with a symbol that represented by mission. I put the symbol in places I see every day. It reminds me of what I'm meant to be doing.

TIP: As you continue to read this book, return to this chapter and define your vision and your goals further. Review what you wrote to make sure it still inspires you. You may decide to add something to your statement or simplify it.

With a purpose, everything in life seems to fall into place. To be "on purpose" simply means you're doing what you love to do, doing what you're good at, and accomplishing what's important to you.

MY "TO-DO" LIST

☑ Realize that we all have a purpose and that we all discover our purpose at different times and in different ways.

☑ Set some time aside (even when life gets really hectic) to think about what I want most from my life.

☑ Appreciate the value of the single days that make up my life and the many things I do each day.

☑ Develop a purpose that inspires me.

☑ Understand that my purpose does not need to be complicated. It can be simple, as long as it excites me.

☑ Write down my purpose statement and think of ways I can remind myself to read it each day—preferably in the morning.

☑ Be aware that I risk the danger of being successful but unfulfilled if I don't first think about and create a purpose that agrees with what I value most.

☑ Think about the times when I was the most happy and see how these moments could be showing me my true purpose.

☑ Revisit this chapter as I go through the book so I can tweak my purpose statement to best reflect who I am.

see the Best to Be the Best

A **pessimist sees difficulty** in every opportunity, but an **optimist sees opportunity** in every difficulty.

—Winston Churchill
Former Prime Minister of the United Kingdom

oo often we meet people who have an enormous list of reasons why they cannot be successful. These reasons can usually be traced back to one underlying belief: *They feel they are ultimately doomed because everyone and everything is working against them.*

The multimillionaire and former publisher of *Success* magazine, W. Clement Stone, was once described as an "inverse paranoid." Instead of believing the world was out to sabotage his dreams, he chose to believe that the world was trying to help him achieve. Instead of seeing every difficult or challenging event as a negative, he saw it for what it could be—something that was going to empower him and help him reach his goals.

What an incredibly positive belief! Imagine how much easier it would be to succeed in life if you were constantly expecting the world to support you and show you new, exciting possibilities. Well, successful people do just that. They search for the best . . . and guess what? The best shows up.

> I've always been the **opposite of a paranoid**.
> I operate as if **everyone** is part of a plot
> to **enhance my well-being**.

> —*Stan Dale*
> **Author and founder of the Human Awareness Institute**

But be careful, this process also works in reverse. If you expect the worst will happen or you expect that people are out to stop you from living your best life, then that is exactly what you will experience. Your mind does not like to be proven wrong, so it will search for evidence that backs up your beliefs and expectations. (Remember the story about Brianna from the *Believe It's Possible Principle* about her expectations and math class? Well, this is the same thing.) If we expect the worst to happen, we will always find negative feedback. And with consistent negativity, we can be sure that we're not going to achieve much or be very happy.

Has your family or someone you know recently bought a new car? Or maybe a new car that you really like was just put on the market. Have you ever noticed that the same model car seems to appear everywhere around you? This is what we call the "new-car syndrome," and it happens because our subconscious mind is constantly searching for it. We are unknowingly looking for that car. And guess what? We continue to find it . . . time and time again.

The same concept works for almost anything, not just cars. Numbers, people's names, types of cell phones, and even good deeds. Try this for one day: Search for the best in every situation! We're sure you'll find it. (Oh, and if it works, you don't need to stop after one day. Feel free to do this every day. The only real side effect is happiness and gratitude. Not a bad deal, eh?)

How can you apply this principle? Here are some simple but practical and powerful ways to approach life:

* If you're going to give a presentation, instead of assuming that the audience wants to see you mess up, assume the audience wants to see you excel and have fun on stage.

* If your car breaks down on the side of the road and a stranger stops to help, instead of imagining a serial killer who's going to harm you, think instead of the possibility that he's a genuinely nice guy who wants to help you . . . perhaps because a year ago someone did the same for him when his car broke down.

* If a friend moves away, instead of thinking you're doomed to a life of loneliness and despair, believe instead that you have a new space in your life for another good friend. You will also have a new place to visit and see an old friend.

In all these situations, the benefits are there. Sure, it's important to be careful and cautious at times, but since we have a choice in every situation, we might as well *assume the positive* and expect that everything will work out. It's all a matter of what you look for. Think about it: Was there a time in your life when something bad happened that later became a blessing in disguise? Of course there was.

Sometimes we hear people say, "Well, this situation sure sucks right now, but one day we'll look back on this and laugh." We always ask, "Why not laugh about it now?" Instead of getting overly frustrated and discouraged for weeks to come, stop yourself, step back from the situation, and ask, "What could be funny and beneficial about this event?" It's all a matter of redirecting your focus. However, we're not suggesting that you become optimistically ignorant. Learn the lesson being offered and get on with your life! Don't take life too seriously. Be willing to have fun and laugh at yourself. Humor and (healthy) optimism are extremely important traits to develop.

> Whatever we **expect** with **confidence** becomes our **own self-fulfilling prophecy**.
>
> Bestselling author and motivational speaker
> —Brian Tracy

5.2 What DO YOU See?

Every **negative** event contains within it the **seed** of an **equal** or **greater benefit**.

—*Napoleon Hill*
Bestselling author and motivational speaker

Jack: I thought my world had ended when the company I worked for unexpectedly shut down. Before that, I had unlimited support, I was working with an exciting team of bright young people, and I really enjoyed my work. Then out of the blue, it was all gone.

At first I was upset at the decision, but while attending a workshop at the W. Clement & Jesse V. Stone Foundation in Chicago, I shared my dilemma with the leader, who happened to be vice president of the foundation. As a result, he offered me a job. But it gets better! They even gave me more money, an unlimited budget, and the opportunity to attend any workshop or convention that I wanted. And now I was working directly with W. Clement Stone, who introduced me to these Success Principles to begin with! Without the loss of that job, this book wouldn't exist, and I certainly wouldn't be the person I am today.

It's odd how life works out when you do your part by living with a positive attitude. Sometimes, when we're facing what looks like a crisis, it can really just be an important turning point in our lives. When "something bad" happens, remember that everything has within it the seed of something better.

Try looking for the upside instead of the downside. No matter how grim things may seem at the moment, there is almost always something positive that will come of it . . . *if* you're looking for it and expecting it. Ask yourself, "What could be beneficial about this event?" If you can't come up with an answer right away, ask the question again . . . and again . . . and again—with an open mind—and you *will* find it.

Things turn out **best** for those
who make the **best** of the **way things turn out**.

—*John Wooden*
Arguably the most successful college basketball coach in history, author, and speaker

Cara, 30, (Vancouver, WA): I wasn't outgoing or confident. Most people would have said that I was very shy—at least compared to my sister, Mairin. She was thirty-nine seconds older than me, and even though she was my identical twin, I still looked up to her a lot. She was confident, funny, and charismatic. Everybody loved her.

But the day after our eighteenth birthday, that all changed. Her new boyfriend had picked her up from the mall, and I was following in a car be-  hind them. He wanted to race me, but I refused. He drove past me going really fast, lost control of his car, and slammed into another car. I watched in horror as rescue crews tried to save my sister, but there was nothing they could do. That day, my friend, my role model . . . my sister died.

I wanted to wake up and realize this was only a bad dream. How could this happen to me? My family? Mairin? How could I live without her?

For months, I denied the fact that anything good could come from my sister's death. I focused on all the things that we could no longer do together; how hard it was to deal with her death; and how my life would never amount to anything now that she was gone. As long as I believed this, I never found anything positive. Eventually, I learned that nothing was going to change until I changed the way I looked at the situation . . . until I changed what I focused on. As hard as it was, I started searching for anything positive about the situation. Within a couple weeks, I began to see things from a different perspective, and I realized that my sister would've wanted me to prevent the same thing from happening to other people. I felt a sense of purpose and set out on a mission.

The following year, I put my fear aside and offered to speak to our high school for the graduation assembly and describe the whole story. The students and faculty were so moved that they suggested I speak at other schools, so I did. I started getting requests from schools around the country and letters from students started pouring in. It was amazing. To date, I've spoken to more than 1 million students in four countries. My confidence has grown immensely, and I've been able to make a difference along the

LIFE IS WHAT YOU MAKE OF IT.

way. I am a completely different person than I was ten years ago, but it all started because I looked for the best in a tragic situation. As weird as it sounds, good things can come from seemingly bad events if you have the right outlook and choose a positive focus.

We're sure that you, too, can think back to several times in your life when you thought that what happened was the end of the world—you had to move, you crashed your car, you didn't get the class you wanted—but later you realized that it was a blessing in disguise.

The trick is to realize that whatever you're going through right now is going to turn out better in the future. So look for the lemonade in the lemons. The sooner you look for the good, the sooner you will find it. And if you expect that something good is coming, you will be less upset and discouraged while you're waiting for it.

5.3 Searching for the Best Creates New Opportunities

Matt Collins received some heartbreaking news at age sixteen, but his optimism and perseverance allowed him to create an alternative outcome. Here's his story:

I attended Esperanza High School in Anaheim, and I was excited because our school had one of the best baseball programs in California. Before the season started, I had a talk with my coach, and he told me that I would not see any playing time in my position as a pitcher. I was devastated. Up until this time, I had played in many competitive leagues and enjoyed being a starting athlete, but now I was about to be cut from the team.

Instead of getting angry or disappointed, I started to think. I wanted to know what I really loved about baseball. I came to the conclusion that it was really the friendships and the camaraderie of my teammates that I enjoyed the most. I decided to embrace the decision my coach had made, but I was not going to let this one piece of news discourage me.

The next day, I spoke with my coach again and told him how much I loved baseball and how I wanted to stay involved in the program. He thought for a minute and asked me if I would be a scout for the team. My job would consist of attending the games of the teams we would play the following week and videotaping them while taking notes about different strategies we could use to beat them.

I took the job, and I did it the best I could. I took notes on every batter and every pitcher, their strengths and their weaknesses. Each week we would meet in the clubhouse and review all of the information I had collected. The team was so prepared that they really looked forward to my reports. I had become an important part of the team—an opportunity that I created because I didn't give up initially.

Together, we ended up going all the way to the semifinals in the CIF playoffs. At the year-end banquet, the coaches called me up to the podium and gave a really nice speech about my love for the sport, their appreciation of my attitude, and how I used my talents to help the entire team succeed.

I had a lot of fun that year, and as I think back now, I can see how that one decision to remain positive has changed my life. I still stop by and see the coaches today, and we'll remain good friends for the rest of our lives.

54) Sometimes It's Hiding, but the Best Is Always There

When **life hands** you a **lemon**, squeeze it and **make lemonade**.

—*W. Clement Stone*
Self-made multimillionaire and former publisher of *Success Magazine*

Imagine your plane is shot down, and you become a prisoner of war for seven years in some of the most crude, harsh, and torturous conditions known to mankind. Well, Captain Jerry Coffee didn't imagine it; he lived through it. He was beaten, became malnourished, and was kept in solitary confinement for years. But if you ask him how he feels about the experience, he would tell you that it was the most powerful transformational experience of his life.

As he entered his cell for the first time, he didn't whine or complain. Instead he asked himself, "How can I use this experience to my advantage?" He told us that he decided to see it as an opportunity rather than a tragedy—an opportunity to get to know both himself and God (the only two beings he'd be spending time with) better.

Captain Coffee spent many hours each day thinking about his life. He began to see patterns that did and didn't work in his life. Over time, he slowly analyzed himself until he eventually came to understand himself at the deepest levels. He fully accepted himself and developed a profound sense of compassion for himself and all of humanity. As a result, he is one of the wisest, most humble, and peaceful people we have ever met.

Of course, he quickly admits he never wants to do it again, but at the same time he also says that he would not trade his experience as a prisoner of war for anything, for it has made him who he is today. Captain Coffee believed that there was "good" to be found in every situation—and his life is evidence that he is absolutely right. If you think that everyone and everything shows up in your life for a reason, then you will begin to see every event—no matter how difficult or challenging—as a chance to become stronger and wiser. You'll find that every step in life can be a step closer to your dreams.

TIP 1: You might want to make a small sign or poster with the question, *"What potential opportunity is this experience offering me?"* Then put the sign on your desk or above your computer so you will be constantly reminded to look for the good in every event.

TIP 2: Although it's a little corny, this method does work. You can train yourself to recognize the best by repeating something like this: "I believe the world is giving me the experiences I need to become the best I can be." It will sound and feel odd at first, but if you do this regularly, you'll see for yourself how powerful it can be.

Use whatever method works for you, but be sure to make an effort to look for the best in every situation. The only way you'll be able to reach your potential is if you're able to see the positive lessons in all of the experiences that life offers us each day. You have to see the best to *be* the best.

MY "TO-DO" LIST

☑ Search for the best in every situation until it becomes a habit.

☑ Remember that the benefits of a seemingly negative experience may not show up right away. But if I look for the positives, I will always find them.

☑ Understand that my mind will search for whatever it believes because it does not like to be proven wrong. This is why it's important that I expect the best and search for positive messages.

☑ Regularly ask myself these questions: "What could be beneficial about this event that I have not noticed yet?" or "What potential opportunity is this experience offering me?"

Unleash the Power of Goal-Setting

Each of us has a **fire in our hearts** for something.
It's our **goal in life** to **find it** and to **keep it lit**.

—*Mary Lou Retton*
American gymnast and first female gymnast outside Eastern Europe to win the "Olympic All-Around Athlete" title

Don't worry. This isn't going to be your usual "set goals to be successful" kind of speech.

Kent: When I was growing up, many people told me that I should "get clear on what I wanted and then set a specific, measurable goal." Well, it may have been a good suggestion, but I heard it so many times that I eventually just shut it out and rolled my eyes every time I heard the phrase "goal-setting." This topic continued to come up in conversations and in all the books I was researching. I couldn't escape from it!

One day, I got sick of seeing it, hearing about it, and being told to "Just do it!" On that day, I finally decided to try this concept to see if it really worked. Well, I wrote down everything I could think of and turned it into a goal. To my surprise, I began to excel in school, sports, and other parts of my life. My business at the time grew fast, and most importantly, I became a more confident person because my outcome was clear and I could see my progress. Something unexplainable happens when you write a goal, and everybody I've spoken to who has put this principle to the test says the same thing.

Quite simply, this could be the most important chapter in the book . . . if you let it! You're not going to want to miss this because goal-setting gives you the opportunity to create your future in advance. How cool is that?!

(6.1) clarity is power

The brain is a goal-seeking mechanism. In other words, to get the most out of ourselves, we need exciting reasons to work hard, stay focused, and get out of bed every morning. Just like a bicycle, we, too, must be moving toward a destination in order to stay upright and work effectively. Otherwise, we fall down, get lost, become frustrated, and then eventually lose our motivation to keep going.

When a goal is set, you set your mind in motion to work day and night to come up with ways to make it happen. But just like the inner GPS system, we need a destination in order to tap into this unique ability.

To make sure your goals unleash all of your potential, they must be measurable (in quantities such as pages, pounds, dollars, points, etc.), and they must have specific times and dates of completion. Here are two examples. Which one is better?

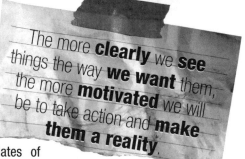
*The more **clearly** we **see** things the way **we want** them, the more **motivated** we will be to take action and **make them a reality**.*

a) I will get good grades.

b) On June 12, 2008, I will have an A in _____ (*list classes*) **with a GPA of** _____(*indicate grade-point average*).

If you chose "a," pay *very* close attention to this chapter. If you chose "b," we congratulate you. It is much more empowering because we are crystal-clear about what needs to be done, and we have a deadline. Here's another example.

a) I will weigh 135 pounds by 5:00 PM on June 30.

b) I will lose ten pounds.

That's right, you guessed it! The answer is "a." Be as specific as possible with all aspects of your goals. Include the make, model, year, features, size, weight, shape, form, texture . . . any specific details. Remember, vague goals produce vague results. For example, if your goal is, "I will lose weight," then you could lose one pound and still achieve your goal—but that result will not change your life.

There is a big difference between those who *hope* for a better life and those who have a better life. You can notice the difference just by listening to the way people talk. When there are no criteria for measurement, it's not a goal—it's just something you want, wish, or prefer . . . it's really just a "good idea." But if you want to engage your brain to help you create a better life, then the goal must be specific. Always answer these two questions in your goal—how much and by when?

Good Idea	Empowering Goal
I'd like more friends.	By August 20, 2008, I will have joined two clubs, organizations, or teams to surround myself with people who share my interests.
I want a car.	I will own a silver 2001 Volkswagon Jetta by January 1, 2008.
I'd like to do well in sports.	I will have scored ten points a game by the end of the season on November 15, 2008, and will be voted MVP of my team.
I want some more spending money.	I will apply for eight jobs and make a courtesy follow-up call for each application by June 1, 2008.

62 Stretch Yourself

Shoot for the **moon**! Even if you miss it you'll **land among the stars**.

—*Author Unknown*

Would you want to repeat third grade again? Would you take basic swimming lessons if you already knew how to swim? Would you re-take the same test you just received 100% on? No way! Why? Because you already know you can do these things. There wouldn't be any challenge. Similarly, it's sad to see people write out goals that don't provide any real challenge to them.

Sometimes a real simple goal is a good place to start, but we also need to write goals that will stretch us to become more of who we can be. It helps to have some goals that require us to grow in order to achieve them. It's okay if some of your goals make you a little uncomfortable. Why? Because the ultimate purpose of goal-setting is not necessarily to just get a result, but rather to shape our characters and grow as individuals.

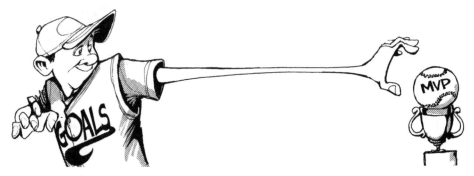

Who we become in pursuit of our goals is the most important part. Big goals help us acquire new skills, expand our vision of what's possible, build new relationships, learn to overcome our fears, and discover what we're really made of. That's the exciting part!

You would never know. What a shame that would be! When we set big goals and charge after them, we often end up surprising ourselves. We say things like, "Wow, that was me? I did that? Cool." Or "Geez, I didn't even know I could do that!" Make your goals realistic, but be sure they also challenge you. There is a fine line here, but you will know what's right for you. Just don't make the fatal mistake of underestimating yourself.

A **dream** is your **creative vision** for **your life** in the future. You must **break out** of your **current comfort zone** and become **comfortable** with the **unfamiliar** and the **unknown**.

—*Denis Waitley*
Author and speaker on high performance and human achievement

Not long ago, we interviewed an incredible individual. Dean Karnazes is the international bestselling author of *Ultra-Marathon Man*, and many people consider him to be the fittest man alive! We found his story to be really inspiring. He knows what it means to set a goal that "stretches" himself. We'll let Dean tell the story:

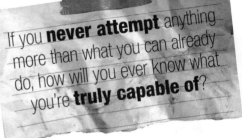

If you **never attempt** anything more than what you can already do, how will you ever know what you're **truly capable of**?

I got sick of living the life that everybody told me I "should" be living, so one day I decided to start living life on my own terms. Frustrated with my job, I came home, put on my shoes, and just started running . . . and running and running. It felt so good to be free. It was the first time I ran in a decade. That first day I ended up running thirty miles without stopping. Yes, I had rediscovered my old passion—and it felt so good I set a goal to support myself and my family from my running alone. I had no idea how I was going to do it, but one thing was for sure: I was committed.

I trained hard every day to get in shape. Since I wanted to be the best I could be, I knew I would have to set some really big goals for myself. A couple of my goals were:

❈ **Run a 135-mile ultra-marathon across Death Valley in 120-degree temperatures.**
❈ **Swim across the San Francisco Bay.**
❈ **Win the Badwater Ultra-Marathon (considered the toughest footrace in the world).**
❈ **Run a marathon (over twenty-six miles) to the South Pole in -40 degrees.**

Again, I had no idea how I was going to accomplish these goals, but they definitely motivated me to work hard. Today, I am really grateful to say that I have accomplished all of them. Shortly after completing these goals, I set one of my biggest objectives: to run fifty marathons in fifty states in fifty consecutive days. Nobody had done anything like this before so, to be honest, I was a little nervous and doubtful. I didn't even know if the human body could be pushed to those limits! But there was only one way to find out . . . so I just started training and preparing to give it my best shot.

I completed that goal one year ago, and it felt great! But for me, life is not all about accomplishing goals. Sure, it feels good to succeed, but the greatest reward for me was learning more about myself and what I was capable of doing. I went from somebody stuck in a boring job to somebody who was living his dreams! It's strange to think that I never would have done any of it if I hadn't first set some big goals that really challenged me to grow.

The only regret I have is not doing this earlier in my life. I challenge you to set big goals that help you break through your comfort zone. Life is too short to chase small dreams that allow us to stay comfortable and safe. Just go for it! You'll probably surprise yourself like I did. Only by stepping out into the unknown and stretching ourselves can we really discover what our true potential is.

6.3 Revisit Your Goals

Don't leave your goals crumpled in your backpack, buried in your binder, or collecting dust in a desk. They need some loving, too! Once you've written down all of your goals, both large and small, the next step is to continually reactivate your enthusiasm and creativity by reviewing your list each day.

Read the list (out loud with passion and enthusiasm) one goal at a time. Close your eyes and picture each goal as if it were already accomplished. What would it feel like if you had accomplished each goal? This may sound like "fluff" right now, but psychologists have proven that this works. They call this process "structural tension." Put simply, here's how it works: Your brain wants to close the gap between your current life and your goals (the way you'd like your life to be), so it will search for ways to close that gap.

Our brains are amazing instruments. The problem is, most people feel "stuck" or dissatisfied with their lives because they haven't empowered their brains to help them change. They haven't designed their lives the way they want them to be or created an imaginary future that inspires them. Here's a tip at no extra charge: *Don't be one of those people!* Just like nobody can do your push-ups for you, nobody can set *your* goals either.

Once you have set your goals and activated your brain to help you make them real, return the favor by doing something each day that will move you closer to your goal.

64 Action Steps

If you want to **be happy**, set a goal that commands your thoughts, **liberates your energy,** and **inspires your hopes**.

—*Andrew Carnegie*
Businessman, philanthropist, and multimillionaire

Since we have so many things that pull our attention in a million different directions, we need to keep guiding ourselves back to our goals. Here are some tools and techniques that can help us do this:

Index Cards

Write your goals on 3" x 5" index cards. Cards make it quick and easy to review your goals. We both keep goal cards next to our beds. We then go through the cards in the morning when we wake up and at night before we go to sleep. Carrying the card in your wallet is another great way to remind yourself.

Day Planner

If you have a diary or a school day planner, write your goals on some of the pages and then write reminders during the week to review them some more. The objective here is to constantly keep your goals in front of you. When Olympic decathlon gold medalist Bruce Jenner asked a room full of Olympic hopefuls if they had a list of written goals, everyone raised his or her hand. When he asked how many of them had that list with them at that moment, only one person raised his hand. That person was Dan O'Brien. Dan went on to win the gold medal in decathlon at the 1996 Olympics in Atlanta. Never underestimate the power of setting goals.

Goals Book

Another powerful way to speed up achieving your goals is to create a three-ring binder or a scrapbook journal. Then create a separate page for each goal. Write the goal at the top of the page and then illustrate it with pictures, words, and phrases (cut out of magazines, catalogues, and travel brochures) that depict the goal you want to achieve. As you come up with new goals and desires, simply start another page and add it to your Goals Book. Don't forget to review the pages of your Goals Book every day.

Write a Letter to Yourself

"What? Are you crazy!? I'm not *that* desperate!" It's okay, this is a different kind of letter. Hey, even Bruce Lee, arguably the greatest martial artist to have ever lived, wrote a letter to himself. He truly understood the power of goal-setting. At Planet Hollywood in New York City, hanging on the wall is a letter written by Bruce dated January 9, 1970. Bruce wrote, "By 1980, I will be the best known Oriental movie star in the United States and will have secured $10 million. And in return I will give my very best acting I could possibly give every single time I'm in front of the camera, and I will live in peace and harmony." Bruce made three films, and then in 1973 filmed *Enter the Dragon*. The movie was a huge success and achieved worldwide fame for Bruce Lee. His dream became his reality . . . and he beat his 1980 deadline by seven years!

Write Yourself a Check

Around 1987, Jim Carrey was a struggling young comic trying to make his way in Los Angeles. One evening, he drove his old Toyota up to Mulholland Drive, and while he was looking over the city and dreaming of his future, he wrote himself a check for $10 million, dated it "Thanksgiving 1995," and kept it in his wallet from that day forth. The rest, as they say, is history. Carrey's optimism and perseverance paid off, and by 1995, after the huge box-office success of *Ace Ventura: Pet Detective*, *The Mask*, and *Dumb & Dumber*, his asking price had risen to $20 million per picture. When Carrey's father died in 1994, he placed the $10 million check he had written to himself into his father's coffin as a tribute to the man who had both started and nurtured his dreams of being a star.

6.5 Triple Threat

We can do **anything** we want to do
if **we stick** to it **long enough**.

—*Helen Keller*
Deaf-blind American author, activist, and lecturer

As soon as a goal is set, three things often emerge that stop most people dead in their tracks. We call these challenges the *Triple Threat*. However, once you know that these three things are just part of the process, then you can treat them as what they are—just "things to handle"—rather than letting them stop you.

The *Triple Threat*, the three obstacles to success, are:

1. **considerations**
2. **fears**
3. **roadblocks**

Most people are surprised when these three visitors show up at their doorsteps. They thought their journey was simply going to be a piece of cake. Everything was going to work out perfectly as planned. We wish! The truth is, life is full of little challenges, and those who ultimately succeed are those who can rise above these challenges. Period.

If you think about it, a goal is a challenge, right? Basically, we make a decision to put ourselves to the test by striving to make our lives better by reaching a specific objective. With any challenge, there are going to be obstacles. Isn't that fair to say? This is just the way life works. So try not to be taken by surprise or discouraged when you encounter

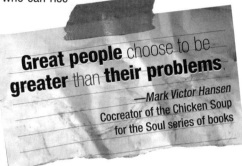

Great people choose to be **greater** than **their problems**.

—*Mark Victor Hansen*
Cocreator of the Chicken Soup for the Soul series of books

a little friction on the road to success. It might just be life testing you to see how bad you really want something.

1. Considerations

Let's say you want to bring all of your grades up to an A within the next three months. Within moments, you start thinking, "Oh, but I'll have to work twice as hard." Or, "I won't be able to spend as much time hanging out with my friends." Or, "What if I put in all of this time and don't get A's?" Or . . . The list goes on. These are all considerations.

You can see why so many people "talk themselves out of something." They're not lacking in ability; they just continually hear negative feedback over and over again—they literally brainwash themselves! But understand this: Everybody—we repeat, *everybody*—has *considerations* in some form or another. No one is 100% confident all of the time. But those who reach their goals treat these "considerations" not as stoppers, but as aids in getting us mentally prepared for the obstacles that might lie ahead.

Keep in mind, considerations can be useful if you let them show you what has been stopping you in the past. Now that you're aware of them, you can confront them and move forward because you'll find that most of these thoughts are *not* based on fact.

2. Fears

It doesn't matter how brave you are; we all have fears. In this case, fears are the feelings you might experience, such as rejection, failure, embarrassment, loneliness, and physical pain. The key thing to remember is that fears are just part of the process.

Trust your **hopes,**
not your **fears.**

—Author Unknown

Allow the fear to cautiously guide you; never let it take complete control. Becoming successful is not about getting rid of fear; it's about learning to read the specific messages that the fear is offering so we can then act accordingly. Remember, fear is really just focusing on what you don't want to happen. Instead, interrupt yourself and imagine how you do want things to be. Visualize everything working out the way you want. See it, feel it, and believe it. If you do this often enough, you will build the confidence you need to face your fear and continue to take bold steps forward.

3. Roadblocks

Finally, you'll probably come across some roadblocks. These are barriers that the world may throw at us—external circumstances that are usually out of our control. But how we handle them is completely up to us.

Potential roadblocks:

- ※ **Nobody wants to join you on your project.**
- ※ **You don't have enough money to start your business.**
- ※ **You don't have a bike for your paper route.**
- ※ **You don't know somebody who could sign your music band.**
- ※ **You don't have the right equipment to play the sport you want.**
- ※ **You don't have a car, and nobody can drive you where you need to go.**

The interesting thing about roadblocks is that they are never permanent; they're only temporary. If you're committed enough, you can find a way around the obstacle in your path.

Taylor, 24 (Salina, KS): I've always loved animals, so when I was sixteen I turned my idea into a written goal to become a zoologist. At first, I was really excited because I felt like I was making a lot of progress. Once I set my goal, what I had to do to reach it became clearer to me. I made some good contacts, spoke with some respected zoologists, and got some great advice. Sounds easy enough, right? Well, I did what I could, but then I faced some unexpected challenges.

How was I going to get to the zoo for an internship? I didn't have a car, my parents were always working, and the bus station was too far away. I didn't have the money to buy all the books and go to the classes. And then my doubt started to creep in. What if I'm not good enough—or smart enough? Roadblocks were all I saw. I wish I could say that I kept trying, but I didn't. I got overwhelmed and scared. Then I convinced myself that I didn't really want to become a zoologist anyway (a complete lie).

For five years, I ignored my goal. In college I did what my dad suggested and majored in business. Then, one semester before my graduation, I attended a business workshop at my college career day. As I was sitting in the crowd listening to the keynote speaker, I realized that my real passion was not business. It was a scary feeling. I knew that my real passion was still zoology. I changed my major, attended my friends' graduations (an awkward feeling), and went back to school for another two years to get the training I needed.

I rewrote my original goal, got my degree, and started to make it happen. Two weeks after graduation, I recognized that the same roadblocks I faced at age sixteen were still there. I laughed to myself as I finally realized that roadblocks are just a part of the process—and they won't disappear until I face them. So that's exactly what I did. I conquered these roadblocks—and many others.

Now, I'm a few weeks away from being a certified zoologist, and I couldn't be happier. Learn from my mistakes and don't look at roadblocks as dead ends. I could have saved myself A LOT of time, energy, and frustration if I continued to pursue my goal the *first* time I faced challenges. There is always a way to overcome roadblocks if you're committed and creative. Take it from me: Don't give up.

We could not have said it better. Thanks, Taylor! Roadblocks can come in different forms. It may rain when you planned a day at the beach, your friend might move away, your new school may not have the best art program, you may not get the teacher you wanted, your parents may not give you all of the support you think you need, and so on. These roadblocks are simply real-world circumstances you need to deal with in order to move forward. Many of these roadblocks may be out of your control, but they're never dead ends . . . unless you choose to give up.

Unfortunately, when these considerations, fears, and roadblocks come up, most people see them as stop signs. But, in reality, they're just a normal part of the process. In fact, if they don't appear, it means you haven't set a goal that's big enough to stretch yourself and grow.

6.6 Mastery is the Goal

You want to **set a goal** that's big enough that in the **process of achieving it**, you **become someone worth becoming**.

—*Jim Rohn*
Self-made millionaire, success coach, and philosopher

It's not about the money, cars, clothes, houses, boats, power, or fame. No, we haven't lost it! We've just seen far too many people betray themselves while chasing after material things. The truth is, at the end of our lives, we leave all of these things behind—no matter how nice they are! And many of these "things" can be taken away from us anyway—sometimes in the blink of an eye!

What matters most in life—and any genuinely successful person will say the same thing—is who we become as individuals in the process of accomplishing our goals. Did we challenge ourselves enough? Did we reach our potential? Did we make a significant difference in someone's life? Did we leave this world a better place? The answers to these questions are what matter most.

The ultimate benefit of overcoming the *Triple Threat* and achieving our goals is that we get to enjoy the personal development and growth we've achieved in the process. It may sound corny, but it's absolutely true. Who we are is our greatest asset. As good ol' Lance Armstrong says, "It's not about the bike." He's right. It's what's inside of us that matters most. Set goals that challenge you to expand, do amazing things, become an outstanding person, and ultimately inspire others to do the same.

6.7 DO It NOW

So this is it. Now it's time to start designing your future . . . the way you want it to be. Before you go on to the next chapter, take a few minutes right now to make a list of goals you want to accomplish. Becoming crystal clear on what you want in life is one of the most important steps to becoming successful. This is your chance to do just that. Below is a goal-setting template that you can use to piece your own goals together.

1. I will _____ by _____ (day, month, year).

2. What will I miss out on if I don't follow through and make a full commitment to my goal?

3. If I reach this goal, my life will be better because . . .

4. What steps should I take or what habits should I create to achieve my goal faster and easier? _____

5. What is one action I can take *today* that will bring me closer to achieving my goal? _____

> There has never been and never will be a **better time** to start designing your **future** than right **now.**

If you are **bored with life**—if you don't get up every morning with a burning desire to do things— you **don't have enough goals**.

—Lou Holtz
Award-Winning NCAA Football Coach

Remember, one goal is never enough. The more goals you have, the more you empower yourself to fully use your creativity, passion, and resources. Make a commitment to yourself to do something each day that will move you closer to where you want to be. All of those little steps add up. Eventually, you will get there. The trick is to get started. Don't delay; make it happen! And start *now*!

MY "TO-DO" LIST

☑ Write my goals on index cards, in my diary, or in my Goals Book.

☑ Keep a pocket-size goal list.

☑ Write myself a letter, or write myself a check.

☑ Write goals that have two things: a measurable quantity and a specific deadline.

☑ Understand that there is a difference between a good idea and an empowering measureable goal.

☑ Write not only small and simple goals but also goals that will stretch me to become more of who I am.

☑ Look at my goals regularly to remind myself of my overall objectives.

☑ Prepare for the *Triple Threat* (considerations, fears, and roadblocks) by realizing that these three obstacles are not stop signs. They are just part of the process.

☑ Remember that the real goal is not to attain a material reward. What matters most is who I become in the process of accomplishing my goals.

☑ Take action! Do something each day that will move me closer to my goals.

Release the Brakes

The only real thing **stopping you** from reaching **your dreams** is **you**.

Let's pretend you want to bike to your friend's house about a mile away. You jump on your bike, start heading down the street, and notice that it's difficult to pedal. When you look down, you realize that the brakes are stuck on full compression. What do you do now?

Do you pedal harder and harder to overcome the drag of the brakes? Of course not! You'd simply adjust the settings, release the brakes, and with no extra effort, you would start to go faster.

Brakes are designed for one thing: to slow you down. But most people drive through life with their psychological emergency brakes on. They hold themselves back because they constantly say, "I'm not capable of this." Or "I'm not good for . . ." They see negative images of themselves struggling, messing things up, or failing to reach their goals. As a result of these mental brakes and restrictions, they keep themselves stuck in the rut of their comfort zone.

QUESTION: What is a "comfort zone"?

Answer: A comfort zone is that place where we feel safe and secure—a place where we can avoid worry, fear, or failure.

QUESTION: So what's wrong with *that*?

Answer: As long as we remain there, we cannot grow, experience new things, or achieve any of our challenging goals.

Everything you **want** is just **outside** of your **comfort zone.**

—Robert Allen
Multimillionaire, author, and motivational speaker

TIP: You will know where the boundaries of your comfort zone are by paying attention to the way you feel. When you're working toward your goals and you feel fear, uneasiness, or butterflies in your stomach, that means you're on the edge of your comfort zone. When the outcome will be beneficial, be willing to face your fears and go for it.

People who stay in their comfort zones live their lives with their brakes on. When they try to achieve their goals, their negative thoughts and images about themselves always cancel out their good intentions—no matter how hard they try. Sadly, they don't even know their brakes are on!

Successful people, on the other hand, have discovered how to recognize when their brakes are on and how to release them, whatever they may be. They've learned that only increasing their willpower is not enough. We also must let go of our limiting beliefs and negative self-images, replacing them with positives so we can achieve success without burning ourselves out.

7.1 steppin' out

The term "comfort zone" is actually misleading. In the short term, the comfort zone feels good because it is stress-free and offers no challenge, but in the long term it's a (self-imposed) prison. Believe us . . . we've met far too many people who have lived their whole lives in their comfort zones. But the cushions always wear out because we've found that these same people feel frustrated, depressed, and regretful in the long term.

Sometimes, we are "trained" to accept our comfort zone as realistic boundaries of our potential. But beware! When this happens, we severely limit ourselves. A popular *National Geographic* show explained how baby elephants are confined to a very small space beginning at birth. The trainer uses a rope to tie one leg to a wooden post planted deep in the ground. The elephant's movement is restricted to the length of that rope, and that area becomes—yep!—the elephant's comfort zone. At first, the baby elephant will try to break the rope, but it soon learns the rope is too strong and will stop trying.

When the elephant grows to be a five-ton giant, of course it could easily break the rope, but sadly it doesn't even try because it now believes that the rope cannot be broken. And so, even the largest elephants are easily confined by the puniest little rope.

Now let's look at *your* ropes. Have you been trained (by somebody else or by yourself) to believe things about yourself that aren't true . . . or things that keep you in your comfort zone? We're sure you don't want to be an elephant confined by a puny rope, right? Be sure to remember that our "ropes" may be invisible. It can be difficult to see our limiting beliefs and those negative self-images we develop of ourselves, but whether we're consciously aware of them or not, they are as powerful as a steel chain.

The good news is that you can change your comfort zone. Here's how:

1. **Change the way you talk to yourself.** Make a decision not to put yourself down by saying "I can't" or "I'm not good enough" or "I don't deserve it," etc. As soon

as you catch yourself saying this, replace it with a positive. You may want to repeat to yourself, *"I can; I am; and I will!"* Allow yourself to know how grateful you are for already having what you want, doing what you want, and being the way you want.

2. **Visualize your life the way you want it.** Create powerful and compelling images of yourself doing the things you want to do and being the person you want to be.

3. **Change your behavior.** Commit to taking that first step toward your goals. The more often you take action, the more confidence you will build. Remember, the first step is usually the most difficult. But if you can get past the first step, you're on your way—you've busted that rope!

Belinda, 16 (Lexington, SC): I never thought I was living in my comfort zone, but I guess I was. I'd always get to a certain point—almost to success—and then something would happen that would stop me from going any further. I didn't realize that the "thing" stopping me was actually myself.

I would subconsciously tell myself that I didn't deserve success or that I wasn't really capable of achieving what I wanted. But that wasn't all. I discovered that I had mental pictures in my head of me messing up on school tests, on the basketball court, and on my driver's license test, etc. It was like I was rehearsing failure. It was really bizarre! I didn't even know I was doing it. Subconsciously, I would not let myself succeed. When I found this out, I made an effort to change my self-talk. Before going to bed, I would visualize how I wanted the next day to turn out.

Since I was trying to change old habits, it took a few weeks of thinking new thoughts and taking new actions, but eventually my subconscious "ropes" got weaker and weaker until I finally started to succeed. I learned that sometimes we can hold ourselves in our comfort zone because we have an unconscious fear of success. I'm just glad I realized this when I did.

For me, thinking the right thoughts and constantly seeing what I want is one of the best to ways to break free of old habits or beliefs that hold me back. If you want to be successful, then try what I learned: *Start thinking about what you're thinking about.* Make sure you release any mental brakes that might be keeping you stuck in the same place.

72 THE ENDLESS LOOP

If you **don't get** the **result you want**, try something else.
If that **doesn't work, try something else.**

—*Anthony Robbins*
Bestselling author and inspirational speaker

o you ever feel like you're *stuck*? The truth is, we're never really stuck. But when we recreate the same experiences over and over by thinking the same thoughts, keeping the same limiting beliefs, and doing the same things, we get sucked into a loop that keeps us in an endless downward spiral. No wonder we feel "stuck"!

*Whatever **we think** about, we **bring about**.*

Our limiting thoughts create limiting self-perceptions, which in turn cause us to do things that don't help us. Then we just end up reinforcing our original limiting thought.

Take this example. Let's say you have to give a presentation in front of the class, and you're worried about messing up and embarrassing yourself. What happens? This thought then creates a picture of you forgetting a key point in your speech. This image now creates a feeling of fear. The fear then clouds your thinking, which makes you forget one of your key points, which reinforces your initial thought: *"I can't give speeches! See, I knew I would forget what I was supposed to say. I just can't speak in front of groups."* And so we find ourselves in that endless loop.

> The significant **problems** we face
> **cannot be solved** by the same **level of thinking**
> that **created them**.
>
> —*Albert Einstein*
> Physicist, inventor, philosopher, and Nobel Prize winner

Have you noticed that some coaches get the most out of their athletes while others don't? One reason points to that "endless loop" process we're talking about. A poor coach will tell you what you did wrong and then tell you not to do it again: "Don't drop the ball!!" Or "Don't miss the shot!" What happens next? The images you see in your head are the pictures the coach just gave you: images of you dropping the ball and missing the shot! Naturally, your mind recreates what it just "saw" based on what it's been told. Not surprisingly, you walk on the court, drop the ball, and miss the shot.

What does the good coach do? He or she points out what could be improved, but will then tell you how you could or should perform: "I know you'll catch the ball perfectly this time," or "I can already see you making the shot." Sure enough, the next image in your mind is you *catching* the ball and *scoring* a goal.

FAILURE

FEAR CLOUDS YOUR THINKING

FEAR OF FAILING

I NEED TO GET OUT OF THIS CYCLE.

Once again, your mind makes your last thoughts, your last images, part of reality—but this time, that "reality" is positive, not negative.

Simple? You bet. A simple process with a massive effect on what we experience and how we perform. As long as we keep complaining about our current situation, our mind will focus on it. This is really important because: If we constantly talk about what we don't want and think about what we don't want, we will get more of . . . *what?* You guessed it: more of what we *don't* want. The good news is this also works in reverse. We can change this cycle by focusing on thinking and talking about what we *do want* to create—what we *do want* to happen.

(73) It's Affirmative!

powerful way to destroy your old comfort zone is to bombard your mind with new thoughts and images of great grades, a fit and healthy body, a big bank account, interesting friends, and peak performance in sports. Then, see all the things you want as though you already have them, as if they're already completed. This technique is called an *affirmation*.

Question: What's an *affirmation?*

Answer: It's a statement that describes a goal in its already-completed state.

Josslyn, 17 (Medford, OR): When I first heard about this idea of saying affirmations, I was thinking, "What the heck is this all about?!" For a long time, I didn't even try it. But I also struggled with building confidence, so eventually I decided to give it a shot.

I wasn't doing very well in school at the time, but I stopped telling myself that I was no good and began saying that I was already smart enough to improve my grades. As odd as it felt at the beginning to say this, over a couple of weeks I could definitely feel a new sense of confidence that I could actually achieve my goal. My affirmations helped me visualize my outcomes and stay motivated because I was constantly reminding myself of all the rewards of taking action and following through.

After a while, I really started to believe my affirmations were true. I think that's where the real power is—instead of just "hoping" I would improve my grades, I expected to do it. I definitely had more confidence than I would have without using affirmations. If you're doubtful about this, just give it a try. You have nothing to lose and everything to gain.

Affirmations give us the fuel, momentum, and positive reinforcement we need to pursue our goals. It may be unexplainable, but what matters is that this technique does get results. It may sound like a far-out concept—some people may even call it magical—but hey, it works. Take it from Jim Carrey himself. This what he said during a Movieline interview back in 1994:

> I've always believed in magic. When I wasn't doing anything in this town, I'd go up every night, sit on Mulholland Drive, look out at the city, stretch my arms and say, "Everybody wants to work with me. I'm a really good actor. I have all kinds of great movie offers." I'd just repeat these things over and over, literally convincing myself that I had a couple of movies lined up. I'd drive down that hill, ready to take on the world, going, "Movie offers are out there for me. I just don't hear them yet." It was like total affirmations. . . ."

(7.4) creating an Effective Affirmation

 eady to experience the power of affirmations for yourself? First, you have to create affirmations that are unique to YOU. There are seven guidelines that will help you create an effective affirmation:

1. **Start with the words** *I am.* The words *I am* are the most powerful words in the English language. They activate your mind as though you are giving it a direct command and calling yourself to action.

2. **Use the present tense.** Describe what you want as though it is already accomplished and you are enjoying it NOW.

3. **State it in the positive.** Affirm what you want (not what you *don't* want). Our subconscious minds do not understand words like *don't* and *no.* This means the statement, "Don't slam the door" is heard in our minds as "Slam the door." The mind thinks in pictures. When it hears "Don't slam the door," it has no picture of what not slamming a door looks like! It has no picture of "don't." Thus, ironically, these words create a picture of us slamming the door. This phenomenon is similar to the good-coach/poor-coach example we used earlier.

For the same reason, the phrase "I am no longer afraid to try out for the volleyball team" still creates images of being afraid. Instead, say, "I am enjoying the volleyball team tryouts." This way, your mind sees images of you *enjoying* your experience.

Wrong: I am no longer tempted to eat junk food.

Right: I am enjoying eating only healthy foods.

4. **Keep it brief.** Think of your affirmation as a TV advertisement. Pretend each word costs you $1,000. Make your affirmation short and memorable:

Goal: I will weigh 128 pounds by February 28, 2009.

Affirmation: I am feeling great with a weight of 128.

5. **Make it specific.** Vague affirmations produce vague results. If you want a specific outcome, make sure your affirmation is also specific. The more precise you are about what you want, the more you empower yourself to get the result you want.

Wrong: I am a student with good grades.

Right: I am a focused student celebrating my 4.0 GPA.

6. **Include an *"–ing"* action word.** The active verb will help your mind create images of you getting started and taking action immediately.

Wrong: I am honest.

Right: I am confidently expressing myself openly and honestly.

7. **Include at least one dynamic emotion or feeling word.** Include the feeling you would be experiencing if you already achieved the goal. Add a word such as *enjoying, happily, proudly, enthusiastically, creatively,* or *confidently.* You want to make this process fun, right? Well, these words will help you create your experience the way you'd like it to happen.

Wrong: I am training hard to be the best runner in my school.

Right: I am enjoying my success as the top runner in my school.

 7.5 DISCOVERING YOUR Affirmation

Don't worry. The journey of discovering your affirmations does not need to be a long, exhausting expedition. In fact, it should be simple and enjoyable. There are two main paths you can take:

1. **Revisit your goals.** Have another look at the goals you wrote in Chapter 7 and reword them as though you've already accomplished them (but don't forget to use the seven guidelines we just talked about). Here's an example:

Good idea: I want more spending money.

Goal: I will apply for eight jobs and make a courtesy follow-up call for each application by June 1, 2008.

Affirmation: I am now enjoying having all the extra spending money I need.

2. Visualize what you would like to create. Here's how:

    a. See things just as you would like them to be. Place yourself inside the picture and see things through your eyes. If you want to be MVP on your sports team, imagine yourself receiving the trophy on stage in front of your school.

    b. Hear the sounds you would be hearing if you had already achieved your goal.

    c. Feel the emotions you will feel when you have created what you want.

    d. Describe what you are experiencing in a brief statement, including what you are feeling.

    e. Now write down what you see, feel, and hear. Then edit it to fit the seven guidelines. Then voila! You have your own affirmation!

7.6 MY OWN GENIE

Kimia, 15 (Irvine, CA): My parents told me that if I strongly believe and persistently say to myself the things I want in life, they'll come to me much easier. I was skeptical at first. "How is this even possible?" I thought. I tried it anyway.

In the seventh grade, I was placed into an introduction to pre-algebra class, and I was disappointed because I knew I was capable of much more. My goal was to exceed expectations and show my teacher that I could enter algebra next year. With my goal in mind, I created an affirmation: "I'm very good at math, and next year I'm going to be in algebra." Along with practicing math problems daily, I constantly repeated my affirmation. By saying this, I boosted my self-esteem so I participated a lot in class and scored 100% on all my tests! I was stunned.

WOW, THAT'S ME?

At the end of the year, I got permission from my teacher to take algebra next year! I decided what I wanted, took action, and I received it! It was like a genie was granting my wishes. But the best part was learning that I was my own genie.

I found that the key to using affirmations is believing they work. I still have the piece of paper on which I wrote my original affirmation. It reminds me that anything is possible as long as I believe. I know it sounds cliché, but it really works. I now use this in all areas of my life. Whether my goals are simple or "out there," my affirmations guide me to success.

MY "TO-DO" LIST

☑ Avoid living life with the brakes on. Change any negative thought or image that I have about myself.

☑ Understand that I might have been programmed to mentally limit myself as I was growing up, but realize that most of these limits are not based on fact.

☑ Expand my comfort zone by changing what I say to myself, what I visualize in my head, and what I consistently do (my behavior).

☑ Realize that I'm never "stuck" in the same place; I just keep recreating the same experiences by doing the same things. When I change what I think, visualize, and do, I will get different results.

☑ Focus on what *I* want to do, be, and have because whatever I focus on, I will get more of. Whatever I think about, I bring about.

☑ Create my own affirmations to build self-confidence and to stimulate my subconscious mind to help me reach my goals.

☑ Review and repeat my affirmations to myself each day, throughout the day.

See What You Want. Get What You See

Imagination is everything.
It is the **preview to life's**
coming attractions.

—Albert Einstein
Physicist, inventor, philosopher, and Nobel Prize winner

lot of people thought Walt Disney was crazy when he described a "magic kingdom" that would span thousands of acres and attract millions of people each year. Disney did get to see many of his visions become reality, but unfortunately he passed away before seeing the opening of the Epcot Center. A reporter at the opening-day ceremony leaned over to Walt Disney's wife and said, "It's a shame that Walt couldn't be here today to see this." Without missing a beat, Mrs. Disney responded, "Oh, he saw it—long before any of us did."

That is the power of visualization, and it is the act of creating vivid pictures in your mind of what you want or the way you'd like things to be—and it may be the most underutilized success tool you have.

Many people have said, "I must see it to believe it." But others, including some of history's greatest leaders and innovators, clearly "believed" *first* and "saw" later. They envisioned great things *before* they actually saw those dreams come true.

The Egyptians envisioned some of the world's most monumental structures—and built them. The Romans envisioned an empire that spread from the Mediterranean to Syria—unheard of! Our Founding Fathers envisioned a free and independent democracy, the first of its kind in the world—and then they collaborated to create the United States of America. Despite the fact that scientists had "proven" the impossibility of man-made flight, the Wright brothers visualized themselves flying the first airplane. They built it and flew it. Edison saw an electric alternative to the candle and invented the light bulb. We could go on forever!

8.1 A World Of Vision

hen you think about it, the world we live in and every man-made object in it started as a dream or a vision: the chair you're sitting in, the book you're reading, the clothes you're wearing, the car you drive, the instrument you play—it was all just an idea at first. And that vision inspired people to create what they first "saw" only in their heads.

The clearer we envision things the way we want them, the more we increase our chances of having things turn out the way we want them to. Many people live their lives just *hoping* that things will turn out for the best, but rarely does life work to our advantage when we leave it all to chance. *Hoping* for the best is not enough. We need to imagine it and visualize it to accelerate the achievement.

Visualizing works in three powerful ways:

1. It activates your creativity.

2. It focuses your brain to help you notice any resources that are available to you.

3. It magnetizes and attracts the people, resources, and opportunities you need to achieve your goal.

Some people live their entire lives never using the power of visualizing. (No, thank you!) Helen Keller's leadership, courage, and persistence still serve as an inspiration to millions of people. She lost her eyesight (and hearing) at a young age, but she never lost the heart to succeed. Although she couldn't physically see, she quickly learned the significance of visualization.

Is there anything worse than being blind? Yes, a **man** with **no sight** and **no vision**. It is a **terrible** thing to **see** and have **no vision**.

—*Helen Keller*

8.2 The Proof

When you perform a task in real life, researchers have found that your brain uses the same identical processes it would use if you were only imagining the activity. In other words, our brain does not recognize the difference between (a) something we have actually done and (b) something we have *vividly imagined*.

Many people used to think that visualizing was just a phony concept that didn't work. But today, we have lots of proof about the power of visualization. A Harvard University study proved that students who visualized in advance performed tasks with nearly 100% accuracy, while students who didn't visualize achieved only 55% accuracy. Amazing!

Put simply, visualization makes the brain achieve more. And although we're not usually taught this in school, sport psychologists and peak-performance experts have been popularizing the power of visualization since the 1980s. Today, almost all Olympic and professional athletes use the power of visualizing.

Jack Nicklaus, the legendary golfer with more than 100 tournament victories and over $5.7 million in winnings, once said:

I never hit a shot, not even in practice, without having a very sharp, in-focus picture of it in my head. It's like a color movie. First I "see" where I want to finish, nice and white and sitting high on the bright green grass. Then the scene quickly changes, and I "see" the ball going there: its path, trajectory, and shape, even its behavior on landing. Then there's sort of a fade-out, and the next scene shows me making the kind of swing that will turn the previous images into reality.

No, you don't need to be an athlete to unleash the power of visualizing. Visualizing works with just about anything. When you imagine your goals as though they're already complete, it creates a conflict in your mind. Your brain now knows there is a gap between what it sees and what it currently has so it will do anything it can to close this gap by turning your visions into reality.

You'll find that you start waking up in the morning with new ideas about how you can reach your goals. You might catch yourself unexpectedly doing things that help you achieve. All of a sudden, you may find yourself raising your hand in class for the first time ever, volunteering to take on new assignments or responsibilities, speaking out in class or sporting events, saving money for things you want, or taking more risks in your personal life—all so you can get the most out of yourself and your life.

Legal Notice: The authors accept no responsibility for sudden changes that create a positive temperament, new levels of motivation, greater serenity throughout the day, etc. Some readers have reported experiencing "light-bulb moments" at random times—such as in the shower, in class, during sports practice, or while driving.

8.3 Picture Perfect

Let's do an experiment. We'll ask you one simple question, and your job is to remember the very first thing that comes to mind. The question is: *What do you think of when you hear the word "money"?*

Do you see each letter spelled out in your head appearing like this: m-o-n-e-y? Or do you see pictures of green pieces of paper, dollar signs, gold, vaults, etc.? The fact is, we all see images and pictures—*not* letters and words. Why? Because our mind does not think in words—it thinks only in pictures.

When you create pictures of your goals in your mind—A's on your report card, getting acknowledged at sports banquets, traveling around the world, pulling up to your brand-new house in your favorite car—your brain will work to achieve those things. But what happens if you constantly feed your mind negative, fearful, and anxious pictures? That's right: It will achieve those, too. How do you view yourself and your life? Hmmm . . .

The good news is that a *positive* mental image accompanied by an inspirational goal is far more powerful and influential than a negative mental image. This is why optimists achieve more and appear to be happier than pessimists. Because optimists constantly have positive thoughts and mental images in their minds, they constantly reinforce working on making constructive things happen in their lives.

Erika, 16 (Riverside, CA): For years, I heard about the power of visualizing. My field-hockey coach used to make the whole team do it the night before big games, but unfortunately, this never really worked very well for me so I decided to stop doing it.

About a year later, I learned about the power of the mind and mental images in my science class, and it inspired me to try it again. I would spend a couple of minutes each night visualizing myself taking tests, accomplishing the things on my to-do list, and seeing myself deal with any challenges I was facing.

The more I did this, the better I got at it. I noticed something interesting begin to happen. My mental pictures became clearer and brighter. I added certain sounds, scents, and sometimes music. Instead of just *thinking* about how I wanted things to be, I started *feeling* different as well—and that's what made the biggest change for me. Since my mind thought in pictures anyway, I just got better at creating more empowering images that made me *feel* better about myself and what I was about to do.

The more detailed and clear my visualizing became, the better my performance was. Not only did I know the outcome I wanted, but I felt motivated to do what was necessary to succeed—and confident that it would happen.

8.4 Training Yourself to "see"

When I **look** into the **future**, it's so **bright** it **burns my eyes**.

—*Oprah Winfrey*
Emmy Award-winning host of *The Oprah Winfrey Show*,
the highest-rated talk show in television history

Here's the best news of all: Visualizing is not only powerful, it's simple and 100% free! All you have to do is close your eyes and see your goals as already complete.

If your goal is to be the lead singer in a successful band, then close your eyes and imagine you're on stage in front of thousands of energetic people. If your goal is to score five shots in the league finals, then see the court in your head. *Be there!* Imagine yourself scoring the goals flawlessly.

And about that college you've dreamed of going to . . . imagine walking on its campus, socializing with your new classmates, and talking with your teachers. What does your classroom look like? What does the landscape look like? What is the weather like? What does your report card look like? How many friends will you have? Imagine as many details as possible. Remember: It's simple, it's powerful, and it's free.

Make the images as clear and as bright as possible. This goes for any goal you make. Each morning when you wake up and each night before going to sleep, read your goals and then visualize the exact outcome you want. Here are two tips to maximize your results:

1. **Appeal to the senses.** As we said in the last chapter, the more "real" we can make our visions, the more we empower our brain to make it a reality. When you visualize your goal, what do you hear? What do you smell? How much does your trophy weigh? What does the ball feel like? Who is next to you? Is there a breeze? What color is your shirt?

   If you want a specific "thing," like a car, then questions that appeal to the senses might include "What is the texture on the car's steering wheel? What do the seats feel like? What color is the interior? Does it have that new-car smell?"

Yes, we're talking about everything! The more, the better!

2. **Make it emotional.** At the bottom of it all, we really want the feelings we will get if we accomplish our goals. You see, it's not about the actual award, the recognition, or even the car—it's about how we feel once we have these things.

What emotions and sensations would you be feeling if you had already achieved your goal? Happiness? Freedom? Confidence? Love? Respect? Researchers know that when accompanied by intense emotions, an image or scene can stay locked in memory forever! We'll bet you remember the day your last pet died. And the day you graduated from elementary school, middle school, or high school. Why can you remember these events? Because you were experiencing intense emotions.

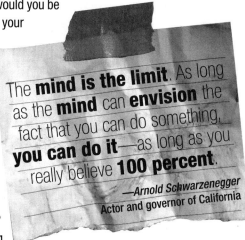

The **mind is the limit**. As long as the **mind** can **envision** the fact that you can do something, **you can do it**—as long as you really believe **100 percent**.

—*Arnold Schwarzenegger*
Actor and governor of California

You can bring the same emotional intensity to your visualizations by adding music, smells, bright colors—and, most importantly, personal feelings. Imagine how you would really feel once you achieved your goal. Exaggerate your feelings, if possible. The more passion, excitement, and energy you create, the more powerful your ultimate result will be.

(8.5) The Power of a Vision Board

Visualization is **daydreaming** with **a purpose**.

—*Bo Bennett*
Author, entrepreneur, and speaker

Not all people close their eyes and visualize images in bright, clear, three-dimensional pictures. If you don't, that's okay. This just means you don't really see an image as much as you just *think it*. It still works just as well. The key to the visualization exercises of imagining your goals as already complete is to do it often. As we said earlier, if you can *feel* the emotions, you will benefit the same as those who actually *see* the image.

If you want to help your brain make the visualizing process more powerful, use printed images. For example, if your goal is to travel to France, then find a picture of the Eiffel Tower and glue a picture of yourself at the bottom as if you were really there.

Jack: Several years ago, I did this with the Sydney Opera House, and within a year I was in Sydney, Australia, standing in front of the Opera House.

If your goal is to start your own business, create a mock newspaper article written about you and your business with a headline such as *Sarah Takes the Tutoring Market by Storm*. If your goal is to get straight A's, create a fake report card on your computer that shows A's in all of your current classes. Then put it on the wall in front of your desk. It will help you stay focused and show your mind the exact outcome you want.

Jack: Mark Victor Hansen and I created a mock-up of the *New York Times* bestseller list with the original *Chicken Soup for the Soul* in the number one spot. Within fifteen months, that dream became a reality. Four years later, we made a *Guinness* world record for having seven books on the *New York Times* bestseller list at the same time.

TIP: You can help your mind visualize by looking at photographs and images from magazines, etc. If you are the type who always likes to push it one step further, then create a vision board—a collection of images and photographs that inspire you.

Kent: There were many times when I almost pulled the plug on my first book. It was really difficult to stay focused for the more than three years it took to finish the project. I needed some newfound motivation, so I started cutting out pictures of places I wanted to go, people I wanted to meet, different things I wanted, and quotes that inspired me. Then I pasted them on a foam-core board in a collage-like layout. It was bright, colorful and, most importantly, kept me motivated because it would constantly remind me of the exciting future I could have if I stuck to my goal.

Now, I drive the same car I pasted on the board, I've traveled to many of the destinations on that board, and I've met some really incredible people who were on my vision board—including Jack Canfield. Who would have thought that I would be writing a book *with* him only a few years later?

Vision boards are extremely powerful tools. When NASA was working on putting a man on the moon, NASA staff members, knowing the power of images, covered the entire wall at their research center with a huge picture of the moon. The goal was clear to everyone. No wonder NASA reached that goal two years ahead of schedule.

(8.6) Start NOW

There is no doubt that visualizing is a powerful technique for success, but like anything else, YOU have to do it— no one will force you to do it, and nobody will do it for you. As you read through your goals, visualize them as though they are already complete. We're not talking about a lifetime— just five to ten minutes. This is one of the most vital things you can do to make your dream come true.

*See it happen so you **can make it happen**.*

**"Time for a pat on the back,
you've made it half way.
You're on the path to success.
Keep up the good work."**

MY "TO-DO" LIST

☑ Visualize what I want because this process engages my subconscious mind, sparks my creativity, and boosts my motivation.

☑ Understand that the clearer I envision things the way I want them, the more I increase my chances of having things *turn out* the way I want them to.

☑ Realize that visualization activates my creativity, helps me notice new opportunities, and attracts the people and resources I need to achieve my goals.

☑ When I visualize, I will remember to appeal to my senses so I can *feel* what it would be like to have my goals already completed.

☑ Take some time to create my own vision board with images and pictures of places I want to go, people I want to meet, things I'd like to have, and quotes that inspire me.

PRINCIPLE 9

Act as If

Believe and act as if it were **impossible to fail**.

—*Charles F. Kettering*
Farmer, teacher, engineer, scientist, inventor, and philosopher

If you couldn't swim, would you jump off a boat just to cool off and get wet? It's highly unlikely. Heck, you probably wouldn't even get on the boat in the first place! If you really believed that all dogs bite people, would you visit the pet store to buy a puppy? Of course not! You probably wouldn't even pet your best friend's puppy.

What we **expect** to happen **shapes** our **future**.

Likewise, if you believe that your dreams are unrealistic or you don't have what it takes to make them happen, how likely is it that you will ever realize your dreams or reach your potential? (No answer necessary!) Instead, what if you believe that your goals are possible—and that you are just the person to make them all happen? Would you go for it then? Of course you would!

One of the first steps to becoming successful at anything is to believe and *Act As If* it were impossible to fail. Think about it: If you believe something is impossible, you are not likely to try it. On the other hand, if you do believe, you will be willing to take the necessary action. Wouldn't you agree?

If you want to be successful, you must act as though you already are successful. This does not mean acting phony or arrogant. *Acting As If* means that we take our positive beliefs about ourselves a step further by thinking like, talking like, dressing like, acting like, and feeling like you have already achieved your goal. *Acting As If* sends powerful

messages to your brain that you are worthy of success and that you are ready to be successful. As you saw in our discussion on visualization techniques, once your mind expects to achieve its goals, it will search really hard to find ways to achieve them.

Jack: I didn't realize the power of this principle until I saw somebody using it. I noticed an interesting phenomenon at my local bank. Several tellers worked there, and I noticed that one in particular always wore a suit and tie. Unlike the other two male tellers who did not wear suits, the young man looked like an executive.

A year later, I noticed he had been promoted to his own desk, where he was taking loan applications. Two years later, he was a loan officer, and soon after that he became the branch manager. I asked him about this one day, and he replied that he always knew he would be a branch manager, so he studied how the managers dressed and started dressing the same way. He studied how the managers treated people and started interacting with people the same way. He started acting as if he were a branch manager long before he ever became one.

Fred Couples and Jim Nantz were two kids who loved golf and had very large dreams. Fred's goal was to someday win the Masters Tournament, and Jim's was to some-day be an announcer for CBS Sports. When Fred and Jim were attending the University of Houston, they used to act out a scene where the winner of the Masters is escorted into Butler Cabin to receive his green jacket and be interviewed by the CBS announcer.

Fourteen years later, they repeated that very scene—but this time, with the whole world watching! Fred Couples won the Masters, and when the tournament officials took him to Butler Cabin, he was interviewed by none other than CBS sports announcer Jim Nantz. Sound fake? It really happened! After the cameras stopped rolling, both Fred and Jim had an eerie feeling. Call it *déjà vu*. Call it whatever you want, but one thing was for sure: They turned their rehearsals into reality. They simply *Acted As If* Fred won the Masters and Jim covered it for CBS. A perfect (but not rare) example of the amazing power of *Acting As If* with the certainty that your rehearsal will be someday staged for real.

The **future we perceive** for ourselves will often **come to pass.**

What should *you* be rehearsing right now? What would your life be like if you were already where you wanted to be? How would you act? What kind of person would you be?

Why not begin right now to *Act As If* you have already achieved any goal you desire? Once you choose what it is you want to be, do, or have, all you have to do is start acting as if you already are being, doing, or having it. How would you act if you already were a straight-A student, your team's MVP, a leader in your school, a successful musician, a world-class artist, or a successful businessperson? How would you think, talk, act, carry yourself, dress, treat other people, handle your money, eat, live, travel, and so forth? Get a clear picture of your future-self and start *being that picture*.

Successful people use the technique of *Act As If* to build their confidence. They also:

※ **Ask for what they want.**
※ **Think anything is possible.**
※ **Take risks.**
※ **Celebrate their successes.**
※ **Save a portion of their income.**
※ **Share a portion with others.**

But here's the best thing of all: You can join them! You, too, can do all of these things right now—before you ever become rich and successful.

In fact, this very behavior accelerates your journey to the life of your dreams. Don't wait until someone tells you that you're talented to feel talented. Don't wait until you're a millionaire to believe that you *can be* a millionaire. Don't wait until you accomplish something outstanding to believe that you can be successful. Start right now. As soon as you start *Acting As If*, you will start attracting the people and the opportunities that will help you achieve it in real life.

Teresa, 16 (Pasadena, CA): I always wanted to be a designer, but I didn't have the confidence. There was a clothing shop in my local downtown area that I thought was really cool. After going there a lot, I knew who the owner was, but I never had the guts to talk to her. When I heard about the *Act As If* concept, I thought it was cool, but I didn't really know how to apply it to my life . . . until a certain situation came up. I was eating lunch at a café when I saw the same fashion-store owner walk in. I nearly choked on my sandwich! I thought, "I should really go up and talk to her about working in her shop. But what if she doesn't like me; what if I say something stupid; what if . . . ?" Then I stopped myself.

I remembered, *Act As If.* I knew this was a time I had to try it. I closed my eyes and pretended that I had already accomplished my goal of being a successful designer. My fear started to go away. I walked up to the store owner and told her about my passion for clothing design. We hit it off really well. She invited me in for another interview. I was so excited. Two weeks later, I had the job. Over the summer, I learned so much from this woman. She even introduced me to some very influential people in the industry. I couldn't believe it.

This taught me that even if you have to "fake it 'til you make it," your mind doesn't know the difference. I acted like the person I wanted to be, and my confidence grew. If I hadn't at least tried it, I definitely would not be where I am today.

9.2 "COME AS YOU WILL BE"

 o you like to go to parties and have fun? Of course! What about a party that can change your life forever? Tell me more . . .

Throw a "Come As You Will Be" party. This is how it works: Tell your friends to think about who and where they would like to be in five years. What is their profession? What have they accomplished? Once they have an idea of their ideal future, they now have to *live* it—they have to come to the party *as they will be* in five years. They must anticipate every part of their future—the clothing, the walk, the talk, the props, and if it's appropriate, the accent. That's right, *everything!* Tell them this is their chance to experience their future in advance.

When they arrive, have someone at the door to remind your guests that they must talk the entire time as if it was five years into the future, focusing on their accomplishments, their successes, what they're happy about, what they're most proud of, and what they plan to do next. The trick is to *stay in character* the entire night. Do you think you could pull it off?

Of course, you must also play your role at the party. If your goal is to be an Olympic athlete, then come dressed in uniform with a replica gold medal around your neck. Are you a police officer? Then dress the part—badge, hat, boots, everything. A millionaire? Then think like one and dress like one. Famous author? Show up with several books with mockup covers. Walk in reading the *New York Times* bestseller list (with your name showing prominently on the list). If you want to be a successful musician, then create a T-shirt with your band name on it. Dress "as if" you're at a concert, and bring your instrument with you to the party.

These parties are obviously good for a laugh and lots of fun. But these parties also have genuine psychological benefits. "Come As You Will Be" parties will flood your mind with powerful images of already having achieved your aspirations. These vivid experiences—combined with all your positive feelings and emotions during the night—strengthen your self-esteem and the way you view yourself. This in turn builds confidence and shows your brain that you *can* live your dreams.

We've experienced "Come As You Will Be" parties firsthand, and we know how powerful (and fun) they can be. Everyone we know who has been to one has said the same thing. If you don't know, there's only one way to find out: Try it! Commit to throw a "Come As You Will Be" party with your friends or graduating class. It will be a night you'll never forget, that's for sure. It's one of those experiences that you can look back on in twenty years and say, "And back then, I was only pretending, but now . . ."

9.4 Party on!

Your party shouldn't stop at the end of the night. To be honest, one "Come As You Will Be" party is not enough by itself to change your entire future. That's obvious. You must still do other things to reach all your goals.

Jamie, 18 (Santa Fe, NM): I thought it was a weird idea, but my friend decided to hold a "Come As You Will Be" party. I wasn't sure if I really wanted to go. One of the reasons was because I didn't know who I wanted to *be*. But this party idea got me thinking. This was the first time I actually thought about what I would be doing in the next five or ten years. I remember wanting to be a detective when I was little, and my recent interest in the TV show *CSI* inspired me.

I attended the party acting as though I was already a forensic detective, and I actually had a lot of fun. It was strange and I can't really explain it, but after that night I found it much easier to believe that I could be a detective if I really wanted to be. I could *Act As If* I were capable of achieving this goal because I had already practiced it for several hours.

Once the party was over, I continued to get into character (my future self), and now I can turn on my confidence when I need it. This has helped me take action toward my goals when I feel doubtful. For example, before the party, I was hesitant to sign up for the appropriate sciences at college. However, by continuing to practice the same thoughts, feelings, and behavior that I did at the party, I slowly developed more confidence and self-esteem. Today, I have chosen my major, my classes, and . . . my future. It feels really good to know that I am in control.

MY "TO-DO" LIST

☑ Realize that what I believe about myself defines who I will become.

☑ Start *Acting As If* I've already achieved all of my goals—today.

☑ *Act As If* by taking the positive beliefs about myself a step further by thinking like, talking like, dressing like, acting like, and feeling like the person I need to be to live my dreams.

☑ Expect with absolute certainty that I will achieve my goals if I work hard and *Act As If* I'm already the person I need to be to make it happen.

☑ Throw a "Come As You Will Be" party for my friends and/or graduating class.

☑ Believe that my expectations about myself and my future will determine my future.

Just Lean Into It

You **can't cross a sea** by merely **staring at** the **water**.

—Rabindranath Tagore
Nobel laureate for literature, 1913

ave you ever rolled a snowball down a big hill? At the beginning, it moves slowly, and it's easy to stop. But as the snowball continues to roll down the hill, it picks up speed and grows bigger and bigger. Eventually, it starts moving extremely fast . . . so fast it seems that almost nothing can stop it!

As you know, this speed and power is called *momentum*. Although it's easy to identify the momentum of the downhill snowball, we often overlook how momentum can be used in our own lives. Once we take action and get started, it becomes much easier to take action next time. In the process, we gain more confidence *and* competence . . . and we become almost unstoppable.

When we commit ourselves to doing something, we've started the process of momentum. Once the process is started, it acts as an unseen force of energy that creates more opportunity, more resources, and more people who can help you get to where you want to be. But it all starts with that first step. We must take that first step . . . and then we must *lean into it*. Martin Luther King, Jr., said it best:

Take the **first step** in faith.
You **don't** have to **see** the whole **staircase**.
Just **take the first step**.

10.1 Take the First Step

hen we lean into something, we're more willing to start on a project or opportunity, even though we may not see the whole pathway from the beginning. We need to have faith that once we get going, the path will gradually reveal itself.

When we have a dream and can't see how we're going to achieve it, we are afraid to start. We become afraid to commit ourselves because the path is unclear and the outcome is uncertain. But leaning into it requires you to be willing to explore—to enter unknown waters, trusting that a port will appear.

Life is full of uncertainties. As a result, in fear of making a mistake, many people go through life waiting for the perfect, no-risk, sure-win opportunity to walk into their lives. Then, if they happen to stumble into this perfect opportunity (which is next to impossible), they decide to take action and go for it. Big mistake! These people end up "waiting" their lives away, sitting on the sidelines just hoping that success finds them.

The truth is, **the only thing that comes without effort is old age!** (Yeah, not such a thrilling reward.) Sooner or later, we must seek out our own opportunities in order to create new possibilities. Sure, life is full of uncertainties, but by doing nothing we can only expect to get nothing.

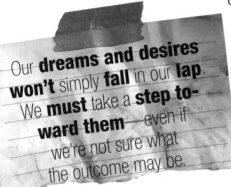

Our **dreams and desires** **won't** simply **fall** in our **lap**. We **must** take a **step to- ward them**—even if we're not sure what the outcome may be.

Those who became super-successful didn't know exactly what the outcome was going to be when they started following their dreams. But you will find that all super-achievers have one thing in common: They commit to giving their best effort—even when there is no promise of success. This commitment and leap of faith is also known as "leaning into it."

Simply start, then keep taking the steps you feel are necessary, and that journey will take you to where you want to go—*or even someplace better.*

10.2 Talking from Experience

There are definitely certain traits that all successful people have in common, and one of them is their willingness to try something without a guarantee of success. This is exactly where this principle comes into play. We've all probably heard of the hit TV show, *MythBusters*, and witnessed the MythBusting Mistress, Kari Byron, putting various legends, fables, and myths to the test. But the story of how Kari ended up on the show is a slightly different journey of self-discovery and persistence. Here's her story:

Sometimes not getting to your **dream right away** helps you **find** your purpose and **leads you** to **your destiny**.

Life as a teenager was not easy for me. I was painfully shy and awkward. But all that began to change in my sophomore year in high school when I decided to start taking new risks. I was using the *Lean into It* principle, and I didn't even know it.

However, not everything worked out the way I had hoped. I tried out for the high-school musical, and everybody but three people made it. Yes, I was one of those three people. I was completely crushed, but as painful as it was, I realized that the experience didn't kill me. And that meant I could try out again for something else.

I didn't pass every test I wanted to, and I didn't make every team I tried out for. I am only human! But each time I tried something new, I grew stronger. I found that the more chances I took, the more my confidence grew. Eventually, I made the auxiliary dance and flag team, where I started making friends with more people who were like me.

It was really important for me to look for people who shared my same interests. We would push each other to step out of our comfort zones and take on new opportunities. This *positive* peer pressure actually motivated me to travel around the world alone—something I had always wanted to do but was once too afraid of.

As soon as I graduated, I packed my bags, bought plane tickets, and began traveling to different countries around the world. This was a big step for me, especially because, until this point, I had never done much traveling—and now I was going to be hopping from country to country around the globe! But taking that trip really broadened my perspective about life and the world we live in. My confidence grew even stronger.

When I returned, I decided to try different jobs that interested me. I knew that I really liked art, but I wasn't sure how I was going to make a living doing it. At first, I took a job at an advertising company that paid really well, but discovered that it wasn't for me. Then I took a really a big risk and left that job to begin working at M5 Industries, a California company that does special effects for commercials, TV shows, and films, with Jamie Hyneman (cohost of *MythBusters*). I went from making a lot of money with a clear and stable career path to working for free and having no idea about how I was going to make a living. But I took the risk to follow my passion anyway, and I'm glad I did.

At M5 Industries, I found that doing special effects and toy prototyping was going to be the way to pursuing my passion for art. By taking the internship at M5 and working really hard I proved to Jamie that I was capable of even more.

Eventually, Jamie offered me the opportunity to be part of a *MythBusters* episode. That was my chance to shine. I gave it my best shot, earned a full-time spot on the show, and the rest, as they say, is history.

Today, I have so much fun working with smart people, conducting fun experiments, and cohosting a TV show! I never dreamed of doing all of this as a kid or even just

HAVE PATIENCE AND YOUR TRUE CALLING WILL BE REVEALED.

a few years ago. It's truly amazing how great life can be if you take risks and follow your heart. If something interests you or an opportunity comes up, be willing to try it—or as Jack and Kent say, *lean into it*.

Life rewards the people who take action. There is no time to waste doing things that don't interest you just because it's easier. There's *not* enough time in life *not* to take chances and go for it! Don't wait for a guarantee of success or for confidence to find you—it won't happen. I've found that success and confidence come by doing something and taking action. I absolutely believe that the key to success is taking chances and proving yourself.

Being a teenager is such an amazing opportunity. It's the perfect time to experiment with your interests and passions. It's so important to have the courage to try something, and then if it doesn't work out, be able to pick yourself up and try something else—that's the reason my life changed. All of the success that I enjoy today began as a teenager. By stepping out of my comfort zone and leaning into new opportunities, I've been able to live life beyond my wildest dreams. And if I can do it, you can do it, too.

10.3 A Noteworthy Journey in Music

For **every failure**, there's an **alternative** course of **action**. You just have to find it. When you come to a **roadblock**, **take a detour**.

—*Mary Kay Ash*
Founder of Mary Kay Cosmetics

 ometimes our dreams don't unfold the way we originally expected. We work hard, but don't seem to make the progress we hoped for. However, this doesn't mean our dreams are out of reach; it usually means that we need to try a different route to get to our destination. At each intersection, challenge, or roadblock, we must be willing to *lean into* it and go for it—otherwise, we'll never know what was possible.

Jana Stanfield loved music and always wanted to be a singer. She didn't know where her dream would eventually lead her, but she knew she had to find out. She *leaned into it* and took some singing lessons, then eventually got a job singing weekends at a local country club. That's when she faced a fork in the road. It wasn't an easy choice to make, but she knew that in order to follow her dream, she needed to move away from home. Jana chose to *lean into* it a little more, so she packed her bags and headed to Nashville, Tennessee.

For three long years, she lived and worked in Nashville. She continued to meet producers who loved her work, artists who considered her song for their next album, and record companies that told her she was great—but, unfortunately, nothing was ever confirmed or finalized.

After working for a record-promotion company, she learned the business from the inside out, and she had to face the facts: There were no guarantees. Finally, she admitted to herself that continuing to try to get a record deal was like pounding her head against the wall. She didn't realize at the time that often, when you lean into it, roadblocks are put in your path that force you onto a different route—one that may be truer to your real purpose.

Even if you're on the **right track**, you'll **get run over** if you just **sit there**.
—*Will Rogers*
American comedian, humorist, and actor

Jana knew that even when you can't move forward, you can turn right or left, *but you have to keep moving*. She realized that sometimes, in the rush to fulfill our dreams, we get caught up in what we think is the only way to satisfy that dream—in Jana's case, a recording contract.

But as Jana soon learned, there are many ways to accomplish your goal if you know what you're really going after. She discovered a deeper motivation underneath her desire to land a record deal. She wrote in her journal: "I want to combine music, comedy, storytelling, and motivation with what I'm here for. I am an artist, and my art is unfolding before me. The roadblock that blocked my path has been lifted."

After this realization, she began to play anywhere people would let her. "Where two people are gathered, I will bring my guitar" became her motto. During this time, Jana was still trying to figure out how to combine her talents for helping people with her need to earn an income. Nobody was doing what she wanted to do, she was charting new territory. There was no known career path to follow and no footsteps to walk in. She didn't know where she was going or how she was going to reach her goal, but she kept *leaning into it.*

Jana began to work odd jobs while she was trying to figure out how to best use her passion for music and people. She called churches and said, "If you let me come and sing two songs, it will give you a chance to get to know me and how I might be helpful."

Finally, a turning point! A few churches invited her to play. After hearing just two or three songs, people asked for a tape of her songs. Jana began making copies of her songs and mailing them to people. All the while, her friends kept telling her to make an album.

Jana thought, "Oh, I couldn't do that. It wouldn't be a real album with a real record company. It wouldn't really count. It would just show what a failure I've been." But her friends persevered. Eventually, she *leaned into it* one more time.

She paid an engineer to put together her ten songs. She printed the cover art at Kinko's and had 100 copies made. "I thought that would be a lifetime supply." As she traveled from group to group, location to location, she set her albums up on a small table to sell after her performances. Then came another turning point.

"My husband went with me to a church in Memphis," Jana recalls. "They didn't feel comfortable having a table with my albums inside the church, so they set my table up in the parking lot."

At the end of the church service, Jana had brought in $300 in sales. This was $50 more than she had earned all week at her full-time job. Holding that $300 in her hand was the first time Jana realized that she could support herself doing what she loved to do.

Today, Jana's company, Keynote Concerts, produces more than fifty motivational concerts a year for groups all over the world. She started her own recording company, which produced eight of Jana's CDs and has sold more than 100,000 copies. Jana's songs have been recorded by some of the most respected names in the industry. She has opened for Kenny Loggins, has been featured on *Oprah, 20/20, Entertainment Tonight*, and radio stations coast to coast, as well as in the movie *8 Seconds*.

Jana Stanfield achieved her dream of becoming a songwriter and recording star—all because she leaned into it and trusted the path that appeared. You, too, can achieve your dreams and get to where you want to be if you'll just trust that when you lean into it, the path will appear. Sometimes it will be like driving through fog, where you can see the road only ten yards in front of you. But if you keep moving forward, you will see more of the road until you eventually arrive at your goal.

10.4 JUST TRY IT

When most teenagers are asked, "What do you want to do in life?" or "What do you want to be when you're older?" the automatic response is usually, "I don't know." Indeed, this can be a tough question. In fact, we said the same thing when we were teenagers. But what separates those who just drift through life and those who set sail and land at an exciting destination is often the willingness to give something a try and just go for it.

The worst thing we can do is sit around and do nothing while we hope that the answer to this daunting question, "What do you want to do in life?" (and similar questions) will one day fall in our lap. Sorry to say, but it's not gonna happen! When people give us the response, "I don't know," we'll often ask a follow-up question, such as, "Well, in a perfect world, what would you want to do with your life?" or "If you knew you couldn't fail, what would you strive to be or do?"

After asking these questions, we usually start to get a different response.

Sometimes the person will say, "I've always thought about acting . . ." or "I think it would be fun to be a chef," or "When I was younger, I really wanted to be a _____ [*fill in the blank*]." This is powerful information! The most useful thing we can do is tap into the interests that we already have and test the water. In other words, try it out and see if you like it . . . *lean into it*. Sometimes, we'll never get a definite answer to a challenging question until we finally take a step in a given direction.

If something has always grabbed your interest or made you curious, then check into it. If you're interested in acting, try out for the school play to see if you like it. If you're interested in owning your own retail store, then interview someone who has their own store—or ask for an internship. If you like art, sketching, and design, then apply for a summer art and design school.

The most powerful part of this principle is taking action. Think about it: We can't lean into something without moving first. Great things don't happen by chance. We must be willing to take a leap of faith and give something a try. As a result of trying different things and experimenting with our interests, we will start getting valuable feedback—information that could affect the overall direction of the rest of our life. That's rather exciting!

Kailani, 18 (Honolulu, HI): I drove my high-school career counselor crazy. Let's just say I wasn't a very decisive person. When it came time to answer the questions, "What do you want to do in life?" and "What do you want to major in?" I was paralyzed.

My grades weren't very good, so I started to unconsciously limit my options. "I would like to be a doctor, but my grades aren't good enough," or "I think it would be cool to be a chef, but I don't know . . . what if I don't like it?" My career counselor finally said, "You're always talking about the possibility of being a doctor, a chef, a policeman, etc. Why don't you try these things and see what you think?"

She was right. I was waiting for a clear and obvious voice inside me to say, "This is what you should do with your life." When I realized that this "voice" wasn't going to speak any time soon, I did what she said. As a junior, I started trying different things. I obviously couldn't just "be a doctor for a day," but I did talk with people who were doctors for many years and bombarded them with questions.

I got a job part-time at a restaurant, and I took some "ride-alongs" with a family friend who was a police officer. Within a few months, I discovered that I didn't want to be a doctor, a chef or a police officer. But, in the process, I did learn a lot! Sometimes the best way to figure out what you *want* to do is to first eliminate the things you *don't* want to do.

This experience opened my eyes to so many other options that I never even considered. After speaking with countless people in different professions, I was introduced to someone who owned a marketing company. Surprisingly, I really enjoyed working for this person. I had never even thought of marketing as a possible option for me, but I liked it so much I decided to major in it. Once I chose my major and started working toward it, I found it was a lot easier to stay focused in class and improve my grades. Looking back, I don't think I ever would have found my interest in marketing if I didn't lean into my other interests first.

10.5 JUSt Lean Into It

A **journey** of 10,000 miles **begins** with that very **first step**.

—*Chinese proverb*

Even though life is uncertain, the future is not out of our control. The only thing we need to be certain about is our own level of commitment and dedication. This has immense power. If you master this principle, you will build the momentum and confidence you need to persevere through roadblocks and challenges in order to reach your wildest dreams and goals. That snowball just keeps going and growing.

Remember, we always have the ability to persevere, change what we're doing, or change our course of direction. But it also helps to understand that success usually happens when you lean into whatever it is you're doing—when you look for opportunities, take that first step, and are willing to do what it takes to make it happen . . . just *lean into it*.

MY "TO-DO" LIST

☑ Understand that nothing worthwhile happens by chance. I must take a step toward my dreams with faith that the right path will continue to appear as I move forward.

☑ Realize that even super-successful people didn't know exactly what the outcome was going to be when they started following their dreams.

☑ Realize that achievers have one thing in common: They are fully dedicated to finding a way to make it happen.

☑ Make a commitment to give my best effort at all times—even when there is no promise of success.

☑ Know that taking the first step is often the hardest. But once I get moving, I will build the momentum that will help me succeed.

☑ When I face a roadblock, realize that it's not a dead-end; it might mean I need to alter my course.

☑ Lean into my dreams and take action toward them *today*.

Face Your Fears Head-on!

Too many of **us** are **not living our dreams** because **we are living our fears.**

—*Les Brown*
Author and inspirational speaker

No matter who we are, where we are, or what we're doing, we all have to deal with fear. Many people think that successful people have simply learned how to shut off their fears. Not true. Fear is natural, and we *all* must deal with it.

Fear is really just our brain doing what it's meant to do—telling us to be cautious of moving traffic while we're crossing a busy street, alerting us that the driver ahead of us is swerving in and out of the lane, reminding us to be careful where we place our wallets or purses. Perfectly natural, and very helpful! Unfortunately, most people let their various fears (even fear of success) stop them from taking the necessary action to achieve their dreams.

Successful people, on the other hand, feel the fear (just as the rest of us do), but they don't let the fear hold them back. They understand that fear is something to be acknowledged, experienced, and taken along for the ride. In other words, they *feel the fear* but do what's required anyway.

Millions of years ago, fear was our body's way of signaling us that we were out of our comfort zone. It alerted us of possible danger and gave us the burst of adrenaline we needed to run away. Today, however, we don't need to outrun bloodthirsty saber-toothed tigers. In fact, many of the fears and threats we face today are not at all life-threatening.

I KNOW YOU MEAN WELL, BUT WE NEED TO WORK TOGETHER.

FEAR

Confront your **fears**, list them, get to **know them**, and only then will you be able to **put them aside** and **move ahead.**

—*Jerry Gillies*
Author

11.1 Take the Leap of Faith

Fear is not something to avoid; it is something we need to learn to live with. Some people will do anything to avoid the uncomfortable feelings of fear. The problem is that these same people run an even bigger risk of never getting what they want in life. Most of the sweetest rewards in life require that we take a risk—and risks create fear of uncertainty. "What if things don't work out?"

At some stage, however, we must be willing to *lean into it* and take that first step.

Hollywood! The movie biz! Talk about risks! There are many stories of "guaranteed hits" that bombed and just as many stories of "long shots" that surprised not only the critics but even the producers. One such example involved Jeff Arch, who had written the screenplay for *Sleepless in Seattle*, a blockbuster movie starring Tom Hanks and Meg Ryan. After writing this hit movie, Jeff decided that he not only wanted to write the next movie he worked on, but produce and direct it as well.

Although he had no background in producing or directing, he was willing to take the risk in order to gain a bigger reward. During an interview with Jeff, he said:

I am about to launch the biggest gamble of my life—writing and directing a two-million-dollar comedy, when I have never directed before, and using my own money plus raising other money to fund it. Really, it's an all-or-nothing situation. And the thing that I'm experiencing right now, which I think is really important (and a lot of people who write about success leave out), is you've got to be willing to be terrified. But it's not immobilizing. It's a good terrified; it's a terrified that keeps you on your toes.

I've learned that you have to believe in your dream because even if everyone is telling you you're wrong, that still might not mean anything—you just might be right. You reach a point where you say, "This is it. I'm throwing everything into this. And it's got to succeed. I'm throwing money, credibility—every single thing there is—into my new project. And it's either going to be a homerun or a strikeout—not a single or a double."

I know there is terror in doing this, but there's also confidence. It isn't going to kill me. It might make me broke, it might leave me in debt, it might make me lose my credibility, and it might make the journey back a whole lot harder. But, fortunately, I'm not in a business where they kill you if you goof up. I think one of the secrets to my success is that I'm willing to be terrified, and I think a lot of people are not willing to be scared to death. And that's why they don't achieve the big dream.

11.2 Fantasized Experiences Appearing Real

You can **conquer** almost any **fear**
if you will only make up your mind to do so. Remember,
fear doesn't exist anywhere **except in the mind**.

—*Dale Carnegie*
American writer, author, trainer, and speaker

ince we don't have to outrun saber-toothed tigers anymore, almost all of our fears are now self-created. Basically, we scare ourselves by imagining negative outcomes to any activity, project, or opportunity we face. Luckily, since we are the ones doing the imagining, we are also the ones who can stop the imagining—and, yes, stop the fear. We can do this by facing the *actual* facts (not the horrifying scenes in our heads). We can choose to be sensible and logical. We choose to look at fear this way:

Fantasized

Experiences

Appearing

Real

Do you bring unrealistic or improbable fears into your life? Here is one way to find out: Make a list of things you are currently afraid to do—not things you are afraid *of*, such as snakes or heights, but things you're afraid to *do*. For example, "I am afraid to . . ."

- ❋ **Pick up a snake.**
- ❋ **Stand at the top of a building or a cliff.**
- ❋ **Raise my hand and participate in class.**
- ❋ **Ask that "hot" person out on a date.**
- ❋ **Go skydiving.**
- ❋ **Give a speech in front of my class.**
- ❋ **Apply for a job at my favorite shop.**
- ❋ **Start my own business.**
- ❋ **Confront a friend and apologize.**
- ❋ **Ask my teacher for feedback that might improve my grades.**

Now go back and restate each fear on a separate piece of paper using the following format:

_____

I want to _____ *, but I scare myself by imagining* _____.

The phrase *I scare myself by imagining* helps you to understand that all fear is self-created by *imagining a negative future outcome.* In the new format, the "raise my hand" example above would be:

I want to raise my hand to participate in class, but I scare myself by imagining myself stuttering or picturing other students laughing at my question or idea.

By rephrasing your own fears, you will find that they are all self-created by simply misusing your own imagination. Our imagination is an incredibly powerful tool, and like all tools, it can be used positively or negatively. When our imagination gets carried away, it can work against us and really hold us back. The simple exercise on previous page shows us that many of our fears are not as bad as they seem. What you'll discover is that your brain is just focusing on what we don't want to happen. When we realize this, we can change our focus and find the courage to look our fears straight in the eyes and take a bold step forward.

Courage is **not** the **absence of fear**, but rather the judgment that **something else** is **more important** than **fear**.

—*Ambrose Redmoon*
Musician and writer

11.3 see a "Brighter" Future

When we're imagining something horrible happening, such as a plane crashing, our mind is using the power of images to heighten our emotions. The more intense the negative mental pictures, the more fear we experience. But what if we could reverse the process by imagining something positive instead? Ah . . . now that has real power.

Scott, 16 (San Diego, CA): When I did the exercise in the last section, I wrote down my fear of speaking in front of my class. This was important for me because I had to give a speech for an upcoming project. When I wrote down my fear in the new format, I realized that I was imagining things that would probably never happen. Then I noticed as I was writing down my

IS THIS REALLY NECCESSARY?

FEAR OF PUBLIC SPEAKING

thoughts that I kept seeing the worst possible things happening—and whenever I saw these images, I could feel my gut knot up.

Instead, I pictured myself at the front of the room talking with ease as people were smiling, laughing (*with* me, of course), and listening to every word I said. At first, I noticed a little change in the way I felt, but by continually imagining myself doing well, the pictures in my mind became clearer and brighter. As this happened, I noticed that my gut didn't knot up the way it used to.

When I finally had to give my speech, I was able to walk up to the front of the room without hesitation and speak. It felt like I had already given my speech. My fear didn't completely disappear, but I was able to gain enough confidence to confront my fear and give my speech anyway. As a result, I did really well, and I felt better about myself for not bailing out.

114 Remember Your Triumphs

Did you ever learn to dive off a diving board? If so, you might remember the first time you walked to the edge and looked down. Your first thought may have been, "Heck, no! I'm not jumping off that!"

The distance from your eyes to the waterline probably looked like a very long way down. A scary moment. You could have looked at your mom and dad or the diving instructor and then said, "You know, I'm just too afraid to do this right now. I think I'll go get some therapy on this, and if I can get rid of my fear, I'll come back and try again."

No way! You didn't say that. Instead, you felt the fear, somehow built up the courage from somewhere, and jumped into the water. You felt the fear, but you still took a bold step forward.

When you surfaced, you probably swam like crazy to the side of the pool and took a few well-earned deep breaths. You felt that little rush of adrenaline, the thrill of having survived a risk, plus the thrill of jumping through the air into the water. After a minute, you probably did it again—and then again and again. Somehow, it got to be fun. Pretty soon, all of the fear was gone, and you were trying crazy, new kinds of dives, cannonballs, and maybe even a back flip.

Remember that experience? How about the first time you drove a car? Or your first date? Use one of these positive experiences as a model that describes how everything happens in life. New experiences will always feel a little scary. They're supposed to. That's the way it works. But every time you face your fear and break through it, you build up much more confidence in your abilities.

You can **control** your **fearful emotions** by **focusing** on what **you can** already **manage**.

(115) SIZE DOWN YOUR FEAR

Recently, we spoke with Amanda, whose goal was to attend Stanford University. She was very driven, focused, and determined, but over the last year, Amanda told us that she had actually become very nervous and fearful. When we asked her a few questions, we discovered that she had a very negative "big picture." The process of achieving her goal was overwhelming her. *"What if I don't make it? What if the school feels like I didn't do enough to qualify? How could I live with myself?"* she asked us.

Amanda described how nervous she felt before tests that

IMAGINATION

AM I REALLY SEEING THIS?

You can't do **everything** in **one day**, but you can do **something every day** to move you **closer** to where **you want to be**.

would normally be simple for her and how she always stressed and worried about not performing to her ability. After we spoke, she realized that many of her fears were either unrealistic or out of her control. To rebuild her confidence, we talked about how to control a great deal of her fear by focusing on the things that she did have control over. We discussed the importance of concentrating on one thing at a time. When Amanda broke down her giant goal into a series of smaller action steps she could take each day, her fear became less paralyzing. As a result, she was able to relax more, perform better, and enjoy the process.

If a fear is so big that it paralyzes you, you can downsize the amount of fear by focusing on smaller, more controllable challenges. When you focus on one step or one milestone at a time, you will find that the fear is much more manageable. Sometimes the size of your goal or dream can feel overwhelming, but it doesn't need to be if you have a clear, realistic plan and focus on the *next step,* not on *everything* you must do to get there.

11.6 Shrink the Risk

Progress always involves **risk**. You **can't steal second base** and **keep your foot on first**.

—Author Unknown

Joel, 17 (Charleston, SC): Last year, I moved to a new neighborhood that had a well-known tennis club. I decided that I wanted to play on this local club team, but I had played very little tennis before. The other team members had been playing tennis for years and were much better than I was. At the start, it was awkward and sometimes embarrassing, but I still set my sights high.

I set a goal to compete in a regional tennis tournament, but every time I thought about it, I doubted my abilities and feared that I would get badly beaten and embarrass myself in front of hundreds of people. Instead of giving up on this goal, I decided to set some smaller goals that would help me accomplish my bigger objective. I focused on learning one skill at a time until I won my first game in practice. Then I competed in my first official competition. After that, I played my first tournament. My confidence began to grow, and my skills also improved.

Eventually, my goal of competing in the regional tennis tournament didn't seem so overwhelming. When the tournament day arrived, I was ready to play. Even though I didn't win this year, I felt good about how I played, and I know I will do even better next year.

It helps to shrink the fear in our own lives by shrinking the amount of risk we have to take to accomplish our goals. If you want to give a graduation speech, focus on giving a great speech in your own classroom first. If you want to learn a new sport, start at lower skill levels until you master them. Then take on a more-challenging skill. *Shrink the risk to shrink the fear.*

How can you shrink the risk and build up to accomplishing your more-challenging goals? Sometimes, additional smaller stepping stones are all we need to reach our biggest dreams. But be careful: Shrink your risks, not your dreams!

11.7 JUSt GO FOR It!

Fear is never a **reason for quitting**; it is **only** an **excuse**.

—*Author Unknown*

Kent: A few years ago, I saw a television commercial that read: "Show up; sign up; and speak out." Hmmm, this was odd . . . I continued to watch. "A new TV show is holding auditions across the country looking for America's next great inspirational speaker!"

"Wow," I thought to myself. "This sounds interesting." I had an eerie feeling come over me. In my gut, I felt that I had to audition. The person with me saw the curious look on my face and said, "You're not thinking about doing that, are you? That's not really you."

My doubts introduced themselves. "Yeah, you're right," I agreed with him. "I couldn't do that." Heck, at the time I had only given about fifteen speeches in my life (if you could even call them speeches). Basically, I had zero experience—and now I thought I was going to try out for a TV show like *American Idol*, but instead of singing I would have to get on stage and deliver a *speech!* What was I thinking? At the time, public speaking was my number-one fear. There was no way I could do this. But then I remembered the quote, "Do the thing you fear most, and the death of fear is certain." The same eerie feeling came over me. I just knew I had to audition. I really wanted to learn how to be a better speaker, and this was a perfect opportunity.

A friend drove with me to the audition. I signed up at 5:00 PM, and by 10:00 PM I still had not been called. My friend was getting frustrated. "This is ridiculous! Look at all these people. Do you really think you're going to make it? Can't we just go home?" I was definitely tempted. My fear over the last few hours had drained my energy, and part of me really wanted to leave.

I felt the fear (no wait, I was *terrified*), but I decided to go for it. Until the time I was called, I was still frantically writing my three-minute speech (which was required for the audition). I could barely hold my pen. "Next!" I heard a voice call out from the dark room in front of me. It was my turn. There was a huge camera in my face and a panel of five judges. "Well, let's hear your three minutes of inspiration," the head judge said. My heart was pounding. I opened my mouth, and the words started to come out. It was the longest three minutes of my life.

A week later, I received a call. "Kent, you've made the top twenty. Can you come back for the final round of auditions?" "Ummm . . . sure," I managed to mumble to the person on the phone. During this round of auditions, things were even more intense, but I faced my fears and followed my passion.

At the end of a long day, the top-ten contestants were named. I was one of them—and, believe me, I was in shock. Who would have thought that I would be a participant on a nationwide TV show speaking in front of a live studio audience and millions of viewers who had tuned in to watch? I couldn't believe it. I competed as the youngest contestant by almost ten years! I didn't win the show, but I learned so much. My confidence grew, and the experience shaped who I am today. Now, I speak to audiences around the world—something that was only a dream three years ago. That experience showed me that we never really know what we're capable of doing until we face our fears and hold tightly to our dreams.

118 Same Situation, New Opportunity

To remain calm and happy, we have to realize that we cannot always control every outcome in our life. We must do everything we can to reach our goals, and then be able to let it go—not letting ourselves feel devastated if we don't get the exact result we want, when we want it.

The truth is, sometimes the outcome we want doesn't show up in the way we anticipate. That's just life. But be ready to look for the lesson or the insight that life is trying to teach us. There may be a new or better opportunity that stems from the same goal.

Rob, 28 (Toronto, Canada): When people asked me what I wanted to be as I was growing up, I always said that I would play in the NHL. But simply talking about doing something is easy. What matters is that you actually do what's necessary to make it happen. For me, this meant facing many of my fears. I felt uneasy playing in front of big audiences, I feared letting my teammates down, and I couldn't stand getting rejected by the goalie, but with time and dedication I pushed through those fears. However, there was one thing I was definitely not prepared for.

While I was in college, things were looking bright. I was playing really well, and the top coaches in the league were impressed. I was then invited to try out for a professional team in the NHL. My dream was unfolding perfectly as planned. Going into the tryouts, I was a favored player. Each day I gave everything I could. I knew that I had a good chance of making the team. But on the second-to-last day of the tryouts, I injured my knee as an intense pain shot through my leg. I couldn't believe it.

I was carried off the ice with my fingers crossed, hoping that I could finish the tryouts. Unfortunately, the damage was severe. I had torn three of my ligaments and suffered some nerve damage. I refused to believe it. After many X-rays and tests, the doctors said that I needed surgery. I was told that my knee would recover, but I would not have the strength and agility needed to play in the NHL. I was absolutely devastated. The thought that my dream was no longer possible was really tough to deal with.

Since I had to spend so much time with doctors and physical therapists, I asked many questions and learned a lot about muscle groups and how the physical body worked. Surprisingly, I developed a passion for it and dedicated the next few years to becoming an orthopedic surgeon.

Now I have my degree, and because of the relationships I made while I was playing ice hockey, I get to work with many professional athletes. Even though I didn't become an NHL player, I still get to stay involved in the sport I love and work with some of the top athletes in the world. It's a blessing every day to know that what I do helps other people reach their goals and dreams.

11.9 GO for It!

When you are **afraid**, **do the thing** you are **afraid of** and soon you will **lose your fear of it**.

—*Norman Vincent Peale*
Bestselling author and inspirational speaker

Fear is something we all have to deal with—no matter who we are, where we're from, or what our goals are. The good news is you're not alone. Everybody gets nervous or doubtful at times. However, the thing that separates an average person from an extraordinary person is how each responds to fear.

Our fear is a fantastic mentor, but it should not be the single force that determines the decisions we make. We must be able to take some risk in order to grow stronger, wiser, and more competent. *Don't let your fears choose your destiny.*

The **biggest mistake** you can make is continually **fearing** you **will make one**.

—*Unknown*

MY "TO-DO" LIST

☑ Realize that my fears are a natural part of life.

☑ Understand that many of my fears are not life-threatening. I may be building them up in my head by simply misusing my imagination.

☑ Write down my fears and restate them using this new format: I want to _____, but I scare myself by imagining _____.

☑ Become aware of the mental images I create in my head when I feel fearful. I can reverse this process by visualizing positive images in bright, intense color and clarity.

☑ Remember the times when I overcame my fears and approach current situations using the same techniques.

☑ I will size down my fear by initially taking on smaller challenges and risks until I develop the confidence and skill necessary to tackle my bigger fears and pursue my larger dreams.

☑ Even though I feel fear, I will still take a bold step toward my dreams and goals. I will not let my fear choose my destiny.

Be Willing to Pay the Price

It took me sixteen **hard years** to be an **overnight success**.

—Nick Nolte
Actor

Before she landed her first record deal, Jewel Kilcher, the well-known singer, lived out of a van while she traveled from city to city playing in coffeehouses. Jim Carrey bounced from one comedy club to the next, just barely making ends meet. Michael Jordan failed to make his high-school basketball team. Sylvester Stallone faced countless rejections before *Rocky* was finally produced. Billionaire Ted Arison went bankrupt twice before making his fortune. Walt Disney went bankrupt seven times; he even had a nervous breakdown before he succeeded with his massive dreams.

The list goes on forever! But the message is simple: Behind every great achievement is a story of education, training, practice, discipline, and sacrifice.

We hear of many people who become well-known, respected, and successful overnight. But we don't often hear about their hard work, sweat, and tears behind the scenes before they achieved their "newfound" success.

The bottom line is: *You have to be willing to pay the price.* True success must be earned. You might have to watch less TV so you can study or practice more. You might have to eat less junk food and exercise more to achieve the body you really want. Maybe you will have to spend less money at the mall to save more money for college. Perhaps you must be willing to take a step out of your comfort zone toward your dream.

Many things are required to reach our personal goals, but the willingness to do what is required instantly increases your chances of success. The willingness to pay the price helps you persevere in the face of overwhelming challenges, setbacks, and even personal injury.

(121) Practice Makes Perfect

Bill Bradley was an all-American basketball player at Princeton University, he played in the NBA on the New York Knicks, he won an Olympic gold medal, and he was inducted into the Hall of Fame. How did he perform so well on the basketball court? Well, for one thing, when he was in high school, he practiced four hours a day, every day.

In his book, *Time Present, Time Past*, Bradley describes his own self-imposed basketball-training regimen: "I stayed behind to practice after my teammates had left. My practice routine was to end by making fifteen baskets in a row from each of the five spots on the floor." If he missed the shot, he would start over from the beginning. He continued this practice all through his college and professional career.

PERFECT! NOW, JUST 99 MORE TO GO.

Bradley says he developed this strong commitment to practice when he attended summer basketball camps sponsored by the St. Louis Hawks' Ed Macauley. Ed said, *"When you're not practicing, someone somewhere is. And when the two of you meet, given roughly equal ability, he will win."* Bill took that advice to heart, and his hours of hard work paid off. Bill Bradley scored more than 3,000 points in four years of high-school basketball. Amazing!

122 Why Not?

It is difficult to thrive in the world of art—difficult, but not impossible, especially if you're willing to pay the price. Just ask Wyland . . .

For many years, Wyland was the classic starving artist who threw everything into his dream. People often asked him, "Why are you doing this? It's almost impossible to make money selling your own paintings!" But that didn't stop him. He painted, and he hustled. He set up art shows at his local high school and sold his original paintings for just thirty-five dollars. One day, even his mother began getting on his case. She said, "Art really isn't a job; it's a hobby. Now go out and get a real job." The next day she dropped him off at the Detroit Unemployment Bureau. Over the next three days, he was fired from three different jobs in a row. He couldn't keep his mind on the boring factory work. He wanted to be creative; he wanted to paint.

A week later, he turned his basement into a studio and worked day and night, creating a portfolio that eventually won him a full scholarship to art school in Detroit. Wyland painted every moment he could, and along the way he managed to sell some paintings, just managing to scrape by for a number of years. But he was determined. After all, art was the only thing he wanted to do, so he continued to practice and practice his art.

One day, Wyland realized he needed to go where other artists flourished . . . where new ideas were nourished. His destination? Laguna Beach, California. With his dreams alive and well, he moved into a cramped, tiny studio where he worked and lived for several years. Then one day he was invited to participate in the annual Laguna Beach Festival of the Arts, where he learned to talk about his art and his work with collectors.

Soon after, galleries in Hawaii discovered his work and sold his paintings—but without paying him!

His frustration grew as he tried to sell high-priced paintings through other galleries. Again, the money disappeared. Wyland decided he had to build his own galleries. In his own galleries, he could control every aspect of selling his art—from how his pieces were displayed and framed, to how they were sold.

Today, twenty-six years after opening his first gallery in Laguna Beach, he produces as many as 1,000 works of art each year (some of which sell for $200,000 apiece), creates artistic collaborations with Disney, owns four homes in Hawaii, California, and Florida, and lives the life he always dreamed of. A long way from the Detroit Unemployment Bureau.

Do you, like Wyland, want to turn your hobby into your career? You can become hugely successful doing what you love if you are willing to pay the price. "In the beginning, you've got to kind of suffer," Wyland says, "giving in to everybody else. But there is nothing better than eventually achieving success on your own terms."

123 A Background Check

I learned that the only way you are going to **get anywhere** in life is to **work hard** at it. Whether you're a musician, a writer, an athlete, or a businessman, there is no getting around it. If you **do**, you will **win**—if you **don't**, you **won't**.

—*Bruce Jenner*
Olympic gold medalist in the decathlon

There are many stories about Olympic athletes who put in hundreds of hours to prepare for success. Well, John Troup, a writer for the *USA Today* newspaper, did some research to reveal the facts. He wrote:

The average Olympian trains four hours a day at least 310 days a year for six years before succeeding. Getting better begins with working out every day. By 7:00 AM, most athletes have done more than many people do all day . . . Given equal talent, the better-trained athlete can generally outperform the one who did not give a serious effort, and is usually more confident at the starting block. The four years before an Olympics, Greg Louganis probably practiced each of his dives 3,000 times. Kim Zmeskal has probably done every flip in her gymnastics

routine at least 20,000 times, and Janet Evans [a world-class swimmer] has completed more than 240,000 laps. Training works, but it isn't easy or simple. Swimmers train an average of ten miles a day, at speeds of five miles per hour in the pool. That might not sound fast, but their heart rates average 160 the entire time. Try running up a flight of stairs, then check your heart rate. Then imagine having to do that for four hours! Marathon runners average 160 miles a week at ten miles per hour.

Becoming an Olympic athlete may not be your goal, but you can become world class in whatever you do by practicing and putting in your best effort every time. To win at whatever game you choose to play—including the game of life—you need to be willing to make the sacrifices necessary to get the result you want.

It's **not the will to win** that matters—everyone has that. It's the **will to prepare to win** that matters.

—*Paul "Bear" Bryant*
College football's winningest coach, with 323 victories,
including six national championships and thirteen Southeastern Conference titles

124 PUTTING IN THE TIME

Even though we don't all have equal talent, education, or support, we do all have the same amount of time. There are only twenty-four hours in a day, 168 hours in a week, and 8,760 hours in a year. How we spend this time is what makes the greatest difference in the quality of someone's life.

Legendary violinist **Isaac Stern** was once confronted by a middle-aged woman after a concert. She said, **"Oh, I'd give my life to play like you!"** "Lady," Stern said without hesitation, **"that I did!"**

Don't make the mistake of waiting until everything is "just right" to get started. Start where you stand. Decide now that you are going to get things done no matter how much work it takes, no matter how long it takes, and no matter what challenges stand in your way. You are responsible for the type of person you are today and the type of life you will be living tomorrow. No excuses. Consider these examples:

※ **At age thirteen, Jasmine Lawrence had a personal experience with a product that destroyed her hair.** She was devastated by the harsh chemical products on the market. But instead of complaining about it, she created a solution, which was the opportunity to start her own company that she called EDEN Body Works—a line of all-natural cosmetic products. Too young? No way! Now at age sixteen, Jasmine is a seasoned CEO making a difference. "It was a lot of work," she says. "I sacrificed numerous opportunities over the last few years to go to the movies and other parties so I could run my business." Has it been worth all the time required? "Absolutely!" she says. In fact, Jasmine's  success even caught the media's attention. She was invited to appear on *The Oprah Winfrey Show*—a huge accomplishment! "I never thought this could happen. I'm so grateful for my success," Jasmine says, "but there is no way that I could be where I am without putting in the time and paying the price over the past few years."

※ **You've probably heard or seen the super-successful television show called** *ER*. Well, the man behind this work is Emmy Award- and Peabody Award-winning Michael Crichton. His books have sold more than 100 million copies, have been translated into thirty languages, and twelve have been made into films, seven of which he directed! His books include *Jurassic Park, Congo, Coma, Twister,* and *Westworld.* He is also the only person to have had, at the same time, the number-one book, the number-one movie, and the number-one television show in the United States. With all of this talent, Michael still says, "Books aren't written—they're rewritten. . . . It is one of the hardest things to accept, especially since the seventh rewrite hasn't quite done it."

※ **Japan's gymnast, Fujimoto, had to land a perfect triple-somersault twist dismount from the rings to win the gold medal in team gymnastics—on a *broken* knee!** It was an extraordinary example of courage and commitment. When Fujimoto was interviewed later, he said that even though he had injured his knee during the earlier floor exercise, he could see that the entire competition would be decided by his performance. "The pain shot through me like a knife," he remembered. "It brought tears to my eyes. But now I have a gold medal, and the pain is gone."

※ **The world-renowned writer Ernest Hemingway rewrote *A Farewell to Arms* thirty-nine times!** This dedication to excellence would later lead him to win the Pulitzer and Nobel Prizes for literature.

Talent is cheaper than table salt.
What **separates** the **talented individual**
from the successful one is a lot of **hard work**.

—*Stephen King*
Bestselling author with more than forty books in print,
many of which have been made into movies

125 It's All About Building Momentum

When a NASA rocket takes off, it uses up a large portion of its total fuel just to overcome the gravitational pull of the Earth. But as soon as it gets beyond the gravitational pull, the rocket can virtually coast through space for the rest of the journey.

Just like that rocket, you'll often find that the hardest part in getting the life you want is getting started. Once you get moving, however, your successes build on each other, creating even more success.

Look at any athlete. When they start off, they put in full days of training, intense exercise, and rigorous self-discipline. Then the hard work pays off. They win a gold medal or a world championship. They get offers for endorsements, spokesperson contracts, speaking engagements, retail merchandise deals. Many other opportunities come pouring in, allowing them to slow down a bit and take advantage of the momentum they created earlier in their careers.

Does this only work with athletes? Definitely not. In school, in business, in any profession, you can create momentum by committing to give your best at everything you do. When this becomes a habit, you get to reap the rewards for the rest of your life.

The **pain** is only **temporary**; the **benefits** last **forever**.

Jack: When I started speaking, no one had ever heard of me. As I delivered more speeches and worked hard to give my best effort, my reputation grew and grew. As a result, new and better opportunities continued to gravitate toward me. The same was true for writing books. It took many years to get good at it. But today, I get to enjoy so much more in my life simply because of the time and energy I invested years ago.

ll successful people know that if you are willing to pay the price in the beginning, you will enjoy the benefits for years to come. Musician and performer Ryan Cabrera knows what it means to "pay the price." Here's his story:

Ryan, 24 (Los Angeles, CA): I was sixteen years old when I saw Dave Mathews play at a live concert. He inspired me to pick up a guitar and learn to play. At that time, I had no background in music, but that day I had a new dream and a new passion to be a musician. I had no idea how I was going to begin a career in music, but I was willing to do whatever it took to become the best I could be.

...AND I OWE THIS TO A SEED OF INSPIRATION AND A LOT OF HARD WORK.

I spent all my money on a vocal coach who helped me improve my singing. It was far tougher than I thought it would be. I called it "The Jean-Claude Van Damme School of Vocal Training." My coach made me do 1,200 bicycles a day (similar to ab crunches), then she had me hold a chair above my head while singing scales. It was like torture, but it really helped.

Since I had no money, I didn't have much freedom either. I basically locked myself in my room day after day and practiced for five months straight. During this whole process, I had heard it all. My parents told me to get a "real job." My friends thought I was "crazy," and other people told me, "You're too old to start playing the guitar." But I still held strong to my dream.

With enough persistence, I was able to audition in front of several big record companies over the next few years. Eventually, I got my record deal. It was such a great feeling. And yes, it took me a while to build my "momentum," but now my life is so different. I have my freedom, a nice house, and some really great friendships. But there's no doubt about it: I would not be where I am today, enjoying this much success, if I didn't pay my dues in the past.

Break Through the Awkward Stage

Anything **worth doing well** is **worth doing badly** in the **beginning**.

—*Marshall Thurber*
Writer and director of *Dodgeball*, the movie

It doesn't matter how talented you are; there is always a learning curve when you try new things. Remember when you first learned to ride a bicycle, drive a car, play an instrument, juggle three balls, or play a sport? It was awkward at first, but part of you understood this in advance—before you even got into it. You assumed that awkwardness was just part of the process. It was simply required to learn that new skill you wanted.

Well, not surprisingly, this initial awkwardness applies to anything we take on. We must be willing to go through the awkward stage in order to become better. When we were young, we accepted this learning curve with no trouble, but as we get older we are so often afraid of making a mistake that we don't let ourselves be awkward. We become so afraid of doing something wrong that we often avoid the very situations and challenges that would make our life fun and exciting. Why? Just to avoid that awkward stage!

Jamie, 26 (Miami, FL): Throughout my teenage years, I always wanted to learn how to snowboard. But living in Florida meant no snow . . . no close place to practice. I'd see pictures of people cruising down perfect snow-covered slopes, but I also heard stories through friends about how difficult it was to learn or how they embarrassed themselves numerous times as they fell getting off the lifts. Part of me wanted to go, but I was also nervous and scared that it would be a painful and embarrassing experience. As a result, I just daydreamed about it and avoided it.

Time ticked by (eight years to be exact) until an opportunity came up that I couldn't refuse. I didn't want to put it off anymore, so I went for it. Did I embarrass myself at times? Yes. Did I have some painful falls? Yes. But was it worth it? Absolutely!

All winners were once **beginners**

I can't believe I waited until I was twenty-four to start! But now that I've taken that first step to learn how to do it, I can't even imagine what my life would be like if I hadn't taken that action. I've made some great friends that I never would have met, and now I feel more confident to try other new opportunities. You have to start somewhere, so there's no point in worrying about things. I've learned that when you start something new, the awkwardness is only temporary, but the rewards are long lasting.

It might be awkward to go on a date for the first time, give a presentation in front of the class, audition for the school play, try out for the talent show, or try out for a new team, but when we understand that it's just part of life (and that everyone goes through it), then we will be much more willing to try new things. To gain a new skill or get better at anything, we have to be willing to risk looking foolish.

All success stories—sports professionals, actors, businesspeople, artists, musicians—have experienced embarrassment, and all learned ways to push past that embarrassment. That's how they became the best at what they do . . . by paying the price, taking a risk, and persevering until they finally got it right. You can, too!

128 What's the Price?

hat price are you willing to pay to reach your dreams? Of course, if you don't know what the price is, you can't choose to pay it. Sometimes, the first step is to investigate what steps will be required for you to achieve your goals. When we know what we're getting into, we can mentally prepare.

Kent: Three years ago, I knew someone who had his heart set on buying a specific car. He was driven, focused, and determined. Sure enough, he saved enough money to finally get it. What he didn't realize were the sacrifices he would have to make to keep the car. He had to take on two part-time jobs just to earn enough money to make his car payments and cover the maintenance and insurance. As a result, he had to quit his baseball team. He slowly drifted away from his friends, and his social life disappeared. In his own words, he "sacrificed my high-school experience." Now, three years later, the car has been sold, and he wishes he could go back and do things differently. In his opinion, the price was not really worth it.

And it's not just monetary costs either. If your dream was to be a professional video-game player, you'd have to ask yourself if it's worth the time it would take. Is it worth the risk of coming up short and having very little to fall back on? How would it affect your family, your friends, your health, etc.? Will you have enough time to do the other things you want to do or must do?

TIP: What costs have others had to pay to achieve dreams similar to yours? You may need to do some research. Make a list of several people who have already done what you want to do and interview them about the sacrifices they had to make along the way.

Your research will show you whether or not some of the costs are more than you want to pay. You may not want to risk your health, relationships, or entire life savings for a certain goal. It's important to weigh all of the factors. The fancy car you want may not be worth your friendships, grades, or the lack of balance in your life.

Only you can decide what is right for you and what price you are willing to pay. It may be that what you want doesn't really help you in the long term. But if it does, find what you need to do, push through the awkward stage, *lean into it,* and get started! With enough momentum, almost anything is possible!

MY "TO-DO" LIST

☑ Realize there is a story of education, training, practice, discipline, and sacrifice behind every great achievement. True, long-lasting success does not happen overnight.

☑ Realize that getting started is the hardest part, but if I'm willing to make some sacrifices and take action, I can build momentum that will help me for the rest of my life.

☑ Even though we all have different levels of talent, education, and resources, we all have the same amount of time. It's how I spend my time that will have the greatest effect on the quality of my life.

☑ Realize that the awkwardness of doing something new is temporary, but the rewards can last a lifetime.

☑ Discover what the real costs will be to achieve my goals.

☑ Interview people who have already done what I want to do and find out what sacrifice they had to make to reach their goals.

ASK!
ASK!
ASK!

You've got to **ask**.
Asking is, in my opinion, the world's
most powerful and **neglected secret**
to **success** and **happiness**.

—*Percy Ross*
Self-made millionaire and philanthropist

There are so many answers, hints, techniques, benefits, and opportunities available in life . . . if we just have the courage to *ask* for them. Throughout history, we see countless examples of how someone's life changed radically simply by asking key questions.

Would Christopher Columbus have discovered the New World if he had not *asked* the queen for a fleet of ships and a crew of men? (And where would we be now? Hmmm . . .) Imagine if Thomas Edison had not *asked* for the funding he needed to finish many of his experiments—including the light bulb. You'd be reading this book in the dark!

And, of course, President John F. Kennedy posed this powerful command to the American people: "Ask not what your country can do for you; ask what you can do for your country." As you see, then, asking for help isn't limited to the weak and powerless; it is a tool of all resourceful, courageous people!

BEHOLD THE POWER OF THE QUESTION.

Tiger Woods became an exceptional athlete because he asked for additional training and coaching. When Bill Murray, the famous Hollywood star, was looking to make a name for himself, he asked John Belushi, a very respected comedic actor at the time, to be his mentor and help him hone his act. The incredible Leonardo DaVinci asked another greatly respected artist, Verocchio, to coach him. Twenty-one-year-old Chad Pegracke asked for $2.5 million to reach his goal. (You'll learn how he did this shortly.)

When we have the courage to ask the right questions, we allow ourselves to use more of our potential to achieve extraordinary results. Asking for what we want or need opens many new doors, behind which are limitless possibilities.

13.1 Asking Creates New Possibilities

Kent: My dreams would have been very short-lived if I didn't ask for help from others. When I first started my publishing company, there were times I couldn't even pay the bills. I approached people who believed in me and what I was doing, and I asked them if they would lend me money so I could stay in business. Although it was not easy and I felt a little uncomfortable, I was motivated to keep my business going—and I knew no one was going to simply start shoving money in my pocket without me first asking. I found that most people, when asked, are interested in helping young people reach their goals.

With enough asking, I did get the funding I needed to keep my business alive. Today, I have paid back all of my loans. I enjoy the satisfaction of owning a successful business that improves the lives of other people, but I definitely wouldn't be where I am now—doing what I am doing today—if I didn't ask for the support of other people.

When we see all of these successful entrepreneurs, musicians, actors, athletes, authors, dancers, and speakers, sometimes we assume they made the entire journey by themselves. This is rarely true. In most cases, we've found the opposite to be true. Almost all successful individuals—as different as they may appear—have asked other people to help them somewhere along the way. And take note: Asking is not a sign of weakness; it's a sign of courage and dedication, demonstrating you are willing to pay the price (remember that?) for long-term success.

Think of all those times in your own life when nothing would have happened unless you asked that first question to get the ball rolling. Maybe you're dating someone who you never would have been with unless you first asked them out on a date. Or maybe you wouldn't have finished an important school paper if you hadn't asked your teacher for advice, hints, or extra time. Or perhaps you received 20% off on your MP3 player because you asked the store to discount the display model. How about that time you were given free tickets to an event simply because you asked for them? Can you see how your requests—as simple as they may seem—really influenced your life?

There are many examples of people who have received incredible resources, opportunities, and benefits simply by asking for them. This is one of the most powerful Success Principles of all, yet surprisingly, it is still a challenge that many of us avoid. Most people hold themselves back simply by not asking for the information, help, support, money, and time they need to reach their full potential and make their dreams come true. But not you—at least, *not anymore*! Let's explore ways to overcome the fear of asking so you can ask for what you need to build the life you really want.

3.2 Me, Afraid to Ask?

o, why are people so afraid to ask? There are many reasons, such as the awkwardness of looking needy, foolish, or stupid. No one wants to experience that! But we've discovered that the most common barrier stopping people from using the power of asking is simply the fear of getting rejected. They are afraid to hear the word no.

The sad thing is, if you start to think about it, these people who are afraid to ask are actually *rejecting themselves* in advance. In other words, they're saying "no" to themselves before anyone else even has a chance to! You might want to read those last two sentences again. Have you ever thought of it that way?

One of the most limiting things you can do is assume that your idea or request will get rejected. Instead, take the risk to ask for whatever you need and want. If you do get a no, you're no worse off than when you started! And if you get a yes, then you are *a lot* better off! Just be willing to ask because you may just land a hot date, get a better assignment, get a part in the play, work with a more exciting group, get a chance to start on the team, or get the help you need to finish a project or start a business. Who knows? The opportunities are unlimited!

TIP: Become aware of the questions you ask *yourself.* Instead of thinking, "What if they say 'no'?" or "What if it doesn't work?" try asking yourself new, positive questions such as, "What if they say *yes*?" or "What if it *does* work out?" Don't let fear of getting a "no" hold you back. When you ask yourself more positive questions, your brain will start searching for and recognizing the benefits of asking others for what you need. The more benefits you're aware of, the more confidence you will have. You'll notice that your fears won't hold you back because all of the positives of taking action will motivate you to approach others and ask for help, support, or resources.

13.3 The Art Of Asking

ow do I ask for what I want?" Very good question. And yes, there is a specific science to asking and getting what you want or need in life, but don't worry—it's not as complicated as rocket science. It's simpler than that! Here are some quick tips to help:

1. **Ask as if you expect to get it.** Don't just cross your fingers and hope; ask as though you absolutely expect to get the outcome you want. Ask with the mindset that you have already been given a "yes" or the resources you need. Act as if it's already a done deal. Assume you can. Don't start with the assumption that you can't get something. If you're going to make assumptions, assume you can— and *will*—get the result you want. With that said, approach people in a respectful manner. Don't be arrogant and in their face. You can be kind and patient while

expecting to get a "yes." Assume that you get to play the position you want on the team. Assume that you can get a scholarship. Assume that he or she will say yes when you ask them to the dance. Assume that you will get to use the car on Friday night, get the part in the play, get the help you need, get the job. When you assume the negative, you are working against yourself. Assume things will work out the way you would like, and you will have much more drive to make it happen.

2. **Ask someone who can give it to you.** Size up the person before you ask. Does he or she qualify? Be intelligent about whom you ask to get what you want. Start by asking yourself questions, such as, "Who would I need to speak with to get . . .?" "Who can give me permission to . . .?" "Who has the resources I need to . . .?" And "What would have to happen for me to get this result?"

3. **Be clear and specific.** When we give speeches, we often ask the audience, "Who wants more money?" Then we'll pick someone who raises their hand and we will give that person a dollar. We say, "You now have more money. Are you satisfied?"

The person usually says, "No, I want more than that."

So we give the person a couple of quarters and ask, "Is that enough?"

"No, I want more than that."

"Well, just how much do you want? We could play this game of 'more' for days and never get to what you want."

The person then will usually give us a specific number, and then we point out how important it is to be precise in your requests.

Remember, vague requests will get you vague results. Your questions and requests must be specific if you want a specific outcome. What do we mean? Here are some examples.

Don't say: *Can I get a better seat?*

Do say: *May I take that seat in the front row?*

Don't say: *Will you support our band by donating some money?*

Do say: *Could you please donate $100 to our band so we can travel to the statewide Battle of the Bands competition?*

Don't say: *Can we spend some time together this weekend?*

Do say: *Would you like to go out for dinner and a movie with me on Saturday night?*

Don't say: *Could you give me some help with my history assignment?*

Do say: *Will you spend an hour with me after school on Thursday to help me with my history assignment?*

4. **Ask repeatedly.** It's not realistic to think that we will get exactly what we want the first time we ask for it. The key is not to see your first "no" as a dead end. One of the most important principles of success is *persistence*—not giving up.

 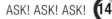

Whenever you're asking other people to help you and participate in the fulfillment of your goals, some people are going to say no. It's nothing personal; they may have other priorities, commitments, and reasons not to participate. It's not a reflection on you or your dreams.

A DASH OF CONFIDENCE. A SPLASH OF VISION. ASK ALL THE RIGHT QUESTIONS, AND... VOILÀ A RECIPE FOR SUCCESS.

Hearing "no" along the way is just part of *paying the price* (remember that?). Accept the fact that there is going to be some rejection along the way. The important thing is not to give up. When you do get a no, don't stop there. Keep on asking. It could just be your timing or some unforeseen circumstances—or maybe it's time to ask someone else.

Kids are excellent at asking for what they want and need. We need to keep that fighting spirit as we grow older and let the word "no" just bounce off us. Those who assume they can get the result they want expect to get it and will enjoy many more benefits and opportunities. The key, then, is to keep our spirits high and persevere.

13.4 "No" Was Not an Option

After watching a documentary in her class about Mexico, twelve-year-old Jessica Wellmont was inspired. She had a new dream. She saw how many Mexicans were living in poverty and wanted to do something to help. She couldn't understand how people just a few hundred miles away from her were living without the basic necessities of life that she enjoyed every day—things such as a solid roof overhead, running water, clean bathrooms, electricity, and so on.

She set a goal to build a house for a Mexican family in Ensenada, one of the cities she saw in the documentary. The only problem was, she had no idea how she was going to do it. But that didn't stop her because she wasn't afraid to ask for help. She made a flyer with her felt pens and coloring pencils that described her goal. She made photocopies and handed them out to her friends, family, and fellow students.

At first, she didn't get much support. People thought her idea was "cute" (as she remembers), but they didn't realize how determined she really was. "The flyers didn't really work because people didn't think I was really going to do it," Jessica said. "I had to find a new way to let them know that I was serious."

Without losing her enthusiasm, she attempted some new approaches to ask for support. She tried mailing out handwritten letters throughout her neighborhood, but that didn't work. She tried gathering donations from students at school, but she didn't bring in enough money. She even held a garage sale, made and sold crafts, and tried selling homemade Christmas cards, but it wasn't working as well as she hoped. The only thing she did not do was give up!

With nothing more than a dream and a desire to make a difference, Jessica wouldn't take "no" for an answer. She then started asking adults, parents, and business owners face-to-face for their help and/or any financial support. Finally, her persistence started to pay off.

She began to convince people that she was committed to making this happen. Not only did she convince some of her friends and fellow students to get involved, but she also won the support of many adults. Some people donated money; some provided their time; others used their vehicles to further the cause.

Nine months later, she—and her crew of sixteen—loaded up some trucks and vans and headed down to Ensenada, Mexico. As a team, they built a modest house and gifted it to a very deserving family that, as she put it, "would not stop thanking us."

Not only did Jessica change the lives of those family members forever, but she learned firsthand how asking—and following your dream with absolute dedication— can forever change your life. Even though she was only twelve, Jessica feels very confident that she can now get the support, help, and resources she needs to realize any of her dreams and goals—no matter how big they may be.

If a twelve-year-old can start with nothing, raise thousands of dollars, assemble a team of sixteen people, and travel to another country to build a house for those less fortunate, then you, too, can certainly ask for what you need to make your dreams a reality!

13.5 some shocking statistics

 veryone knows that it can be really difficult to be a door-to-door salesperson. But what exactly are the statistics here? Check this out: Door-to-door salespeople get rejected 90% of the time—and that's not to mention the crazy dogs, creepy people, and unexpected obstacles they encounter along the way. This means they get turned down at least nine out of ten times before making a sale. Imagine that! The successful ones choose to focus on the 10% that do buy. They realize that they must visit 100 houses to make ten sales.

Kent: By the time our first book was finally published, my brother and I were in desperate need of income to cover our expenses. We had asked people for financial support to help us start our business, but now we needed to ask people to buy our books so we could *stay* in business. We hit the streets running with boxes of books to sell door-to-door. Little did we know what we were getting ourselves into . . .

On our first day, we convinced our friend to join us in hopes of selling a large number of books. Well, we barely made enough money to pay for our gas! In most cases, we were asked to leave people's houses and offices before we even had a chance to show them our book and explain what it was about. Sometimes guard dogs forced us to keep our distance. Other times, people just didn't want to have anything to do with salesmen—but we knew if we could just get people to see the book and hear our explanation, they would have to have it!

The second day, our friend chose not to join us, and sadly, the results were the same: only a few sales. On the third day, we had similar results again. By now we were tired, confused, and frustrated. We were ready to call it quits, but we weren't in a position where we had that choice. We needed to earn money to keep our dream alive. "Just keep asking," we told ourselves.

The fourth day, we talked to a church, a bank, and a motorcycle company that collectively ordered hundreds of books! They absolutely loved the book! We had several more small orders as well. In that one day alone, we earned a few thousand dollars! The money we earned that day, and in the following weeks, allowed us to pay off some of our loans and grow our business—and pay for gas! Although those first three days were tough, we learned a lot, but perhaps the most important lesson was learning not to give up when we heard a "no."

Herbert True is a marketing specialist at the University of Notre Dame. In an extensive study, he found that:

※ 44% of all sales people quit trying after the first sales call

※ 24% quit after the second call

※ 14% quit after the third call

※ 12% quit trying to sell their product to a customer after the fourth call

It doesn't matter if you're making sales calls to sell a product or asking people to help you reach your goals—the game is the same. It involves the willingness to take risks and to pay the price. If you total the numbers on the left, you see that 94% of all salespeople quit by the fourth call. But here's what's really interesting: 60% of all sales are made after the fourth call! This shows that 94% of all salespeople don't even give themselves a chance at 60% of the selling opportunities they have! Incredible!

Don't be one of these statistics. Keep asking until you get the result. If you think about it, we are all salespeople in our own way. We sell people on our ideas, dreams, goals, and our own capabilities. Even the top achievers in the world still have to sell people on their visions and aspirations. It's all part of being successful. We all have the capacity to ask questions and succeed, but we must also develop the tenacity to follow through. To live the best life you can, you'll have to ask, ask, ask, ask, ask!

13.6 JUSt ASk

In 1997, twenty-two-year-old Chad Pregracke set his sights on a really big dream. He wanted to clean the shores of the Mississippi River. To say the least, he was a man on a mission. He started with a twenty-foot boat and his own two hands. Since that time, he has navigated thousands of miles of our nation's mightiest rivers, pulling more than 4 million pounds of debris from the riverbanks.

To achieve these remarkable results, Chad used the power of asking to raise more than $2.5 million in donations and enlisted more than 40,000 people to help him with his crusade.

When Chad first realized there was a garbage problem on the Mississippi River, he asked state and local offices to help, only to be turned down. Refusing to get discouraged, Chad grabbed a phone book, turned to the list of businesses, and called Alcoa—"because," as Chad said, "it started with an A, and it was the first listing in the phone book."

Armed with only his passionate commitment to his dream, Chad asked to speak with the "top guy." Eventually, Alcoa gave him $8,400 to work by himself for one summer. Not a bad start! A year later, working his way through the A's, he called Anheuser-Busch. As reported in *Smithsonian* magazine, Mary Alice Ramirez, the Director of Environmental Outreach at Anheuser-Busch, remembers her first conversation with Chad:

"Will you give me some money?" Chad asked.

"Who are you?" replied Ramirez.

"I want to get rid of the garbage in the Mississippi River," Chad said.

"Can you show me a proposal?" Ramirez inquired.

"What's a proposal?" Chad replied.

Ramirez eventually invited Chad to a meeting and gave him a check for $25,000 to expand his Mississippi River Beautification and Restoration Project. With this extra money, Chad was able to get another boat and hire some friends to help clean up the enormous river.

Chad's knowledge of how to effectively ask for money began to grow, but what was even more important was his desire to make a difference, his constant enthusiasm, his complete dedication to his project—and yes (you knew it was coming), his willingness to *ask*.

Eventually, Chad gathered everything he needed by asking the right people the right questions, and not stopping until he achieved the result he wanted. He now has a board of directors made up of lawyers, accountants, and corporate officers. He has several full-time staff members and thousands of volunteers.

Chad's journey has literally transformed his life. He has not only removed trash from the shorelines of the Mississippi, Illinois, Anacostia, Potomac, Ohio, and Missouri Rivers, but he's also developed a newfound passion to preserve the health and beauty of all rivers. His vision and dream has inspired thousands of people to help make a positive difference by showing them the responsibility we all share in keeping our environment clean.

Chad was proactive and took to heart what President John F. Kennedy said, "Ask not what your country can do for you; ask what you can do for your country." He asked himself, "What can I do, and how can I do it?" As a result, he recognized a solution and felt a sense of responsibility to take massive action and improve the situation. So what questions can you start asking yourself and other people to begin shaping your life and your world in a positive way?

13.7 Start Asking NOW

To unleash the power of asking, you must first be *willing* to ask—and we know from experience that this can be a scary process. But the good news is, it doesn't have to stay that way. You may be wondering, *"So, how do I overcome my fears of asking for what I want?"* Ah . . . now that's a great first question. Fill out your answers to the questions on a piece of paper to build the confidence you need to ask the questions that will help you create the life you want.

1. **List the things that you want—but don't usually ask for—at home, school, practice, or work.**

2. **Next to each item describe how and why you are stopping yourself from asking. What is your fear? What do you normally feel before you ask for what you need?**

3. Now, write down what it is costing you *not* to ask. What are you missing out on by not asking for what you need?

4. Finally, write down how your life would be better if you were to ask for what you need. What benefits would you enjoy? How much faster would you reach your goals?

5. Write one brief sentence for each thing you listed in number one describing why you *should* ask for what you want. What would you say to convince yourself to start asking for more in your life?

Remember, the first time you do anything is often the most difficult. Then, after that first time, you will get better and better at asking for what you need, and you will get the results you really want. We hope you took the time to do the above exercise. If it's done right, it's very powerful. Don't let another day go by before you get clear on what you need and want. Then begin to take charge by asking for it. Make it happen!

MY "TO-DO" LIST

☑ Realize that more opportunities and benefits come to those who are assertive and ask for what they need to reach their goals.

☑ Understand that many of the greatest achievers in the world are great because they have learned to ask effective questions that have encouraged other people to help them.

☑ Make a habit out of asking *myself* new, positive questions, such as, "What if they say yes?" and "What if it *does* work out?"

☑ Take the risk to ask because even if I get a "no," I'm no worse off than when I started. But if I get a "yes," then I am a *lot* better off.

☑ When I ask for what I want, I should assume and expect that I *can* get it.

☑ Qualify each person to make sure he or she is the right person to ask.

☑ Make my requests clear and specific so I can increase my chances of getting what I really need.

☑ Ask repeatedly. Getting a "no" is no reason to stop asking for what I need. I will keep asking until I get the result I want.

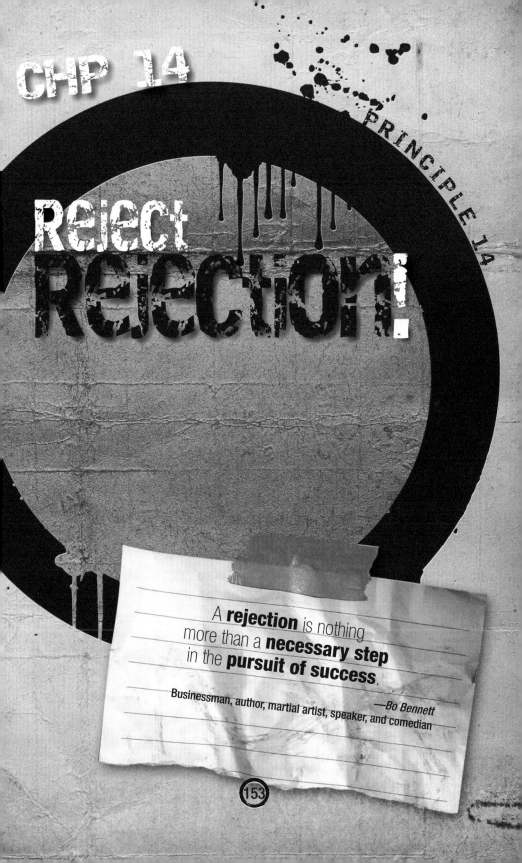

Reject Rejection!

A **rejection** is nothing more than a **necessary step** in the **pursuit of success.**

—Bo Bennett
Businessman, author, martial artist, speaker, and comedian

When Henry Ford came up with the idea to build an automobile on an assembly line, he knew that his cars would increase comfort and convenience, cut down on travel time, and boost the economy. Sounds impressive, right? But no matter how good his idea was, people still told him it was ridiculous. He was rejected when he looked for funding, and he was constantly criticized in the media. But that didn't stop Mr. Ford. He rejected the rejection . . . and persevered.

When we see successful people, we don't see their past history and all of the obstacles that were in their way. All we see is their current success. It's easy to think that successful people didn't have to deal with rejection, but in fact, the opposite is true. We've interviewed countless great achievers, and they ALL agree: Rejection is a prerequisite for success. You see, it's not something to be feared; it's something to be welcomed, because the lessons we can learn from rejection make us stronger, wiser, and more skilled.

Even Sir Isaac Newton, now considered one of the most influential scientists of all time, was considered nuts by his own generation. His ideas and theories were constantly being rejected.

And who said women cannot fly planes? Apparently, most people did! When aviation was still in its infancy, Amelia Earhart heard what everyone had said: Women can't fly airplanes! But Amelia wasn't afraid to break down barriers. In 1932, she pushed aside all doubt and disbelief and became the first woman to pilot a plane across the Atlantic Ocean. By her actions, she motivated other women not only to become pilots, but to follow their dreams, no matter what they were. She faced incredible rejection and resistance—enough to break most other people—but she still broke through long-standing social barriers.

Who knows what our world would be like today if Ford, Sir Isaac Newton, Amelia Earhart, and other groundbreakers had given up on their dreams because they were rejected by their peers!

14.1 Rejection Is a Myth!

Let's look at this topic from a completely different perspective and pretend that rejection is a myth. How would our lives be different? Well, let's see . . .

First, we'd have to believe that rejection is simply a concept that exists in our heads—and if we stop and think about it, we'll discover that's true. Look at it this way: If you ask somebody out on a date and the answer is "no," you didn't have a date before you asked, and now you don't have a date after you asked. Did the situation really get any worse? No, it stayed the same.

It gets worse only if *you* make it worse—only if you tell yourself something extra like, "Yeah, that kid in my sixth-grade class was right. No one will ever like me. I am the slug of the universe!" Only if you build on that negativity does the rejection become worse. In other words, *you* must add to that "no" and *allow* yourself to feel rejected in order to feel lousy. Rejection is just something we create in our heads. When we realize how this process works, we can take control and make sure that rejection doesn't hold us back.

Here's another example: If you try out for the soccer team and you don't make it, you weren't on the team before you tried out and you aren't on it after you tried out. Again, your life didn't get worse; it stayed the same. You cannot lose something you don't really have. This is why rejection is a myth.

The truth is, you have nothing to lose by asking, trying, or being proactive. Rejection is dangerous only when:

1. It is taken personally,
or
2. You let it cause you to stop taking action.

Let's take a closer look at number one: Taking rejection personally. Most people would agree that rejection is painful, but they never stop to understand why—they just think it's out of their control. But it's not. You see, in order to feel or experience the pain that comes from rejection, we must be taking something personally—as though it is an attack on us, which in most cases, it's not.

Jasmine, 17 (Newark, NJ): I'm the type of person who likes to talk and discuss everything. Ever since I can remember, my teachers, parents, and friends have told me to join the speech and debate team. Finally, in my sophomore year, I took their advice. I spent a few months just learning the basics of public speaking and how to correctly present my thoughts in a formal debate.

At my first debate competition, I did really well and won the contest. Some people said it was beginner's luck, but I set out to prove otherwise. I worked hard to win my next competition and the one after that. I ended up winning eight in a row. I felt unstoppable—as though I could never lose.

However, everything changed on my ninth competition. I thought I did well until the judges opened their mouths. They said my "information was inadequate and poorly arranged, and my thoughts were disjointed." I felt like I was on *American Idol* getting grilled by Simon Cowell!

"What?" I said to myself. I couldn't understand it. How could they think that? How could they reject my thoughts, my opinion, my efforts—me? I was really devastated. But these questions only deepened my pain. I began to focus on the wrong things, and I overanalyzed what the judges said. During the next few days, my confidence almost disappeared, and my self-esteem went with it. I remember thinking, "Maybe everyone was right. It was probably just beginner's luck anyway. Maybe I'm just a good talker and not such a good debater."

I told my speech and debate teacher that I wanted to quit the team. She laughed at me and said, "You're not serious, are you?" I guess I was really affected by the judges' comments. After speaking with my teacher, she made me realize that I was not using the feedback; it was using me. The real problem was not the judges—they weren't trying to embarrass me. The real problem was *me*. I was the one taking it personally. I was blaming other people, complaining about losing, and feeling sorry for myself. And as long as I did this, I couldn't see the lesson it was offering me. I was rejecting myself because there was no way I could use the feedback to improve.

I soon realized that there actually was no "rejection" involved in this process at all. The only rejection I experienced was what I was creating in my head by telling myself that I was no good. I learned how easy it is to turn feedback into rejection by taking things personally.

It doesn't matter if you're on the speech and debate team, a sports team, in a marching band, in the classroom, at work, or just hanging out with your friends—you will at times hear people say things that may not make you feel so great. That's not being negative; it's realistic. Wouldn't you agree? So if it is realistic, then it definitely helps to be prepared for that type of feedback. Try this: Look at your results as merely a reflection of what you're doing—not who you are. You can always change how you act and what you're doing. Remember, when you change what you do, you will get a different result. Henry Ford once said:

Failure is the opportunity to **do something again** . . . more intelligently.

If you get feedback that appears to be rejection, just remember that this is just your signal to do something differently and try again. Take yourself out of the equation. We have to be careful to take only the lesson that is being offered—nothing more.

> We should be careful to **get out of an experience** only the
> **wisdom** that is in it—and **stop there**;
> lest we be like the cat that sits down on a hot stove-lid.
> She will never sit down on a hot stove-lid again—
> and that is well; but also she will never sit down
> on a cold one anymore.
>
> —*Mark Twain*
> **American humorist, lecturer, and writer**

Rejection can also be dangerous if it stops us from taking action and prevents us from moving toward our goals. We've found that rejection is the one of the most common barriers that stops people from reaching their potential and becoming successful. But rejection is not a stop sign or a dead end—unless that's how you *choose* to look at it.

Kent: One of my friends was an extremely talented athlete. His goal was always to become a professional baseball player—and he was definitely capable of it. But he solely relied on his natural ability to succeed, and that was his downfall.

Since he wasn't used to making mistakes, he didn't take feedback very well. Every time a coach, a teammate, or his parents tried to give him suggestions, he felt a sense of rejection—as though he wasn't good enough. The problem was, in order to perform at the next level, he needed the insight his coaches, teammates, and parents were offering him. But instead of listening and working on his weaknesses, he just quit the team and started playing a different sport.

Everyone thought he would eventually come to his senses and start using the feedback to improve, but he never did. As soon he felt rejected, he would stop taking action and focus on something else. At the time, he didn't see any major consequences. But ten years went by, and he never developed enough skill in any sport to reach a professional level. In fact, he never even made the starting lineup on his college baseball team. He always had the ability, but it didn't matter because once he felt any sort of rejection, he would pull back and stop trying. From his example I learned that in life, it doesn't matter what you're doing; if you don't continue to take action and work through challenges, there is no way you can grow to become better and use your full ability.

If our attitude is "I'm not trying that again!" whenever we face rejection, then chances are we will never reach our dreams or accomplish our goals. Don't allow that to happen! You always have this choice: (1) to stop trying and give up when you face rejection OR (2) look at the rejection as an opportunity to prove to yourself that you can and will be successful. In the end, you choose whether rejection will stop you or motivate you to become more of what you can be.

My **drive** came out of my **reaction to rejection**.

—*Harrison Ford*
Actor

SW-SW-SW-SW

What on Earth do these letters stand for? No, we're not stuttering. These eight letters are just an abbreviation for an extremely powerful concept you should apply to your life. Interested? We thought so.

Here's how it works: Whenever you ask anyone for anything, remember the acronym SW-SW-SW-SW, which stands for *"some will, some won't, so what?— someone's waiting."* In the last chapter we talked about the power of asking for what we need to reach our goals. We also mentioned that one of the main reasons people don't ask is that they are afraid of being rejected. The truth is, when we ask other people for anything, some are going to say yes, and some are going to say no. *So what!*

This doesn't mean that everyone will say no. In fact, out there somewhere, someone is waiting for you: your ideas, your passion, your drive, and your skills. It's simply a numbers game.

The next time you share your goals with someone and ask for help or participation in your dreams, remember SW-SW-SW-SW. What you want or need is available to you; you just have to hang in there long enough to eventually get a "yes."

What you want wants you,

—*Mark Victor Hansen*
Inspirational Author & Speaker

14.3 REJECTION MOVES YOU CLOSER TO A "YES"

If **someone says your idea is wrong**, then it might be **too fantastic to be understood**.

—*Author Unknown*

Jack: A graduate from one of my seminars said the event helped her so much she wanted to volunteer to make phone calls to enroll people in an upcoming seminar of mine. She made a commitment to talk to three people every night for a month. She made a total of ninety phone calls. The first eighty-one people decided not to take the seminar, but the next nine people all signed up.

What if she had given up after the first fifty people and said, "This just isn't working. It's not worth my effort." If she had that attitude, she would have had zero sales and wasted all of her time. But because she was committed to sharing this life-transforming experience with others, she persevered in the face of rejection, knowing that if she made enough calls, she would eventually get a "yes." Not only did she help me by bringing nine new people to my seminar, but she also helped those nine people by inspiring them to transform their lives by attending the event.

> **You have** to **be passionate.** You have to be **able to take rejection** and disappointment at first and **not let your confidence** be **undermined.**
>
> —Juliet Mills
> Actress

We never know when we're going to get the "yes" that opens up countless new opportunities for us. Success comes when you least expect it—often after you've overcome many challenges and persevered through each one. Sometimes, following one rejection after another, you reach a certain point where you notice that the successes you were working for seem to come to you all at once.

14.4 JUST SAY "NEXT!"

hances are, you've heard of KFC. But how could this be? Is it really possible, given all our readers in different parts of the world who have read this book, that almost all have heard of KFC? *Everyone?* That's rather impressive, don't you think?

There is no doubt that KFC has become incredibly successful around the world. But the success of this restaurant did not come easy. Colonel Harlan Sanders, the founder of KFC, started by cooking food for customers in his living quarters at a small auto-service station. From there, he headed up a restaurant in a hotel. Over the next nine years, he perfected his recipes and gained a lot of popularity, but he still wanted to take his business to the next level.

Almost sixty years old, Colonel Sanders left home with his pressure cooker and his special recipe for cooking Southern fried chicken to sell his mass-marketed chain-restaurant idea. Well, after he received more than 300 rejections, he finally found someone to believe in his dream. But because he rejected rejection more than 300 times, there are now 11,000 KFC restaurants in eighty countries around the world!

The reason Colonel Sanders became so successful in his life was because he didn't stop when other people didn't share his same thoughts, ideas, and dreams. We need to get used to the idea that there are going to be a lot of rejections along the way to achieving our goals. The secret to success is to not give up. When someone says "no," just say "Next!" and keep on moving toward your dream.

Most of the **important things** in the world
have been **accomplished by people** who have
kept on **trying** when there seemed to be **no help at all**.

—Dale Carnegie
American writer, author, trainer, and speaker

Jack: Mark Victor Hansen and I were so excited to travel to New York City in the fall of 1991 to begin the process of selling our first Chicken Soup for the Soul book to a publisher. With our agent, Jeff Herman, we met with every major publisher that would grant us a meeting. All of them said they weren't interested. "Collections of short stories don't sell." "There's no edge to the stories." "The title will never work." We heard it all!

After being rejected by more than thirty publishers, our agent gave our book back to us and said, "I'm sorry; I can't sell it for you." What did we do? We said, *"Next!"* We knew we had to think outside of the box. After weeks of intense thought, it finally came to us. We printed a form that was a promise to buy the book when it was published. It included a place for people to write their names, addresses, and the number of books they promised to buy.

Over a period of months, we asked everyone who attended our speeches or seminars to complete one of these forms if they would buy a copy of the book when it was published. Eventually, we had pages and pages of promises from people who agreed to buy a total of 20,000 books! Now we really had some bargaining power!

The following spring, Mark and I attended the American Booksellers Association convention in Anaheim, California. We walked from booth to booth, talking to any publisher who would listen. We were shocked to discover that even with our thousands of signed pledge forms, we were turned down again and again. But again we said, "Next!" At the end of the second very long day, we gave a copy of the first thirty stories to the co-presidents of Health Communications, Inc., a struggling publisher who agreed to take it home and look it over.

Later that week, Gary Seidler took the manuscript to the beach and read it. He loved it and decided to give us a chance. Those hundreds of "Nexts!" had paid off! After more than 140 rejections, that first book went on to sell 8 million copies, which led to a series of 115 bestselling Chicken Soup books that have been translated into forty-seven languages. That's a lot of books!

NEXT...

What happened to the pledge forms? Well, when the book was finally published, we stapled an announcement to all of the signed forms, sent them back to the person at the address on the form, and closely watched the sales list. Almost everyone who had promised to buy a book came through on his or her commitment. In fact, one entrepreneur in Canada bought 1,700 copies and gave one to every one of his clients.

This is just proof that extraordinary success comes as a result of handling rejection with a positive attitude—and the reason we say "attitude" is because it's a *choice*. On an ongoing basis, we choose how we deal with the rejection we experience. We're all going to face rejection at various times in our lives—especially if we dare to set big goals and have big dreams, but it's what we do in the face of that rejection that matters most.

Remember, there are more than 6 billion people on the planet! Someone, somewhere, sometime will say "yes" to your ideas, your dedication, and your ultimate objective. Each "no" brings you closer to a "yes." Don't get stuck hesitating in one place in fear of having someone, somewhere, reject your request or your goal. Move on to the next person, and keep your eyes on your target. It is just a numbers game. Remember, someone is waiting to say "yes."

14.5 Keep on Keepin' on

I take **rejection** as someone blowing a bugle in my ear to wake me up and **get going**, **rather than retreat**.

—*Sylvester Stallone*
Actor

Shortly after graduating, Rick Little didn't want anybody else to go through what he went through. He had a rough upbringing and struggled to get through high school. Rick wanted to help other students by offering practical class lessons that would help them to succeed both in and out of school.

At only nineteen years old, Rick had a dream of starting a program in high schools that would teach young people how to deal with their feelings, handle conflicts, set powerful goals, and learn communication skills and the values that would help them live more effective and fulfilling lives. That's a really big vision.

Inspired by the passion and enthusiasm of his new goal, Rick wrote proposals and approached 155 different foundations and donors to ask for support and funding. All 155 said, "no." Rick did whatever it took for over a year to make ends meet—sleeping in the back of his car and eating peanut butter crackers—but he never gave up on his dream.

On his 156th attempt, he approached the W.K. Kellogg Foundation and asked for $55,000 so he could start developing his idea. Two weeks later, he received a call from the chairman of the foundation; "Rick, you asked us for $55,000, and we collectively voted against it." Rick's heart was shattered. He couldn't believe it. *Another rejection?!* he thought to himself. But before he could say anything, the chairman continued, "However, we did vote to approve a grant of $133,000."

Rick was ecstatic! He couldn't believe his ears. He ended up with more than twice what he had asked for! And if you do the math, that's almost $1,000 for each "no" he endured.

Now, during every school day, Rick's Quest programs are taught in more than 30,000 schools around the world, reaching millions of young people with important life skills because one nineteen-year-old rejected rejection and kept on going until he got a "yes."

A few years later, because of his perseverance and demonstrated success with Quest, Rick received a grant of $65 million—yes, you read that number correctly! At the time, this was the second-largest private foundation grant ever given in U.S. history! Rick used this money to start the International Youth Foundation, where he and his team have been able to positively impact even more young people in seventy countries.

Since then, Rick has gone on to create even another organization called the ImagineNations Group—a collection of some of the world's leading social entrepreneurs, foundations, companies, and organizations all working together with young people to bring positive change to the world.

What if Rick had given up after the 100th rejection and said to himself, "Well, I guess this just isn't going to work out?" Just think about the consequences of that one decision. If Rick had given up on his original dream at age nineteen, there might never have been a Quest, or an International Youth Foundation, or now an ImagineNations Group—together bringing hope and opportunity to millions of young people every day across the world. What a loss that would be!

14.6 carry on . . .

Where there is **no struggle** there is **no strength**.

—*Oprah Winfrey*
Emmy Award-winning host of *The Oprah Winfrey Show*,
the highest-rated talk show in television history

The journey to your dreams may not be easy, and the path to success may not be paved, but never let your dreams slip away when you encounter some friction along the way. Rejection does not need to stop you . . . unless you allow it to stop you by giving up.

Whenever you take a step toward our dreams, you risk facing rejection. It's just part of life. But it's how you handle all of these situations that ultimately shapes your future. Learning to deal with rejection effectively means learning how to deal with life.

IT'S CLOSER THAN YOU THINK.

When people have a dream and work hard to achieve it, they also inspire the people around them to be at their best. In the end, everyone benefits from their optimism, passion, and enthusiasm. Who knows? Maybe one day your story of perseverance will be written in a book or told to other people as an example of what's possible if you don't give up.

I think that you have to **believe** in **your destiny**;
that **you will succeed**. You will meet a lot of rejection
and it is not always a straight path,
there will be detours—so enjoy the view.

—*Michael York*
Actor

MY "TO-DO" LIST

☑ Understand that rejection is just part of life, but those who learn to deal with rejection effectively are always the ones who ultimately become successful and accomplish their goals.

☑ Realize that rejection is really just a myth. It's simply a concept that I hold in my head—nothing more.

☑ Recognize that feedback only becomes rejection if my mind wanders and I tell myself something extra like, "I knew I was no good!" Only then can I make rejection negative. In other words, I must first allow myself to feel rejected in order to feel lousy.

☑ I will remember SW-SW-SW-SW whenever I ask anyone for anything: "Some will, some won't, so what?—someone's waiting."

☑ Realize that every rejection I face can move me closer to a "yes."

☑ When someone says "no," I will just say "Next!" and keep on moving toward my dream.

USE feedback to Fast- FORWARD

> **Feedback** is the **breakfast of champions**.
>
> —*Ken Blanchard*
> Self-made millionaire and bestselling author

It's amazing how accurate modern missiles can be. Shot from thousands of miles away, they have been reported to strike within inches of their target destination. Now that's precision! What is it that makes them so accurate? Despite what many people think, it's not their initial setup or trajectory. What makes a smart missile "smart" is its ability to adjust its course while in flight by using feedback to its advantage.

The same could be said about smart and successful individuals. Top leaders and high performers are excellent at receiving and processing the feedback they get on an ongoing basis. Like smart missiles, top leaders and high performers must make important alterations and adjustments in flight if they are to accurately reach their target.

Too many people go through life doing the opposite. They spend far too much energy worrying about perfecting their action plan, in constant fear of making a mistake (which is really just feedback anyway). Often, the fear of this "feedback" paralyzes them and stops them from doing anything at all.

Caitlyn, 17 (Las Vegas, NV): My best friend Jamie was far more talented than I was. She was a naturally gifted athlete and student. Even when we were in elementary school, she was faster, stronger, and smarter than the other students in our class—including me. It seemed that I was always in her shadow. But as time went on, she was no longer the top performer in class or in sports. Although she still had a lot of natural ability, apparently it wasn't enough.

For years I couldn't figure out why she wasn't performing well . . . that is, until I saw her arguing with her teacher after class one day. This was nothing new. She argued all the time. And suddenly it clicked: Jamie spent a lot of time arguing with people. She was easily offended by anyone who didn't agree with what she thought or didn't compliment her. It finally made sense: *She simply couldn't take feedback very well.* I tried to explain my thoughts to her, but there was nothing I could do. After all, she looked at my advice as "feedback," too.

Now, I'm going to the college of my choice on a soccer scholarship while Jamie, frustrated as always, decided not to go to college at all. I always thought she was a "natural" for college, the one who would get great grades, the winner of a sports scholarship—not me. It was interesting to see how things turned out. The only difference between my situation and Jamie's was the way we each looked at the feedback we received from our friends, teachers, coaches, and parents. I was open to it, and she was not.

Once you begin to take action toward *any* goal or objective, you *will* start getting feedback in the form of advice, data, help, suggestions, direction, compliments, and yes, even criticism. And that feedback will help you constantly adjust your course as you move forward. The question is, *How will you respond to it?* By using feedback to your advantage, you will excel much, much faster at whatever you are doing.

15.1 TWO KINDS OF FEEDBACK

hat kind of feedback will you encounter on your journey to success? Two kinds:

1. Positive

2. Negative

This may seem rather broad, but there's really no need to complicate it. Not surprisingly, most people would rather get the positive feedback. Great grades, certificates of achievement, trophies, awards, acknowledgments, results, praise, compliments, happiness, and so on. (That's right, the good stuff!) We like this feedback . . . it feels better . . . it tells us that we are on course, that what we're doing is the right thing.

And now, for that other type of feedback: negative. This is the feedback we don't like very much. Criticism, poor results (or none at all), low grades, frustration, disappointment, complaints, unhappiness, loneliness, pain, problems, being fired, being cut from the team, confusion, lack of support—*you name it.* These are definitely

There is **no** such thing as fail- ure. There is **only feedback**.

—*Adage*

things most people would rather avoid—but don't pass it all up just yet! There is actually A LOT of useful information hidden in negative feedback—in fact, there is just as much here as there is in positive feedback. Negative feedback can give us all kinds of helpful hints, tips, advice, and guidance. It tells us if we're headed in the wrong direction or doing the wrong thing. This is all valuable information!

One of the most useful and powerful things we can do in life is to change the way we view negative feedback. Instead of thinking that negative feedback means you've failed, look at it as information that can improve your life. You might think, "The world is telling me where and how I can improve what I am doing. This is an opportunity to learn and get better. This is where I can change my actions to get even closer to my goals." It may sound a little corny, but just think how re-interpreting feedback this way could boost your performance in all areas of your life.

To reach our goals quickly and accurately, we need to welcome all feedback and realize that no matter what type of feedback we're currently getting, there is always something positive in it—that is, if we look for it . . . and view the feedback as something valuable to us.

15.2 "on course, off course"

When we receive feedback, we have many choices about how we'll respond to it. Some responses take us closer to our goals and others keep us stuck in one place or take us even further from our goals.

When we give training sessions and speeches on the Success Principles, we like to show people exactly how important feedback is. First, we ask for a volunteer to stand at the far side of the room. This person represents the goal we want to reach. Our task is to walk across the room to where they are standing. If we get to where the volunteer is standing, then we have successfully reached our goal.

The volunteer's job is simple. He or she acts as a constant-feedback machine. Every time we take a step, he or she says "on course" if we are walking directly toward him or her and "off course" if we are walking even the slightest bit off to the side. We're not blindfolded, but for the sake of the exercise we sometimes purposefully walk in the wrong direction, and as soon as we hear "off course" we immediately correct our direction. Every few steps, we veer to the side again, listen to feedback, and then continue. After a lot of zigzagging, we eventually reach our goal.

We then ask the audience to tell us what they heard more often: "on course" or "off course." The answer is always "off course." But here's the interesting part. Even though we were off course *more than* on course, we still reached our goal . . . simply by continually taking action and adjusting to the feedback. The same is true in life. All we have to do is get started and then respond to the feedback. If we do this enough, we will eventually get to our goals.

If it all comes down to how we react to feedback, then it would be helpful to be aware of some of the responses that *don't work* so we can avoid them whenever possible. Here are some responses that simply *do not work*:

> If you're **going through hell**, keep **going**.

1. Caving in and quitting. Think about the previous exercise we just described. What if every time we heard "off course" we just broke down and cried? "I can't take it anymore. Life is too hard. I can't take all of this negative criticism. I quit!" What would happen? We would just be stuck in one place—listening to the very feedback we want to escape. Not such a great idea. When you find yourself in a place you don't want to be, remember what Winston Churchill once said:

It becomes easier to persevere and face challenges when you remember that feedback is simply information. It's "course-correction information"—that's all. Just like an airplane's automatic-pilot system constantly tells the plane that it has gone too high, too low, too far to the right, or too far to the left.

As a result, what does the plane do? Does the plane freak out all of a sudden and break down because of all the feedback? No way! It simply corrects its course. Feedback is just information presented to help us adjust our actions and get to our goals a whole lot faster. (When you look at it that way, it doesn't seem so bad, does it?)

2. Getting mad at the source of the feedback. Think of the volunteer in the last exercise. What if every time the volunteer said "off course" we just started yelling, "Who do you think you are?! Why do you always say 'off course'? What's wrong with you?" It's obvious, isn't it? Nothing would get better. In fact, the situation would just get worse because when we act out of anger, it's rare that we actually come up with useful solutions. Think about it. Has reacting with anger toward someone ever helped you in the past? Probably not.

USE FEEDBACK TO FAST-FORWARD

You may want to remember this quote: *"Speak when you're angry, and you'll make the best speech you'll ever regret."* Keep in mind, the source of the feedback is never the problem. If you find yourself getting heated about the feedback, step back, breathe, and ask yourself why you feel that way. Chances are, you're just taking things too personally.

3. **Ignoring the feedback.** Once again, imagine the volunteer in the exercise saying, "Off course." What if we stuck our fingers in our ears so we couldn't hear anything? Is that better than not adjusting our direction?

Not listening to feedback or simply ignoring feedback is another response that does not work. We all know people who tune out everyone's point of view but their own. They are simply not interested in what other people think or say. The sad thing is, it's the very feedback that they ignore that could radically change their lives for the better . . . if only they would listen.

So, those are the three possible reactions to feedback that don't work. Remember that feedback is only information—nothing more. Just welcome it and use it. That's what really successful people do every day. If you really want to have some fun with this and throw people off guard—including surprising your own brain—you could say something like, "Thank you for the feedback. Thank you for caring about me enough to take the time to tell me what you see and how you feel." Say what?! Bet you never heard *that* before! Why not try this the next time someone offers you feedback?

Imagine their shock! You might just have to help them scrape their jaw off the ground because you know they won't be expecting it. And the best part is that your brain will instantly start searching for ways to apply the information it was just given. But don't take our word for it . . . *try it*!

TIP: Need to know what feedback to listen to and what not to? Keep reading, and we'll explain soon.

15.4 Ask for It!

If you really want to be skyrocketed toward success, then don't just wait for feedback to find you. Instead, go out there, be proactive, and *ask for it*. Yes, to many people this sounds like a crazy idea, but this is still—and always will be—the best and most powerful way to get lots of important information that can transform your life.

Try asking this powerful question to family members, friends, teachers, and coaches: "How do you see me limiting myself?" Their responses might tell you some things that you weren't aware of—and it's those little tweaks we make that can dramatically change our results. Imagine a missile traveling through the air making small, three-degree adjustments as it goes along—adjustments so minor it seems like nothing. But as the missile continues to travel over thousands of miles, those little alterations make a really big difference and completely change the final destination.

In the same way, the feedback we get and how we choose to use it can also make critical course adjustments in our life paths.

Some people are uncomfortable offering feedback. Maybe they don't want to hurt your feelings. Maybe they are afraid of your reaction. Maybe they don't want to risk disapproval. Maybe they are insecure or just feel uncomfortable. Whatever the reason, there are people who will never *offer* you feedback; they will give it *only* if you ask for it, because only then do they feel "safe" telling you. This is why it's important to ask for it. By asking, you are letting them know you won't take it personally and you won't be angry.

Here are more powerful questions you could ask other people:

※ **How could I be more effective?**

※ **How could I be a better friend, brother, sister, student, teammate, athlete, employee?**

※ **What could I do differently to improve my results?**

※ **What have you learned that has really helped you to _____**

If you look closely at these questions, you'll notice something interesting. None of these questions allows for one-word answers such as a simple "Yes" or "No." Yes-or-no answers can be helpful, but an explanation always offers more information and greater detail.

By the way, you might think that the answers would be hard to listen to, but most people find the information so valuable that they are grateful for what people tell them. Remember, you're getting information that will make *your life* better. That's rather useful, don't you think?

15.5 The Most Valuable Question You May Ever Learn

 he restaurant business can be really tough, but restaurant owner Robert MacLellan was determined to succeed. When he began researching what it took to start a successful restaurant, what he found was very interesting. He discovered that many restaurant owners and chefs were really sensitive about getting feedback. They didn't want to hear anything negative, so they never asked customers for their comments. Big mistake! After interviewing various customers at different restaurants, Robert found that most customers had very good suggestions, but they felt uncomfortable sharing their ideas with the manager or the chef.

Not surprisingly, Robert focused on this discovery when he opened his first restaurant, Newport Bay Seafood Broiler, in Portland, Oregon. He made a vow to be different. As a very proactive man, Robert created a new custom in his restaurant by bringing the chef out from the kitchen and to the customers after they have finished eating. He then asked the customer an extremely powerful question: "On a scale of 1 to 10, how would you rate your meal?"

At first, many of the customers gave 9s and 10s because they didn't want to hurt the chef's feelings. However, Robert realized that the 9s and 10s offered no ways to improve, no ways to change! He was excited to get the 9s and 10s, but he was even more eager to get really honest feedback, Robert said, "I'm looking for the 4s and 5s so we can make this meal the best it can be and satisfy our customers to the fullest." Whoa! This usually surprises customers because they are not used to meeting people who are so open and willing to hear feedback.

Once Robert gets the honest feedback from his customers, he follows up with another compelling question: "What would it take to make it a 10?" The feedback, Roberts says, is "invaluable"! "We learn exactly what customers want. And when we know what they want, they will always leave satisfied." Robert also explained how customers feel more appreciated when their comments are asked for and valued.

As a result, they tell all their friends and continue to come back again and again. Today, Robert has 2,800 employees and twenty-five very successful restaurants, along with many awards and rave customer reviews. He says that most of his success has come as a result of asking for and using feedback to his advantage. Robert's lesson is clear: *Ask for it!*

Do you need to own a restaurant to use these two powerful questions in your life? No way! You can adapt Robert's "How would you rate . . . ?" and "What would it take . . . ?" to your life. Here are some examples that will help you get priceless feedback.

First, start by asking *yourself*:

On a scale of 1 to 10, how would I rate my . . .

✻ **Academic performance?** ✻ **Family and personal relationships?**

✻ **Health?** ✻ **Financial situation?**

✻ **Athletic performance?** ✻ **Level of happiness?**

✻ **Friendships?**

Then ask others (friends, teachers, parents, coaches, boss, etc.) something like this:

On a scale of 1 to 10, how would you rate me . . .

✻ **As a friend?** ✻ **As a son or daughter?**

* **As a student?**
* **As an athlete?**
* **As an employee?**

Or you could ask:

On a scale of 1 to 10, how would you rate . . .
* **Our game last night?**
* **My homework?**
* **This meal?**
* **My cooking?**
* **Our weekend together?**

Are you beginning to see the limitless possibilities? With these questions you will definitely get some interesting feedback. But it's the follow-up question that gives you the most power. Here's how it works: Any answer less than a 10 gets this follow-up question:

*What would **it take** to make it a **10**?*

This follow-up question will open the floodgates of feedback and valuable information. There are so many ways these two questions can improve the quality of your life! You just have to be willing to do three things:

1. Ask.

2. Don't take the feedback personally.

3. Adjust your actions and what you're currently doing so you can get different results (that is, 10s) next time.

If you really want to excel fast, use these on a weekly basis—or even a daily basis. First, ask them of yourself, and then ask other people.

156 Take the Lead

 eel your fear and take action anyway . . . *just lean into it.* Remember those principles? Well, this is a great opportunity to put them into practice. Sure, asking for feedback can make anyone a little uncomfortable, but there's really nothing to be afraid of. The truth is the truth—and you're much better off knowing the truth than not knowing the truth at all. Once you know it, you can do something about it. You cannot fix what you don't know is broken. You cannot improve your life, your grades, your health, your friendships, your relationships, your game, or your performance without feedback. Yes, it's *that* important.

But we're just getting into it. Do you want to know the worst part of *avoiding* feedback and *ignoring* the truth? You are the only one who is "not in on the secret," as Whitney pointed out. Ouch! You see, other people have already noticed the truth, and maybe those people have already told their friends, their family, their teacher, and their coach what they are dissatisfied with. So whether you ask for the feedback or not, other people already know the truth. Just like Agent Mulder and Scully said in the old hit TV show *The X-Files*, "The truth is out there." The question is, *Will you accept it and then use it to your advantage?* We sure hope you do.

The people who gossip to others should really be giving that "feedback" to us directly, but they're often afraid to. As a result, we don't get the very feedback we need to improve our life. *We lose out!* However, there are two important things you can do about it:

1. **Intentionally and actively ask for it.** Approach your friends, parents, teachers, coaches, bosses, and mentors and ask the two questions: (1) "How would you rate _____ on a scale of 1 to 10?" and "What would it take to make it a 10?" Get used to asking these questions regularly so you get the corrective feedback you need.

2. **Be grateful for and appreciative of the feedback.** Let the other people know that you are open to it, that you will not take it personally, that you will not get angry at them. Remember, they are only messengers. They are not pirates out to destroy your life and steal your dignity. Thank them for their thoughts and for caring about you enough to notice. Be grateful for it.

(15.7) Listen Up!

Whether we ask for it or not, we're going to get feedback—and it will come to us in various forms. Maybe it will come from a short chat with your coach. Or in the form of an e-mail from your friend. It might be a letter from your manager at work. A certain look on your parents' faces. Maybe a note indicating that your college application was denied. Or it could be a new opportunity that comes your way because you persevered.

Whatever it is, it's important to *listen* to the feedback. Simply take a step . . . and listen. Take another step and listen. If you hear "Off course," then take a step toward "on course" (guess the direction if necessary!) . . . and then listen again. Listen to what other people tell you, but be sure to pay attention to what your gut feeling and instincts may be telling you as well.

Is your gut feeling saying, "I'm happy; I like my classes, my teachers, and my friends"? Or is it saying, "I'm scared; I'm emotionally drained; I don't like this as much as I thought; I don't have a good feeling about this person"? Whatever feedback you get, don't ignore the yellow alerts. Pay attention to all forms of feedback you get so you can make any necessary changes.

Andy, 17 (Santa Fe, NM): We were put into groups of five for our next big history assignment. I was happy to be part of a group with some of the top students in the class. We had one month to finish the project and hand it in. At our first meeting, we outlined the project and divided the responsibilities. A few days later, we had our second meeting. Everybody showed up with his or her research, but I only had my notes from the first meeting. I explained to the group that we had enough time and that I would bring my work next time.

The next few days flew by, and I realized that I missed the third meeting. Oops. When I showed up to the fourth meeting, I came with some research and explained it to the group. I knew I wasn't doing much, but I thought I was doing enough. A week before the assignment was due, my teacher called me to his desk and said, "Your group wants you out. Do you know why they would say this?" I was shocked. "What? They never said anything to me!"

But as I was forced to look back on things, I could see the subtle feedback I failed to notice. When I spoke at that fourth meeting, not everyone listened. Sometimes their eyes seemed to be glazed over as though they were thinking about something else. Eventually, they simply didn't ask for my ideas, opinions, or input. I wasn't given any new tasks or responsibilities. I thought I was just getting off easy, but the real reason was they didn't trust me to finish the job. I wasn't even told about the final meeting.

I was angry at the rest of group for not telling me sooner, but I also knew the real cause of the problem was me—not them. I wasn't doing my part, and I wasn't picking up on the feedback that I was getting. I learned that sometimes feedback is not always obvious, and sometimes people won't tell you how they feel so it's up to me to seek it out.

(158) Hit and Miss

Before you readjust your course, change your methods, and take a different action, it's important to know that not all feedback is accurate. It's hit and miss, meaning sometimes it's true and factual, and other times it's incorrect. So before we apply the feedback and make changes, we need to consider the source. Sometimes the people giving you the feedback do not have all the facts—or worse, they might be emotionally charged so their judgment is clouded.

For example, if a student tells you that you're not smart enough, not good enough, not talented enough, how accurate or useful is this "feedback"? Not at all! Just the fact that they would say something like that shows they are lacking self-esteem. By putting down others, some people feel better about themselves. Clearly, when someone lacks self-esteem, their judgments won't be accurate—that is feedback you should not listen to.

If you really stop and think about the feedback you get, you will know in your gut whether it is truthful or not. Be aware of the source and remember:

Don't try to make sense out of nonsense.

159 Get the Positive from the Negative

 ince we won't get only positive feedback, it helps to learn how to pull the positive lessons from negative feedback. Sometimes the feedback will indicate that we've failed—meaning we didn't get the result we set out to achieve. That's okay . . . it happens. No one is perfect. But there are certain things we can do to respond appropriately and keep moving forward:

1. **Acknowledge that you did the best you could with the knowledge and skills you had at the time.**

2. **Recognize that you have survived and that you can definitely cope with the current situation.**

3. **Write down everything you learned from the experience.** You may want to start a journal called *Insights & Lessons* where you jot down all of the life lessons you learn. Imagine how valuable that journal would be! When we work with individuals who have just faced a devastating challenge, we often have them write, "I learned that . . ." at the top of a piece of paper and then write as much as they can think of in five minutes. Then we make another list under the heading "Ways to Do This Better Next Time."

4. **Make sure to thank everyone who gives you feedback.** If someone gets really angry and intense when giving you feedback, remember that it's a reflection of that person, not of you. Blaming and justifying are a waste of time. Just take in the feedback, use whatever is valuable, and discard the rest.

5. **Clean up any messes or mistakes that have been created—including any apologies or regrets that should be given.**

6. **Take some time to go back and review your earlier successes.** It's important

to remind yourself that you've had far more successes than you've had failures. You've done many more things right than you've done wrong.

7. **Find support.** Spend time with positive friends and family who can build your self-esteem, help show you your strengths, and remind you of your past triumphs.

8. **Revisit your goals and objectives.** Once you've taken your lesson to heart, recommit to your original plan (or create a new plan of attack) and then get started. Stay in the game. Keep moving toward your dreams.

THIS IS YOUR CHANCE TO TURN WEAKNESS INTO STRENGTH.

9. **Set your expectations straight.** No one is perfect. All you can do is give your best. That is the most anyone can ask. You're going to make mistakes along the way, so be prepared to dust yourself off, get back on your horse, and keep on ridin'!

15.10 Look for Patterns

While talking with a very successful entrepreneur, we asked him, "What is the number-one thing that has contributed most to your success?" He immediately said, "Feedback. I always pay close attention to the results I am getting—specifically, to any patterns that continue to show up."

What a great answer! One of the most important things we can do when we go through life is to train ourselves to notice any *recurring* patterns of feedback that we continue to get. These little patterns can be BIG clues.

There is an old saying: "If one person tells you you're a horse, then he might be crazy. If three people tell you you're a horse, then be suspicious. If ten people tell you you're a horse, then maybe it's time to buy a saddle." In other words, if you continue to get the same feedback again and again, there is probably some truth in it. So why resist it? Of course, we'd all rather be "right" instead of listening to the feedback, but the real question to ask is, "Would I rather be right or be happy? Would I rather be right or successful?"

Once we met a sixteen-year-old guy who would rather be "right" than happy or successful. He got mad at anyone who tried to give him feedback. "Don't talk to me that way!" he'd often say. "Don't tell me how to live my life. It's my life, and I will live it the way I want to! I don't care what you think."

"It's my way or the highway" was his life philosophy. He wasn't interested in anyone else's opinion or the feedback anyone else had to offer. In the process, he lost many of his friends and alienated his teachers, coaches, and even his parents.

A year later, we were not surprised to hear that he ended up in summer school because he didn't have enough credits to graduate the previous spring. He had very few friends. He got kicked off the football team. And he nearly died after totaling his car driving home drunk from a party. But in his mind, he was "right"—he thought he always knew best. So be it. But don't get caught in this trap yourself. It's a dead-end street . . . literally.

What feedback have you been receiving from your friends, family, coaches, teachers, and the opposite sex that you need to pay attention to? Are there any patterns that stand out? No matter how we're performing, there is almost always some constructive feedback we can use to improve our lives . . . but first we must be open to it and willing to make the necessary changes.

If you're **not willing to listen** to **feedback** and apply it to your life, then you must also **accept** the fact that your **life** will **not get any better**.

What's the bottom line?

No one can make you use the feedback that you're getting. In the end, it's your choice how you react to it. Realize that the fast track to success requires that you seek out feedback, live with an open mind, and make an effort to adjust your behavior to get more of the results you want. If you want to be a missile to success, feedback is your rocket fuel. Good luck.

MY "TO-DO" LIST

☑ Ask for feedback and show others that I am open to receiving it.

☑ Be willing to use the feedback I receive so I will excel much faster at whatever I am doing.

☑ Understand that there is no such thing as failure, only feedback.

☑ Realize that the first step in getting and using feedback is getting started. Once I start moving, I will know if I'm on course or off course so I can adjust my approach.

☑ Understand that feedback comes to me in different forms so I will be better prepared to recognize it.

☑ Understand that not all feedback is accurate. I must consider the source!

☑ Notice the *patterns* of feedback that I continue to get.

PRINCIPLE 16

Stop Hanging With Turkeys and Soar With Eagles

You **can't soar like an eagle** when you **hang with turkeys.**

When people ask us, "what's the fastest way to become successful?" we always say, "Choose to hang out with people who are successful or those who are working hard to become successful . . . people who challenge you to grow."

This can sound so basic, but it's true. The friends you hang out with are the number-one most powerful factor that will determine the quality of your life. Yes, it's that important! Your friends influence your attitude, opinions, and the way you handle situations.

Whether you like it or not, you will rise or fall to their level. Take sports, for example. When a good team plays a better team, they usually rise to the challenge and play better. And when a good team plays a weaker team, they often play down to the weaker team's level. We cannot emphasize this enough: Who you hang out with will affect your potential!

Kent: I had a tight group of friends growing up. But when my family moved to New Zealand, we lost touch. Two years later I visited them and they didn't even appear to be the same people. It was as if I never knew them. Why? One simple reason: They had a new group of friends. They had changed so much—and not for the better.

The interesting thing was they were completely unaware of it. I was recently shocked to discover where two of my closest friends recently ended up. One developed a serious drug addiction, and the other ended up at San Quentin High-Security Prison. It's odd to think about it: We grew up in the same area, went to the same school, and at one point in time, enjoyed doing the same things together. The one element that changed it all in the end was the group of people we chose to hang out with.

(16.1) YOU Are Who YOU Hang Out With

You are the **average** of the **five people** you **spend** the most **time with**.

—*Jim Rohn*
Self-made millionaire and successful author

At age twelve, Tim Ferriss checked his answering machine and heard a message from a mystery caller. The message? It was the Jim Rohn quote above! According to Tim, this quote changed his life forever. For days, he couldn't get the idea out of his mind. At twelve years old, Tim recognized that the people he was hanging out with were not the ones he wanted influencing his future. So he went to his mom and dad and asked to change schools. A bold move . . .

Four years later, in his junior year of high school, he decided to continue his education abroad in Japan. Later, he attended Princeton University, where he became an all-American wrestler and a national kick-boxing champion. At age twenty-three, he started his own company. Tim had learned what every successful person knows: We become like the people we hang out with. It's that simple.

Kent: After attending nine different schools—four different high schools—I could see first hand how my friends impacted my performance. When I took a closer look, I found that I also shared their same level of achievement. In fact, this similarity was easily measurable in our grades. How are your friends influencing your performance? Find out now . . .

The Five Friends' Factor

Step 1: On a sheet of paper list five friends you spend the most time with. Then write their GPAs (grade point averages) next to their names. You may make an estimate if you don't feel comfortable asking your friend this information.

Friend 1: _____ GPA: _____

Friend 2: _____ GPA: _____

Friend 3: _____ GPA: _____

Friend 4: _____ GPA: _____

Friend 5: _____ GPA: _____

Step 2:

GPA 1 _____ + GPA 2 _____ + GPA 3 _____ +

GPA 4 _____ + GPA 5 _____ = _____

Step 3: Now divide the total by 5

Total GPA _____ / 5 = Average GPA _____

Step 4: Enter *your* GPA here: _____

Step 5: Now compare your GPA to the average GPA.

What did you discover? Is the average GPA close to yours? Below yours? What does this comparison tell you about your friends' influence? Do they challenge you enough to succeed? Also, look at it from the other side: Are you challenging your friends to be the best they can be?

16.2 You Are Always "In the Making"

A person can look in the mirror, but if they really want to **know themselves**, they should **look** at the **friends they choose**.

As you know, we're always being influenced, always adjusting, adapting, and changing. The question is this: Are we growing in a positive way or a negative way? We won't be the same person a year from now that we are today—and next year's "you" will largely be the result of the type of people you choose to spend your time with from now until then. In fact, the friends you choose are a reflection of you. Spooky, huh? An old Jewish proverb states:

John, 46 (San Diego, CA): The path I was on was either going to lead me to jail or the morgue. Either way, it wasn't good. I grew up in a rough environment, and my parents were always arguing about money, so I thought that money would give me happiness. I thought that if I had money, then I was a person of value. This drove me to do anything possible to get money. As a result, I met the wrong group of teens and started shoplifting, getting in trouble at school, and rebelling against authority.

I still wanted more money, so I started delivering newspapers, pressing clothes, and working at a pharmacy, until I ended up with a job at a men's health club. In addition to earning $1.65 an hour, I got an unexpected education. Every night after work from 9:15 to 10:00 PM, I'd go to the sauna and listen to successful businessmen tell their tales of success and failure. I was fascinated by their challenges and accomplishments. Their stories of what went wrong with their businesses, families, and their health gave me inspiration because my own family was experiencing challenges and difficulties. I learned that it was normal to have challenges—and that other people also went through similar crises and still made it to the top.

This group of men taught me never to give up on my dreams. "No matter what the failure," they told me, "try another way; try going up, over, around, or through, but never give up. *There's always a way.*" I also learned that it makes no difference where you're born, what race or color you are, how old you are, or whether you come from a rich or a poor family. For the first time I realized that success was not reserved for those born with every advantage. These men had become my mentors, my friends, and my own private business school—and, as a result, my life was never the same again.

There's something else you should know about John Assaraf. He is a very humble guy. Today, it's obvious that his time spent learning from his adult mentors has had a major impact on his life. John has built four multimillion-dollar companies. He has operated a franchise company with annual real-estate revenues topping $5 billion! He also helped build an Internet company that now nets millions in monthly sales.

He has written a bestselling book titled, *The Street Kid's Guide to Having It All*. And his most recent endeavor is a new company, *OneCoach*, which shows thousands of small- business owners and aspiring entrepreneurs how to take their current business or ideas and grow them into thriving businesses that provide with financial freedom. But after looking back over all he has accomplished, he claims that his new groups of friends and his mentors have been the greatest influence of his success. That is the power of relationships!

16.3 Leave the "Pity Party"

The "Ain't It Awful Club" . . . have you heard of it? Every school has at least one chapter—and countless numbers of these clubs spring up not only on campus, but also in homes, at work, etc. In fact, you've probably experienced it firsthand.

One person starts off by saying, "This sucks! I can't wait until this day, this class, this meeting, or this practice is over! My parents yelled at me this morning, *and* I forgot to hand in my homework." Then someone else cuts in and says, "Yeah, I feel your pain. Brian called me a loser, and Heather dissed me during lunch. I hate the jocks!" In comes the third person: "Ha! You think you have it bad?! Well, you have no idea. Wait till you hear what happened to me!"

Whoa! What the heck is going on? By the end of that conversation, you're bound to feel miserable, drained, and uptight. Unfortunately, every school, every neighborhood, every team has members of this club. There are certain people and certain groups who seem to always find something negative to talk about. Their conversations are just a constant stream of criticizing, blaming, and complaining. The good news is that membership isn't mandatory. You don't have to be part of the "Ain't It Awful?" club. You have the choice to drop out—and it might be one of the best decisions you make.

Stephanie, 19 (Fresno, CA): I had the same group of friends for years. The problem was I didn't notice the little changes that were happening over time. In middle school, my grades started to get really bad, but I knew my friends had similar grades so I didn't worry about it. I thought, "Oh well, they're getting the same results, so at least we're in this together."

Our mentality became "Things will get better. Somehow it will work out." We all just sat back, did enough to get by, and then hoped that things would improve. Of course, they didn't. When nothing got better, we just complained to each other about how horrible our teachers were, how mean the principal was, how stupid the other students were, and how lame the school was.

We didn't even notice it at the time, but as I look back now, I can see we became really critical and negative. We never missed the chance to say something sarcastic or point out what someone did wrong. The weird thing was it seemed normal—I guess because my closest friends all acted the same way. We were slowly bringing each other down, but we didn't know it. We just reinforced each other's behavior.

During the summer before my senior year, my parents decided to move about three hours away. I was devastated and angry. "How could they do this to me?" I kept saying to myself. When the new school year started, I didn't know anyone, so I decided to try out for the field hockey team. Some of the girls were really nice, so we started to hang out together. I noticed that I was much happier when I was with this group, even though I had known them for only a couple of weeks.

For the first time since I could remember, I felt a drive to work hard—like that was the "cool" thing to do. It was kind of strange, but in a good way. At times I felt like a completely different person. I couldn't believe how this new group of people was affecting me. I felt better about myself because I wasn't constantly criticizing other people. Not only did my grades improve, but my confidence and self-esteem did as well. Now I can see there are way more opportunities available to me than I once thought. I never dreamed that just by hanging around positive people my life could be so different.

16.4 Plus or Minus

There are two types of people—**anchors** and **motors**. You want to **lose the anchors** and get with the motors because the **motors are going somewhere** and they're having more fun. The anchors will just drag you down.

—*Robert Wyland*
World-renowned marine artist

Here's a simple but very powerful exercise. On a piece of paper make a list of everyone you spend time with on a regular basis—your family, friends, neighbors, relatives, members of your band, people involved in your club or your youth group, individuals at your work, and so on.

Name: _____ (+) or (-)

Name: _____ (+) or (-)

Name: _____ (+) or (-)

Name: _____ (+) or (-)

Now, are these people adding to your life or bringing you down? Are you hanging out with positive people or negative people? Let's find out. Next to each person's name enter a (+) and a (-). Your job is simple: Circle the minus sign (-) next to those people who are negative and unsupportive, and circle the plus sign (+) next to the people who are positive and encouraging. (Sometimes it helps to do this based on your initial gut reaction.)

As you make your decision about each person, you might find that a pattern begins to form. What do you see more of, pluses or minuses? Now, this is very important feedback worth listening to. If you do this exercise properly, you might discover that you're spending too much time with the "anchors"—people who are bringing you down. Maybe it's your friends who naysay everything you do. Or could it be your family, your band members, or your club members who are breaking down your self-esteem and confidence.

Be careful! Remember this is *your* life and *your* future. Here's the next step: Stop spending time with those people with a minus sign next to their name (we'll explain how to do this soon). If you think that is impossible (and remember, nothing is impossible; it's always a choice), then severely cut down the amount of time you spend with them. You have to free yourself from those who are limiting your potential.

6.5 What Do You Expect?

Two twin brothers were born into a rough life. One brother became an alcoholic who was constantly in trouble with the law, and the other brother grew up to be a successful student, athlete, and singer.

When the troubled brother was asked what happened to him, he replied, "What do you expect? I was born into poverty, violence, and drugs. I just acted the same way

STOP HANGING WITH TURKEYS AND SOAR WITH EAGLES 185

everyone else did." When the successful brother was asked the same question, he replied, "What do you expect? I was born into poverty, violence, and drugs. I saw how my parents ended up, so I decided to surround myself with a different group—people who were happy and successful."

Here's how it works: Naturally, we want to fit in with and excel in whatever group we spend the most time with—whether it's positive or negative. If we hang out with negative and destructive people, then we, too, will feel the need to be negative and destructive. However, if we hang out with positive and successful people, we will be motivated to do positive and constructive things.

So we ask you, what kind of people do your peers and friends expect to become? Do they expect to work hard and become successful, or do they expect to just "get by"? Do they expect that life will be a painful struggle, or do they expect life to be an exciting adventure full of unlimited possibilities?

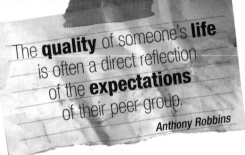

The **quality** of someone's **life** is often a direct reflection of the **expectations** of their peer group.

Anthony Robbins

These are very valuable things to think about, because we usually won't exceed the expectations of those we spend the most time with.

Choose to be with people who have high self-standards and expectations for themselves, because chances are that you will rise to their level. Remember, our peers are not "assigned" to us. We *choose* who we hang out with. There is an old saying: "Love your family, but pick your friends." We can't do that for you. All we can say is . . . *choose wisely.*

We will rarely **exceed** the **expectations** of **those** we spend the **most time with.**

TIP: Take this one step further: Ask yourself, "What do I expect from myself?" Both of us choose to live by this philosophy (and you might want to as well): **Demand more from yourself than anyone else would expect.** This means we not only hang out with positive and successful people, but we also make the choice to *become* positive and successful ourselves.

Remember the *Act As If* principle? Well, this is where it can really come in handy. When you think and act like a happy and successful person, you will become one.

16.6 Avoid the Vampires

Have you ever been around someone who seemed to suck the energy right out of you—someone who walked into a room and drained the liveliness? We call them "psychic vampires." They suck the life right out of you! What's the solution? Stop spending time with them.

Do you have friends who constantly try to bring you down to their level? You know, people who, simply by calling you, can make you feel frustrated, stressed, depressed? And the dream-stealers who tell you that your dreams are impossible and try to make you believe that pursuing them is ridiculous? If so, then it's time for some new friends!

These people hold you back with their victim mentality and their mediocre personal standards. In our opinion, you're better off spending time alone than spending time with negative people. Instead, make an effort to surround yourself with those who are supportive and uplifting—people who believe in you, encourage you to go after your dreams, and congratulate you when you succeed.

We are *not* saying that you should *only* talk to and appreciate happy and successful people. No way! It's very important to make an effort to treat *everyone* with respect—that's not a choice. We should always respect others, but the choice we do have is deciding who to spend the *most* time with. There is a big difference.

Question: "If I know that my friends are bringing me down, how do I get involved with a better group of people?" First of all, there doesn't need to be a formal "Good-bye, I can't be your friend anymore." (Isn't that a relief?) We recommend that you make other commitments that require time apart from them. For example, by joining a club, a team, or an after-school organization, you can gradually make the transition to a new group of friends. By joining clubs or teams that interest you, you'll also find more people there who share your same goals and aspirations.

School clubs, key clubs, builder's clubs, Circle K, ASB, music clubs, sport enthusiasts' clubs, hobby clubs—these are just a few of the many places to find happy and successful people. Join a group! Start attending youth events in your area (and yes, there are lots of them if you do some research to find them).

Join the Boys and Girls Club after school, sign up for Junior Achievement, Key Club, The Congressional Youth Leadership Council, 4-H, or the FFA. How about your local

Toastmasters? Or volunteer to serve with other leaders at a church, temple, or mosque. Consider teen seminars or youth camps. Ask your school counselor. The opportunities are out there! There are always ways to find a better group of people to hang out with.

*If you want to **find people** who are proactive, **successful**, and **passion-ate** about life, then you, too, must be proactive and take that first step to **seek them out**.*

16.7 Soar With the Eagles

Success leaves **clues**.

—Anthony Robbins
Bestselling author and inspirational speaker

hile we were speaking at a high-school assembly, we asked the audience of 400 high-school seniors some specific questions: "Do you know who the top student in your class is? Do you know who the best athlete is? Do you know who the student body leader is? Do you know who the best teacher is?" We asked them to raise their hand if they had an answer. Almost everyone did.

We then asked them to raise their hands again if they had ever gone to any of these people and asked them to share their secrets of success. This time, not one hand went up. Almost everyone knew who the top performers were, but nobody ever asked these leaders to share their secrets. How crazy is that? The answers were there, but the students didn't seek them out. Learning from others and modeling success is one of the smartest things you can do.

The great thing about living in today's world is there are A LOT of "answers" that have already been revealed. Chances are, almost everything you want to do (or, at least, something very similar) has already been done by someone else.

*The **smart man learns** from **his mistakes**, but the **wise man learns** from the **mistakes of others**.*

It doesn't matter if it's getting straight A's, losing weight, starting a business, writing a book, getting into college, earning millions of dollars, running a marathon—someone has already done it and has left "clues" in the form of books, manuals, audio programs, documentaries, university classes, online courses, seminars, workshops . . . you name it!

For virtually anything you want to do, there are people and resources that can give you the answers and insights you require to become more successful and better at what you want to do. When you take advantage of all of this information, you'll discover that life is simply a connect-the-dots game, and all of the dots have already been identified and organized by somebody else. All you have to do is follow the blueprint, use their system, or work their program to achieve similar results. If you want to soar like an eagle, learn from those who are already doing it.

Too often, we automatically ask people we're comfortable talking to instead of approaching those who have already "been there, done that" and have valuable advice for us. Why not take advantage of all the wisdom and experience that already exists by finding a mentor who has already been down the road you're traveling?

QUESTION: How do you find such a mentor or personal coach? You can start by doing two things:

1. **Look around for leaders in your school, your community, and your everyday life.**

2. **Ask, ask, ask! Politely ask these leaders and role models if they will share their insight with you.**

Sometimes we just need someone to help us see the possibilities available to us—and that's exactly what coaches and mentors can do. They can help open doors, offer expert advice, train us to recognize new opportunities, and give feedback about whether or not we're on the right path. For Jason Dorsey, a mentor changed the course of his life.

Jason, 28 (Austin, TX): I was an eighteen-year-old college student with good grades and excellent career options, but I still felt I was missing something. One day a guest speaker named Brad challenged my class to define success by more than money. I was so inspired by what he said that I took a huge risk and asked him to be my mentor. He agreed. Little did I know the effect this one relationship would have on my life.

Brad helped me realize that I was working hard to achieve a goal (making lots of money) that ultimately wouldn't make me happy or fulfilled. He then challenged me to write a book about how I ended up with great job options at age eighteen, so other young people could do the same. The idea of writing a book was way out of my comfort zone. However, Brad believed so strongly that I could write this book that I eventually believed it myself. On January 7, 1997, at 1:58 AM, I started my book. Five months later, I self-published *Graduate to Your Perfect Job*. I was soon $50,000 in debt! I had to move out of my comfortable dorm room and into a garage apartment where I slept on the floor for a year on $4 a day. I got really good at cooking Ramen noodles.

But once again, Brad showed me a new possibility. He challenged me to start speaking to young people. This launched me into speaking at schools, colleges, and conferences across the United States and as far away as India, Finland, Spain, The Netherlands, and Egypt—sometimes in front of audiences of more than 13,000 people! Along this journey, I met other mentors who supported me and helped me grow in new and different ways. I even ended up on *20/20*, NBC's *Today Show,* ABC's *The View*, in *The Wall Street Journal*, and in *Fortune* magazine. These were all things that only a few years ago I never dreamed were possible. All I needed was someone to believe in me and share their hard-earned secrets to success.

Now that I am older, I have several mentors. I've learned so much from them. Every time I talk with them, I feel energized and empowered—and I have a new group of people to hang out with . . . a group of experienced, knowledgeable, courageous, and successful people. I didn't plan on writing a book, starting my own business, or speaking in foreign countries, but my mentors have shown me a world of opportunity that I didn't even know existed—all because I found the courage to ask Brad to be my mentor when I was eighteen years old.

Jason is also author of *My Reality Check Bounced*, www.jasondorsey.com.

168 Get a Coach

hink about it. You wouldn't expect an athlete to reach the Olympic Games without a world-class coach, right? Well, today, coaching is no longer only for athletes. Peak performers in all areas of life—academic, athletic, business, music, *anything*—take advantage of the power of coaching.

In many cases, we need someone who can help us clarify our goals, break through our fears, and inspire us to give our best effort. A coach can also help you discover what you truly want to do and how you can get there. And here's the best news: Most people will be happy to share what they've learned because they will feel a "sense of importance" and will interpret your asking as a sign of respect to them.

Of course, not everyone will be able to mentor you, but many will . . . *if* you ask. You have nothing to lose. You simply need to make a list of people you would like to have as mentors (teachers, athletic coaches, business owners, community leaders, family friends, etc.) and start asking if they would be willing to devote a few minutes a month to you.

TIP: When mentors do offer their advice to you, be sure to follow it. No one likes to waste time. Once your mentors share their strategies with you, try them on and see if they fit you. Try doing what they do, reading what they read, thinking the way they think, and so on. If these new ways of thinking and behaving work, then adopt them and make them *your* habits, too. If not, drop them and keep looking for new and better techniques.

Need to know what to say? Here's what Christina, a sixteen-year-old reader from Houston, said to get her first mentor. Maybe you can use some of her ideas.

Hello, Mrs. Warren. My name is Christina. We haven't met, but I really respect what you've accomplished with your clothing business. I know you're really busy, so I'll be brief. I'm a high-school student with a goal of starting my own clothing line. I can see that you are very knowledgeable about the fashion industry. Mrs. Warren, I would really appreciate it if you would consider being my mentor. This would require only about ten minutes of your time every two weeks, when I would ask you a few questions. Would you be open to that?

Christina faced her fears, asked Mrs. Warren, and got a coach— and hasn't looked back. In your request, explain why you'd like them to mentor you and what kind of help you're looking for. Be brief, but be confident, too. If Christina did it, you can, too!

> **Surround** *yourself* **with the best**, *and* *you'll* **achieve more** **than** *the* **rest**.

If someone you ask says no, remember SW-SW-SW-SW. Ask someone else. Don't be discouraged. You will eventually get a yes. Remember, the more people you ask, the faster you will get a yes.

MY "TO-DO" LIST

☑ Realize that I cannot soar like an eagle when I hang with turkeys.

☑ Accept that I will become who I spend the most time with. If I want to understand myself better, I should look at the friends I choose.

☑ Understand that I will often perform only to the expectations of my peers.

☑ Drop out of the "Ain't It Awful?" club and surround myself with happy, positive people.

☑ Avoid "psychic vampires"—those people who suck the energy I need to succeed.

☑ Approach people who are the best at what they do and ask them for their success formulas.

☑ Find a wing to climb under, and get a mentor who will challenge me to grow.

Keep score of your success and Build on It

> You **can't build on failure;** you **can** only build **on success.**
>
> —*Anthony Robbins*
> Peak-performance expert and bestselling author

id your mom or dad ever record your height as you were growing up? Maybe they kept track of your growth by marking the wall near the pantry or inside your closet door. We didn't *need* to see the measurements to know we were growing, but keeping track of our growth gave us something visible so we could actually *see* the progress—and that was the best part!

The measurements let us know where we stood compared to our past and compared to our future goal (which was usually to be as tall as our mom or dad). "Keeping score" of our progress motivated us to eat right, drink our milk, and so on, so we could keep growing. In other words, our positive results encouraged us to continue doing constructive things so we could continue progressing.

Well, successful people also record measurements; they keep scores that show their progress, victories, positive behavior . . . anything they want more of. Charles Coonradt, author of *The Game of Work*, made a powerful observation while he was studying success. He said:

You have to **measure** what you **want more of**.

Naturally, we always want to improve our score, break our own records, and perform better the next time we try something. That's how scorekeeping motivates us to create more and more of the positive outcomes we're keeping track of. This is a great way to reinforce the behavior that created these outcomes in the first place. And that's where this principle comes into play.

(17.1) measure what you want

hink back to when you were just a little kid. Chances are you counted the number of times you skipped the rope, the number of gold stars you collected in class, the number of hits you made in Little League, the number of boxes of Girl Scout cookies you sold, the number of anything you valued. Basically, you kept score mostly of the good stuff because that was what you wanted more of.

But as you got older, maybe you started comparing yourself to others and being more critical of yourself. Maybe you started noticing more of your flaws and mistakes. It's okay, of course, to acknowledge our mistakes and weaknesses—we must do that so we can improve. However, it's not good to overemphasize the negative and make it our central focus.

Remember, you get more of what you focus on—and in order to measure something, we first have to focus on it. Many of us do this unknowingly. We subconsciously keep track of our results. The problem is, many people tend to focus more on their past failures, screwups, and weaknesses than on the many things they did well and the strengths they have developed. So, as you can imagine, this causes even more trouble. However, if you do the opposite and measure the positive, the effects on our self-esteem and performance can be invaluable.

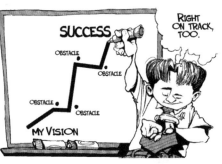

Tyler, 18 (Park City, UT): At age twelve, I joined my local junior basketball league. When my dad would come to watch our games, he noticed something interesting. The coaches appeared to be concerned about what the players did wrong, such as dropping the ball, making a bad pass, missing a shot, and getting a foul. My coaches thought my dad was crazy when he decided to counteract the usual negative focus of youth sports. He created a scorecard that kept track of what I did right and how I was becoming a better athlete. He tracked seven different ways I contributed to the team's success. On this scorecard, my dad awarded points for virtually everything positive I accomplished during the game.

Sure enough, I found myself sprinting over during timeouts to check on my "contribution points," as my dad called them. When I arrived home after a game, I would mark the chart I had on my wall to plot my progress. With this simple graph, I could see where I was improving. As the season went on, I worked hard to make sure the graph kept going upward. It was cool, because by the end of the season I improved so much that I amazed myself—and I did it without a single harsh word from my dad. I definitely became a much better player in the process because I worked on developing my strengths. I focused on what I did well, and as a result, my confidence grew as well.

Today, I still do something similar. I've made a habit of tracking my growth and my successes. I am very careful about what I choose to focus on. I'm aware of my weaknesses, but I focus on my strengths and what I do well so I can build on them.

17.2 Appreciate Your Positive Past

Why do most people put more emphasis on their failures and their limitations than on their successes and strengths? Well, it's really no surprise when you think about it. Just look back to how you were raised. When you were just a child and you "behaved," what happened? You were probably left alone to twiddle your thumbs. But when you misbehaved by being a nuisance and making too much noise, you got yelled at and punished. Hmmm . . . When you got an A on your report card, you might have received a simple "good job," but God forbid what happened when you got an F!

Do you see the trend here? There's often more attention placed on negativity. It is true that there are consequences to poor performance—and that's what our parents, teachers, coaches, and bosses are emphasizing when they get mad at us. But it's important that we take it upon ourselves to emphasize our own strengths and past successes so we can build on them (and then experience more of them).

When we speak, we often ask the audience to do something very simple: "Just turn to the person next to you and share a success you've had in the past week." It's amazing how many people struggle to do this. Many people don't think they have had any successes at all. But if we ask them to list ten failures they've had in the past week . . . "Well, that's easy!" they say. People have a much harder time identifying the victories.

What about you? What great things have you done in the past? The truth is we all have past successes and victories that we can build on. The question is, will we remind ourselves of our progress and measure it so we're driven to create even more successes?

Stacy, 17 (San Francisco, CA): In middle school, I became really critical of myself. I was never happy with my effort or performance. As time went on, things just got worse and worse. One of my teachers could see that I was really frustrated and talked with me about it. I didn't notice it, but apparently it was obvious to him. He said that I was constantly focusing on the negative—my weaknesses, failures, and problems. "Well," I told him, "that's because everything I do is wrong, and it turns out to be negative."

Then my teacher asked me a question: "What have you done well in the last week?" "Ummm . . . nothing," I said. "Don't you see? I mess up *everything*." Then I continued to list all of my problems again. He just smiled and nodded. This got me more frustrated. Once I finished talking, he surprised me with an assignment: "For one week, focus on what you do well and the successes that you have."

A few days later, he checked with me. I told him I didn't do it because it would just be demoralizing. "Trust me," he said. "Do it for one week. Write down what you find in this notebook." I wasn't excited about it, but I gave it a shot.

The first and second day, I didn't have many things to write down, but by the third day I noticed things that I hadn't recognized before. At the end of the week, I was getting really good at it. Each day my list grew longer and longer. I wrote down everything I could think of, from not pushing my snooze button on my alarm, to declining junk food at lunch, to giving someone a compliment, to improving my test scores.

When I finally made an effort to search for the good things I was doing, I could see that there were actually a lot of positive things I was doing all along. Once I noticed them, I started feeling better about myself. I know it sounds cheesy, but it really did work. Today, it's become a habit. Instead of always having a long list of reasons why I am no good or why I shouldn't try something, I now automatically search for reasons why I can do something and why I *should* take action.

173 There's a Lot at Stake

 o what is the big deal about acknowledging our past success, and why is it so important? The answer is simple: It builds our self-esteem. But wait, hold the eye roll. *Self-esteem* is a word that's often tossed around as something that only the shy, timid, and weak need. Not true!

Look at it this way: Imagine if your level of self-esteem was measured in poker chips. Then imagine we are sitting at a table about to play a game of poker. But here's the catch: You have only ten chips, and we have 200 each. Who do you think is going to be more confident? And who do you think is going to be more hesitant, doubtful, and cautious? Easy answer, right? You are going to be much more hesitant and reserved because you only have ten chips. For example, if you lose two bets of five chips each, you're out of the game. We could lose five chips forty times before we would be out of the game! As a result, we would be much more willing to take risks because we can afford to take the losses.

Our level of self-esteem works the same way, but unlike the chips, we can have an unlimited amount. The more self-esteem we have, the more risks we're willing to take and the more confidence we will have to achieve our goals and follow our dreams. There is a massive amount of research that proves the more we acknowledge and appreciate our past successes, the more confident we'll be in taking on new challenges and enjoying our new successes. We will know that even if we face temporary defeat, it won't destroy us because our self-esteem is high. This is vital because *the more we risk, the more we will win in life.* In other words, the more shots you take, the more chances you have of scoring.

For me, winning isn't something that happens suddenly on the field when the whistle blows and the crowds roar. **Winning** is something that **builds physically** and **mentally** every day that you train and every night that you dream.

—Emmitt Smith
The NFL's all-time leading rusher

 n army has an arsenal of weapons. A professional basketball team has a playbook of various plays. Even a squirrel collects a stash of food for the winter. How are these related? The army, the team, the squirrel—each has prepared resources to help them survive, thrive, and succeed. Believe it or not, our arsenal of past successes and victories is essential if we are to achieve great things.

The more victories we can remember and build on, the better off we're going to be. So here's our challenge to you: On a separate sheet of paper, make a list of 100 or more of your life successes. Yes, we said "100 or more." Maybe you're thinking, "This is a piece of cake!" or perhaps you're thinking, "100? Yeah, right! Are you serious?" Whatever your response may be, we challenge you to give this exercise a shot. The benefits are extremely valuable, and you're the one who gets to enjoy the rewards.

Our experience has shown us that most people have no trouble coming up with the first thirty on the list, but after that, it becomes a little more difficult. To come up with 100, you are going to have to list things like learning to ride a bike, singing a solo in the school play, getting your first summer job, getting your first hit in Little League, getting your grandfather's old car to run again, making the cheerleading squad, getting your driver's license, writing an article for your school newspaper, getting an A in Mrs. Bennett's history class, bringing up a C to a B in Mr. Carter's biology class, learning to swim or surf, winning a ribbon at the county fair, and so on. If you need to, it's okay to resort to writing down "passed first grade, passed second grade, passed third grade." These are victories, too! The goal is simply to get to 100. Can you do it?

There's no doubt about it—life moves so fast! It's easy to lose perspective. For example, if somebody hasn't seen you in a little while, he might say, "You've really grown up." Meanwhile, you're thinking, "I have? I don't feel any different." Sometimes it's difficult to measure the progress of our own lives because we're so immersed in them. We have so much going on that we don't always see the big picture. We're always growing. Six months from now, we won't be the same person because we've experienced new things and learned new important life lessons. But if we don't acknowledge our progress, our growth, and the success we have each day, then it won't have the same positive impact it could have.

To keep stacking up those poker chips, try keeping a written journal of your successes—both big and small, as Stacy explained earlier in this chapter. It can be a simple list in a spiral notebook, a document on your computer, or a leather-bound diary—it's up to you.

> **Appreciate your strengths,** and they will **get stronger.** **Acknowledge** your **successes,** and they will **multiply.**

175 Put It on Display

It's a fact: What we see in our environment influences our moods, our attitudes, and our behavior—and that means our overall performance is affected as well. But here's an even more important fact: We have almost complete control of our environment. We get to choose what pictures to hang, what quotes to tape to our bathroom mirror and our locker door, and what rewards, certificates, and trophies we place on our desk and shelves.

It may sound a little ridiculous, but putting evidence of our success on display (awards, certificates, trophies, photographs, letters, medals, etc.) psychologically reinforces our willingness to focus and work hard. Why? Because we're reminded of the rewards and benefits we received in the past. When we constantly see things that remind us of our past success, we become programmed to see ourselves as a winner—someone who has *consistent* success in life! Not only does this build confidence in yourself, it also causes other people to put their confidence in you as well.

Confidence is contagious. So is lack of confidence.

—Vince Lombardi
Head coach who led the Green Bay Packers
to six division titles, five NFL championships, and two Super Bowls

 # Life is a Journey, so Enjoy the Progress

Have you ever noticed how some people accomplish remarkable feats—like breaking a sports record, starting a successful business, writing a book, or graduating top of their class—but still remain unsatisfied? How sad!

> **Success without satisfaction is senseless.**

These people often think they're "pushing themselves" beyond their "real" capabilities to reach a higher level of performance, but the truth is, they're cheating themselves of the confidence and fulfillment they could be experiencing (the very confidence and happiness they could use to accomplish even more). In reality, we'll never be successful if we don't feel successful.

It's nice when people appreciate our accomplishments and our efforts, but the true rewards come from within ourselves. We determine whether or not we feel unsatisfied or successful. Relying on our next accomplishment or on other people to make us feel good about ourselves only sets us up for disappointment.

How good are you at sports, academics, hobbies? How do you measure your performance? By grades? Other people's opinions? Past accomplishments? Personal evaluation? This is extremely important. The most significant criterion of all should be your own personal evaluation. Why? Because in most cases, people who don't think they are skilled or competent will not change their opinions of themselves regardless of their personal achievements. You might want to read that last sentence again! This means that if we're not careful, our self-doubts can blindfold us from seeing the evidence that clearly indicates we *are* already competent and successful.

Value *all* of your successes because your self-worth and self-esteem are not shaped by grades, trophies, certificates, or other people's opinions. They are, however, dependent on how you evaluate your own accomplishments. If you've done something well, you should feel good about it—and, yes, this is a conscious choice you must make. Be sure to stop and appreciate yourself, your talents, your skills, and your results. All of these things help build your confidence and strengthen your self-worth. Simply by acknowledging what you do well, you will feel a sense of accomplishment and recognition.

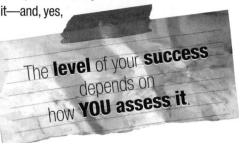

The **level** of your **success** depends on how **YOU assess it**.

Recently, we were talking to Monica, a seventeen-year-old student who was greatly respected by her friends and the rest of her school. She was very popular, not to mention a straight-A student, captain of the volleyball team, winner of several art contests, and to put the icing on the cake, she was also crowned homecoming queen.

By most people's standards, Monica was very successful, but through her own eyes, she was never quite good enough. Last year, after her team's victory in the volleyball league finals, we congratulated her: "Great job! You must feel pretty good!" She replied, "Well, I could have done better." Then she rattled off a long list of all the mistakes she made in her final game and how she could have played better. We were shocked!

After talking with her some more, we discovered that Monica's self-criticizing didn't stop at the volleyball court. Although she had accomplished so much and had many reasons to feel good about herself, she knew more about her weaknesses and mistakes than she knew about her accomplishments. Why? Because that's what she chose to focus on. It's important to have high standards and work on our shortcomings, but if we don't appreciate the many great things we do, we will eventually suffer from a horrible side effect known as "burnout." Will this happen to Monica? Possibly, but one thing is for sure: She will never experience the maximum exhilaration and satisfaction she could until she stops to fully appreciate herself, her strengths, and her accomplishments. And no one else can do this for her.

We are the only ones who can allow ourselves to feel like we are valuable, competent people. If we don't value ourselves, no reward, certification, or compliment will change that perception. It all begins by acknowledging the things we do well.

Your **happiness in life** is **not determined** by what you **achieve, but** rather by **how you assess** what **you achieve**.

Are there any successes—big or small—that you haven't fully acknowledged? Think about it. It's the fuel you need to persevere and continue to work hard. Don't rob yourself of the happiness, confidence, and self-esteem you could build on for future success.

MY "TO-DO" LIST

☑ Realize that keeping score of my progress will help me stay motivated and understand that my scorekeeping will reinforce the behavior that created these outcomes in the first place.

☑ I will focus on and track my strengths and successes because I now know that I will get more of what I focus on.

☑ Create a victory journal where I keep an ongoing record of my accomplishments, victories, and successes.

☑ Make a habit of focusing on and appreciating what I do well each day.

☑ Understand that my environment influences the way I feel and my performance, so I will choose to create a positive environment by hanging inspirational quotes, photos, awards, certificates, and trophies where I can regularly see them.

☑ Realize that building confidence in myself also helps other people to put their confidence in me.

☑ Understand that the level of my success depends on *how I assess it.* I must appreciate my abilities and my victories in order to build on my successes and strengthen my self-worth.

PRINCIPLE 18

Perform With Persistence by Keeping Your Eyes on the Prize

It's **always too soon** to **quit**!

—Norman Vincent Peale
Bestselling author and inspirational speaker

**e**'ve all heard it before: *"When the going gets tough, the tough get going"*—and it's absolutely true! After years of researching success, we've found that persistence is probably the single most common quality of high achievers. They simply refuse to give up. And since challenges are inevitable, only those who persevere can ever fully enjoy all the rewards that life can offer.

Here's how it works: The longer you hang in there, the greater the chance that something will happen in your favor. No matter how hard it seems, the more you persist, the more likely your success.

Despite what some people believe, persistence is not something you're born with. It's something you develop by deciding to follow through and making an effort to keep your eyes on the prize.

Here comes the Disclaimer!

The slogan **"press on"** has solved and always **will solve the problems** of the human race.

—*Calvin Coolidge*
Thirtieth President of the United States

As much as we'd like to deny it, the journey to our goals and dreams is not always going to be easy. Sometimes we're going to have to persist in the face of obstacles—challenges that we don't even expect to show up; obstacles that no amount of planning or forethought could have predicted. But guess what? That's just life, and no one is an exception to the rule. The sooner we accept that our journey to success will not always be easy, the more we can mentally prepare ourselves to persevere and "keep on truckin'" when life's challenges show up—and, inevitably, they will.

Our willingness to persevere is much like our muscular strength: We need to work at it every day to build this much-needed "mental muscle." And the more we do, the stronger and stronger our focus, determination, and ability to persevere will become. In other words, the more often we work through challenges, ignore temptations, and refuse to quit, the easier it will be to persevere "next time."

Sometimes we'll experience what appears to be unbelievably bad luck, or we'll encounter what seem like overwhelming odds. In these situations, our commitment will really be put to the test, and as usual, it's how we react that matters most. In the face of challenges, winners step it up, dig in, and commit to giving their best. They don't complain about it; they act with determination.

If you want to see a great example of extreme willpower, simply observe ants. Yes, ants . . . those little creatures that (according to fascination.com) outnumber us by about 1,666,666 to one! There are good reasons why ants have been so successful. Have you noticed that ants *always* persevere? Think about it. When rain washes away their nests or humans stomp on them, you will never see ants mope around, pout, get angry, and start complaining. If ants could talk, you would never hear them yell, "I just spent 75% of my life building that

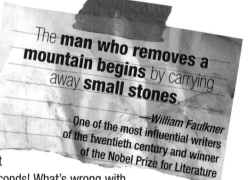

The **man who removes a mountain begins** by carrying away **small stones**.

—*William Faulkner*
One of the most influential writers of the twentieth century and winner of the Nobel Prize for Literature

nest and now you destroy in a matter of seconds! What's wrong with you? I can't believe it! What am I going to do? Poor me. Poor me. Poor me." No way! They just deal with it! In a matter of seconds, they're already fixing the problem and rebuilding their nest. Now that's impressive!

18.2 Against All Odds

Effort only **fully releases its reward** after a **person refuses to quit**.

—*Napoleon Hill*
Bestselling author of *Think and Grow Rich*

ur friend Bruce Kennedy faced some devastating odds early in life. He was born in the small African country of Rhodesia (now Zimbabwe), which was on the brink of war. He saw sports as his ticket to freedom.

Working really hard to be the best javelin thrower he could be, he won a track scholarship to Cal Berkeley in 1969. His future was looking bright. His personal best javelin throw at the time was 222 feet, 3 inches. The next year, he threw even farther—249 feet, 10 inches, and he was thrilled when he qualified for the Rhodesian Olympic team.

After arriving at the 1972 Olympic Games in Munich, the Rhodesian team received news that they could not compete because of apartheid and other political issues. "They moved us out of the Olympic Village and into an army base nearby so we could watch as spectators," Bruce recalls. "It was still a great experience, but it was also a bitter disappointment."

In 1973, Bruce was able to improve his throwing distance by 17 feet and 1 inch, but at the 1976 Olympics in Montreal, the Rhodesian team wasn't even allowed to travel to Canada. Bruce couldn't compete for a second time. "I couldn't believe it, but there was nothing I could do about it. I had the choice to quit and sulk or keep my head high." And yet, he wasn't willing to back down.

After getting married in 1973, Bruce became a U.S. citizen. When he won the national javelin championship and qualified for the U.S. Olympic team, he thought his troubles were behind him. But three years later, right before the next Olympics in 1980, President Carter ordered a U.S. boycott of the Olympics—the *third* time in a row Bruce could not compete. Imagine qualifying for three different Olympic teams and never having the chance to compete in the Olympic Games! Bruce felt devastated—especially since he threw his personal best of 287 feet, 9 inches just before the 1980 Olympics. (By the way, before throwing his personal best, he had gone from June 1973 to March 1980 without improving an inch! Seven years . . . how's that for perseverance?)

"A lot of people can't believe it, but I don't regard my experiences as negative," Bruce says. "I was just a regular kid growing up in Africa. Athletics helped me go to a university for free, meet my wife, and become a citizen of the world's greatest country. Otherwise, I would have been stuck in Africa fighting a war."

What an incredible example of how the right attitude mixed with persistence can positively shape your life. Even though he didn't get the results he wanted, he did meet the person of his dreams, and he did earn his American citizenship, all because he had built up his psychological muscles, remained focused, worked hard, and persisted through life challenges.

Today, Bruce remains extremely focused and determined. At age fifty-six, he gets up at 4:00 AM to travel to work each morning; he always keeps his commitment of biking twenty-five miles every day; he owns his own investment management business; and he has an incredible family, house, and lifestyle in the hills of Santa Barbara, California. Not bad! Ask him, and Bruce will tell you that his many successes are the direct results of his valuable life lessons.

"You must have a goal and believe in yourself if you want to live your dreams," Bruce says. "There must be an end result. You can't just turn your efforts on and off when it's convenient. Pursuit of a worthwhile goal is a 24/7 prospect, and persistence is key. Look at it this way: A journey without a destination is just wandering."

> Our greatest **weakness lies in giving up.**
> The most certain way to succeed
> is always to **try just one more time**.
>
> —*Thomas A. Edison*
> World-renowned inventor

18.3 Keep Your Eyes on the Prize

> **Obstacles** are those things you see
> when you **take your eyes off of your goals**.
>
> —*Henry Ford*
> Entrepreneur and founder of the Ford Motor Company

When was the last time you wanted something really bad? We're talking about a desire so strong that you could feel butterflies in your stomach just by thinking about it. Maybe it was a certain toy when you were little, a puppy, a starting position on the team, a trip to your favorite city or campground, an opening gig at a local concert, a date with that special someone, a certain sports title, or that dream car.

YOU DON'T HAVE A CHANCE, TORTOISE.

IT'S ALL ABOUT PATIENCE AND PERSISTENCE.

Whatever it was, do you remember how you constantly thought about it? How you were always focused on the result, the achievement, the prize? When your eyes are dead-set on a target, the obstacles in your way seem insignificant and easily conquerable. Your ability to reach that specific outcome has not changed. The only thing that changed was where you chose to focus. When you're focused on the outcome and keep your eyes on the prize, determination will follow—and with that determination comes the natural drive to persevere through the roadblocks on your path to success.

Successful people keep a positive focus no matter what is going on around them. They focus on the next action steps they need to take to get them closer to their goals, rather than all the other distractions that life presents to them. They are very aware of how and where they spotlight their attention and energy. On the other hand, those who never take action and always have reasons why something "can't be done" have simply developed an unconscious habit of focusing on all the obstacles in their path.

To unleash the power of persistence, we must know what the prize is at all times and give it the majority of our attention and thought. Why? Because discipline and persistence are naturally created when we know that our efforts will directly contribute to a specific reward or outcome. All successful people know this, and now you do, too:

Those who consistently follow through with their goals and objectives know exactly why they should take action—the reward gets them excited. If you're struggling to find a reason to persevere or you want even more determination, continually ask yourself these three questions:

Discipline comes by convincing yourself that the **rewards are** worth the **sacrifices**.

1. **What is the outcome I want?**

2. **How will my life be better if I persist and make this happen?**

3. **What will I miss out on if I do not persist through my challenges and obstacles?**

Caroline, 15 (Oceanside, CA): I was never good at finishing things. I could get started, but when things got tough, I usually backed out. But what bugged me most was that I didn't know why. One day, I meant to go running with my friend to train for a 5K race, but I decided not to show up. My friend got annoyed because I used to flake out a lot. She said, "You always have a reason not to do something!"

I got angry and instantly responded, "No, that's not true—" But this wasn't the first time I had heard this, so part of me stopped and thought, "Maybe she's right." It seems so obvious now, but I didn't notice it then. After that, I started recognizing things about myself that I didn't see before. I caught myself thinking about the wrong stuff. I was focusing on everything I had to do and go through rather than all the benefits of just sticking with it and following through. So I wrote down the three questions that Kent and Jack talked about [*see questions above*] and constantly reminded myself to ask those questions every time I faced a challenge.

I was really surprised: It worked! Now that I know the benefits of persevering, I don't see as many obstacles in my way. I'm excited to say I committed to running another 5K race with my friend, and I did it! I proved to myself that it feels so much better to take action and complete things rather than avoid them. Today, I actually get excited about finishing everything I start. It's become easier and easier to follow through.

18.4 Don't Eat That Marshmallow!

Great things are not done by impulse,
but **by a series of small things** brought together.

—Vincent Van Gogh
Maverick nineteenth-century painter

magine if someone placed a piece of your favorite candy on a table in front of you. Then before leaving the room, he said, "You can have one piece of candy right now or wait fifteen minutes and have two pieces of candy." What would you do? Your answer might say more about your long-term success than you think.

In the 1960s, Dr. Walter Mischel at Stanford University led an extensive long-term study that became known as the "Marshmallow Tests." A group of researchers put a marshmallow in front of four-year-old children and said: "You can have one marshmallow right now, but if you can wait fifteen minutes while I go run a quick errand, you can have two marshmallows when I come back. It's up to you."

Some kids ate the marshmallow as soon as the researcher left the room; others thought about it, waited for a few minutes, and then they also ate the marshmallow. In the end, despite the discomfort of waiting, about one third sat patiently until the researcher returned so they could enjoy the double reward.

Years later, Dr. Mischel interviewed the same kids again, this time to measure their current success and happiness in life. The results were incredible! Now in high school, the same individuals who had declined the first marshmallow now had better grades and higher SAT scores. They were also more confident, self-reliant, motivated, socially competent, and personally content. The study also found that they were more effective at solving problems and more likely to follow through with their goals during challenging times—and the list goes on and on! The one thing these students had in common was the ability to control their impulses and delay gratification in pursuit of larger goals.

How about "the grabbers"—those who ate the first marshmallow? Their results were just as interesting. The researchers found that the grabbers were more stubborn, more easily influenced by others, less decisive, had lower self-esteem, and were easily frustrated and discouraged. According to the study, even years later these individuals still could not delay their gratification. In other words, they would settle for less in the short term rather than be persistent and work for a greater reward in the long term.

Life today moves fast, and in a fast-moving world, most people don't like waiting for results. Just think about it: It takes seconds to send an e-mail message around the world. Using only our tiny cell phones, we can take a quality photo and send it across the world instantaneously to a friend. We can read our most recent bank balance online virtually the moment the bank posts it. And in minutes we can get a meal twenty-four hours a day! Yes, we have become used to immediate results.

The bad news: This "I want it now" mentality is a severe handicap that stops many people from getting the life they really want. It's easy to overlook the fact that some things take time. Period. Many people know what they want "right now," but very few people are willing to make the sacrifices necessary to get the maximum benefit and reward in the future.

In order to be persistent, we must control our impulses and be willing to work for a result that may not be immediate. Easier said than done, but as the Marshmallow Tests show, those who can control their focus and delay their urge for instant gratification will drastically increase their long-term chances of success and happiness. So is it worth it? What do you think?

Here's a great example: education. Would you agree that education is extremely valuable in today's world? Of course, you do. Otherwise, you wouldn't be reading this! Even though it's not always easy to stay in school and remain focused for years and years, education obviously does have a long-term payoff. A quality education invariably means a much bigger paycheck later in life.

Don't let **pleasures** of the present **take advantage of your future**,

18.5 Redefine "Problem"

If it weren't for **challenges**, would we ever really know **what we're capable of doing**?

—*Author Unknown*

"**W**ow, just the man I need!" said the young high school student as he pointed across the busy street to the billionaire businessman he recognized in the news.

Without thinking, the student immediately ran across the busy intersection, almost causing an accident. As he approached this businessman, he grabbed his sleeve and said, "You've got to help me! I have some big problems in my life and I can't deal with them any longer." The businessman very calmly removed the stranger's hands from his suit jacket and said, "I'm on my way to an important meeting, but if you'd like, I can direct you to a place where people have no problems."

"You'd do that for me?" the student said. "Thank you, thank you!" The business man pulls out two pieces of paper. On one piece he writes the direction to an address nearby. While writing on the second piece of paper, he says to the student, "Don't read what is on this second piece of paper until you arrive at the address I have given you."

The student tries to hold in his excitement as he nods his head. The businessman waves to him and winks as he steps into his limousine.

As the student followed the directions he ran as fast as his feet would take him, passing by the massive city buildings chasing down street after street. As he got closer to the address, the student noticed an opening in the skyline and saw what appeared to be a park with trees and green grass.

As he neared the park, seeing nothing else around, he begins to think the address must be wrong. The student quickly realizes that this was no ordinary park—it was a cemetery. He takes a big gulp of air after noticing the entrance gate bears the correct address. Confused, the student grabs the second piece of paper from his back pocket and reads it aloud, "There are over 5,000 people buried right here . . . and not one of them has a problem."

What an interesting way to look at life, don't you think? Most people believe that success means not having any problems at all. This couldn't be further from the truth! It doesn't matter who you are today or what you've accomplished in the past; we will all face problems as we move through life. In fact, problems and challenges are signs of life. So, if this is the case, then one of the best things we can do is redefine what "problem" means to us.

Let us explain: Instead of getting discouraged and overwhelmed when something unexpected happens, choose to view your obstacles as a sign that you're still alive! And better yet, remember that every situation you face gives you a chance to grow stronger, wiser, and more experienced—everything you need to be more successful! Would that make a difference in the way you approach your difficulties in your life? Absolutely!

Try eliminating the word "problem" from your vocabulary entirely. As soon as we did this, we noticed a big difference in our willingness to persevere. Why? Because nobody enjoys facing a problem. And since the words we use affect the way we think and feel, it makes sense to rename the word "problem" and redefine it as "challenge." Now we can approach the same obstacles— make that "challenges"—with a completely different outlook. This new definition is better because we all enjoy taking on "challenges." Just think about it; this is why we enjoy sports, board games, video games, crossword puzzles, and so on—things that test us and help us see what we're capable of doing. We like to challenge ourselves, push our luck, and observe our progress.

> **Problems** are to the **mind** what **exercise** is to the **muscles**; they toughen and make strong.
>
> —*Norman Vincent Peale*
> Bestselling author and inspirational speaker

18.6 The 90/10 Rule

It's easy to persist when things are going well, but our true colors shine through during challenging times. What do you do when you face an unexpected challenge? Would you choose to take the easy way out by complaining about it, stressing about it, or whining about it? Or would you do something different? If you're reading this, you certainly know that complaining about something never makes it go away. In fact, situations get worse and worse the longer we stare at them.

Have you ever noticed how small problems start looking like really big problems the more we talk about them and focus on them? Overanalyzing a roadblock can make the situation or challenge look like a dead end—and when we don't see any options, that's when we lose our drive to persevere. On the other hand, successful people don't give problems too much attention, allowing them to grow out of control. They use the 90/10 rule: They give only 10% of their focus and attention to the problem and 90% to developing a solution and taking the action needed to take care of the challenge. It sounds simple—*and it is*!

Yet many people do the opposite. They know everything there is to know about their problem, but they never get past that stage to create a solution. That is a recipe for disaster!

The next time you catch yourself facing an obstacle, create a limit for the amount of time you can think about the problem itself. Then, when the time runs out, immediately shift your focus and start creating a plan of attack to handle the situation. Here's the math: For every one minute you spend looking at the problem, spend nine minutes developing a solution and implementing it.

TIP: Try coming up with three ways to get around, over, or through the block. For every obstacle, come up with three different ways you could handle it. There are many ways that will work, but you will find them only if you spend time looking for them. Always be solution-oriented in your thinking . . . persevere until you find a way that works.

When you spend the majority of your time developing a solution, you will have the energy and creativity you need to move forward. Persistence is easy when we know the benefits of following through. When we know what to do next, we're much more motivated to get started and work through the challenge. Why? Because *we know what to do!* Your vision of the outcome you want will help you take action and work your plan.

Sara, 16 (Seattle, WA): It's not that I enjoyed facing problems; I just wasn't aware of how much time I spent focusing on them—and, not surprisingly, they never went away. Whenever something came up, I would instantly think, "Why me?" or "Oh, great, not this again!" And these responses only prolonged the problems because the longer I focused on them and thought about them, the more daunting they became and the more often I put things off.

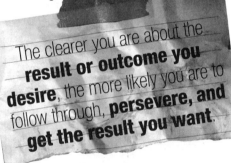

The clearer you are about the **result or outcome you desire**, the more likely you are to follow through, **persevere, and get the result you want**.

I always felt like I was *forced* to change things in my life—and I was! But only because I waited so long that eventually I *had* to. The 90/10 rule helped me change my focus. Instead of identifying the problem and dwelling on it, I instantly started thinking about what I could do to fix things. Big difference! I recognized way more solutions—and once I saw the solution, I immediately felt better because I knew what I had to do next. Believe me, it's so much easier to take care of things right when they happen. Focusing on problems only makes things worse.

18.7 Avoid Insanity!

> The majority of men meet with **failure** because of their **lack of persistence** in creating new plans to take the place of those which fail.
>
> —*Napoleon Hill*
> Author of the all-time bestseller *Think and Grow Rich*

Do you remember our definition of *insanity?* "Doing the same thing over and over again and expecting a different result." We've seen many people who persist and persist, but continue to get the same outcome. They convince themselves that if they implement the same strategy enough times, eventually it will work. While it's important to be optimistic and keep our eyes on the prize, we must be able to look around long enough to see if what we're doing is working. As we've already discussed, we are constantly getting various forms of feedback, and this information can give us very important insight.

Sure, there are times when we have to persist and keep repeating our action steps, but we must also be able to notice patterns in the feedback that we are receiving. Ask yourself, "Am I getting close to where I want to be, or am I just digging a deeper rut?"

It's one thing to be **persistent** in **overcoming challenges**, but it's another to do the **same** thing **over and over** again when it **clearly isn't working**.

If you continue to get the same undesirable result, do not blame your lack of ability. When you get a result you don't want, it's seldom a reflection of you; rather, it's a reflection of your current strategy. This is where flexibility comes into play—and no, we're not talking about your ability to touch your toes. We mean that you must be able to adapt your behavior. In the real world, a "one-size-fits-all" strategy" to achieve a goal does not exist. If something isn't working, we must be willing to change our actions and let go of a strategy that doesn't work. It's okay to change your course— that is not quitting. We're not talking about giving up, but rather trying something different to get the same result. This is key for long-term success.

Is YOUR STRATEGY WORKING?

If what you're doing isn't working, then try something

else. If that doesn't work, then (yes!) try something else. Like a combination lock, we simply need to find the right sequence. Be persistent in *getting the result*, not persistent in continuing to work a plan that doesn't work for you.

18.8 The Wrap

Winners never quit, and **quitters never win**.

—*Unknown*

Nelson Mandela once said, "The greatest glory in living lies not in never falling, but in rising every time we fall." Life is full of unsuspected challenges. Sometimes we'll fall down a couple of times on our journey to success, and sometimes we won't achieve our goals as soon as we'd like to. That's okay . . . it's just life. But we must be willing to persevere and give our best even when things aren't going our way. Just because we don't see a result right away does not mean we won't see it eventually.

> I WILL MAKE THIS CATCH!

Perhaps you've heard the saying, "Failure is the path of least resistance" but we look at it this way: "Failure is the path of least persistence"—and it's absolutely true. Failure comes only after we stop, give up, or quit. Persistence helps us to stay in the game long enough to give ourselves a chance to win.

MY "TO-DO" LIST

☑ Realize that the longer I persist, the more likely it is that I will achieve my goals.

☑ By accepting that my journey to success will not always be easy, I can mentally prepare to persevere through challenges.

☑ Focus on the outcome and keep my eyes on the prize, because determination will follow.

☑ Control my impulses and be willing to work for a result that may not be immediate because I drastically increase my chances of long-term success and happiness.

☑ Look at "problems" as "challenges" and understand that these obstacles only make me stronger and wiser.

☑ Spend only 10% of my time analyzing a challenge and devote 90% to developing a solution and implementing the plan.

☑ Look for patterns in the feedback that I am constantly receiving and be willing to try something different to get the results I want.

CHP 19

Give your best to be your best

Excellence comes by caring **more than others think is wise,** **risking** more than **others think is safe,** **dreaming** more than **others think is practi-** **cal,** and **expecting** more than **others think is possible.**

—*Author Unknown*

217

Are you someone who consistently goes the extra mile and always over-delivers on your promises? Well, successful people do . . . it's a characteristic of all high achievers. In fact, you cannot be your best if you're willing to settle for a half-effort.

Here's the truth: Even a 99% percent commitment will not do. Even one reason not to do something is often enough to stop us from doing what's necessary to get what we really want in life.

The difference between luck and success is consistency—and the way you truly get the best, experience the best, and become your best is by consistently *giving* your best effort. Such a simple concept, right? Yet it's amazing how many people wake up every day and fight with themselves over whether or not to keep their commitments, live up to their word, and follow through with their action plans.

Those who enjoy the best in life are those who have a "no matter what it takes" attitude. They give it their all; they put everything they have into achieving their goals—whether it be winning the league finals, getting straight A's, selling the most magazines for a school fundraiser, exercising, working at their job, starting a business, keeping healthy relationships—yes, even doing the dishes, cleaning the car, completing homework, and so on. High performers are completely dedicated to excellence, and, as a result, the quality of their lives is also excellent.

19.1 What's "Cool"?

What's the secret to an extraordinary life? Do more, be more, and give more than other people expect.

Here's the basic challenge: There seems to be an unspoken law that says, "It's not cool to try hard." Where did that concept come from? It's not said, but it's often implied. However, if "cool" means not trying, then it must be cool to struggle through life and barely make ends meet, because that's what happens to those who decide to give a half-effort.

> *Those* **who give more, become more.**

(And please note that it *is* a "decision"!) Just where are those so-called "cool" people twenty years after high school? You'll find them working for those people who were busting their butts in the classroom, on the field, in the music room, and in all other areas of their life.

It's a choice we all make: (1) Exceed expectations and work hard, or (2) cut corners, look for the easy way out, and slack off. It's purely up to us; nobody can force us to do either one. And, by the way, what is "cool" anyway? You might find that it's actually something different than you originally thought. Sometimes, when we're giving presentations, we'll do an exercise called "The 'Cool Element.'" Instead of boring you with an explanation, try it out yourself. Here it is:

The "Cool Element"

Step 1: Select five people you think are "cool"—five people you admire. They can be famous or people you know personally. (There is no wrong or right answer.) Write all five names on a piece of paper.

Step 2: Next to their names, list their traits and the reasons why you think they are "cool."

Step 3: Look over your list and circle any recurring words. The traits you circle are typically what you define as "cool."

So what did you discover? Did the outcome surprise you? Our answers sure surprised us the first time we did this exercise. We found that what we admired was different from what we thought was cool initially. The trend became obvious: The people we respect and look up to are the same people who work hard, stay focused, persevere, and think about other people—whether they're well-known or not! So it seems that trying hard and doing what you can to succeed is pretty "cool" after all. Interesting . . .

19.2 Exceed Expectations

Four short words sum up what has lifted most **successful** individuals above the crowd: **a little bit more**. They did all that was **expected of them** and **a little bit more**.

—*A. Lou Vickery*
Writer

Seventeen-year-old Brian McMurray was visiting his grandmother's gravesite at the Gate of Heaven Cemetery in Cupertino, California, when a tall, elderly man carrying a bouquet of flowers fell while walking on some uneven ground. Several people cringed as they witnessed this—including a group of Brian's friends.

Refusing to be a bystander, Brian immediately ran over to the man to make sure he was okay and helped him get back on his feet. The people watching were stunned that Brian reacted so quickly. They certainly did not expect that—and neither did the old man.

Brian initiated a conversation and discovered that the man was on his way to his wife's gravesite, but he couldn't remember where it was. Instead of just leaving him there, Brian offered to help him find it. After they did, Brian patiently waited for the man and then walked him all the way back to his car. Over? Not quite. He didn't stop there! Brian asked for the elderly man's phone number so he could call him in thirty minutes to make sure he got home safely.

Wow! The onlookers—all of his friends and even his father—were absolutely blown away. But Brian didn't do it to impress anyone; he gave no thought to whether it was "cool" or not. He admits that he was a bit surprised by the way people responded to his actions. The old man was overwhelmed with Brian's thoughtfulness and could not stop expressing his gratitude. He told Brian that he had "made his week." His friends were also impressed by his leadership, and his father couldn't have been prouder.

Brian's actions didn't cost him a penny. Anybody could have done it, but nobody else did. Nobody was expecting it, and everybody loved it. For the rest of the day, as Brian explained, he was on a natural high. He put other people before himself, and ironically he felt he was the person who received the biggest gift of all. Today, Brian is always looking for ways to exceed expectations and overdeliver. As a result, he has become a natural leader . . . someone other people look up to.

19.3 GO the Extra Mile

Do more than is required. What is the **distance between someone who achieves their goals consistently** and **those who spend their lives** and careers merely following? **The extra mile**.

—*Gary Ryan Blair*
Author, speaker, coach, and consultant

When Mary Jacobs, age sixteen, agreed to be the bartender's assistant for a family friend's house party, she had no idea what she was getting herself into. In fact, she had no experience at all, but she had one thing going for her: the willingness to go the extra mile.

That evening, she not only worked hard; she also looked for ways to exceed expectations. She started by listening closely to everyone's name as she was introduced to all the guests. In addition, she paid attention to what drinks people ordered. Mary was very proactive and didn't wait for people to come to her. The moment she had a break at the bar, she walked around the house searching for empty glasses and antsy guests to see how she could make their evening better.

Even though it wasn't in her job description, she retrieved people's coats, delivered drinks directly to the guests, picked up trash around the house, and refilled the snack bowls. She didn't ask for more money or expect any special treatment in return.

As the party proceeded late into the night, Mary started to get tired. She was up early in the morning for swim practice, but you never would have known because she constantly made an effort to smile and focus on the guests, not on herself.

When the guests began to leave, she called each of them by name and said good-bye. The guests were so impressed with her efforts throughout the night that she was flooded with more requests to work at other parties and events—and she began the night only as an assistant! Yet, through a choice in attitude, she created a leadership role, making herself valuable. Mary says, "I didn't have any special talents. I just wanted to deliver the best service possible, and I noticed different ways I could do that."

Today, four years later, Mary runs her own event-planning company out of her "headquarters" (her dorm room at college). She has several people working for her, and she still has to turn down requests because she is so busy. Due to her extra efforts, she has been asked to organize parties for many community and business leaders. As a result, she has been introduced to some very powerful individuals who are scouting her to work at well-respected companies that are willing to offer her "big money."

There is always an important place in the world for those who **overdeliver**. Their worth is **invaluable**.

Who knows what Mary would be doing today had she not gone the extra mile? New opportunities were presented to her because she took that extra step, searched for ways to give more, and made it happen.

If you really want to excel at what you do—we mean become a supersuccess in school, in sports, at work, or in life—then do more than is required, something that is not expected.

What's the payoff for you? A lot! When you give more than is expected, you are more likely to consistently get better results, achieve your goals, receive promotions and pay raises at work, and gain respect from those around you. You are more likely to be viewed as a valuable leader in your classroom, on your sports team, at the workplace, and in your group of friends. You won't need to worry about keeping a job either. You'll be the first hired and the last fired. You'll also find that you feel more satisfied at the end of each day. But if you want all of these rewards to start appearing in your life, you have to start now.

If you focus only on your own needs, you may think that giving more than is expected is unfair. "Why should I give an extra effort without extra compensation or recognition?" You have to trust that, eventually, it will get noticed, and will be worth it. If anything, you will earn a respectable reputation, and that is one of your most valuable resources.

19.4 Why 100% Is So Important

Why is it so important to exceed expectations and give a 100% effort at everything we do? Well, because if everyone gave even a 99.9% effort, it would mean:

- ※ **Two unsafe landings at the O'Hare International Airport each day**
- ※ **16,000 lost pieces of mail per hour**
- ※ **114,500 mismatched pairs of shoes would be shipped each year**
- ※ **20,000 incorrectly filled drug prescriptions every year**
- ※ **500 incorrect surgical operations performed each week**
- ※ **50 newborn babies dropped at birth by doctors every day**
- ※ **315 entries in *Webster's Dictionary* would be misspelled**
- ※ **22,000 checks deducted from the wrong account each hour**
- ※ **Your heart failing to beat 32,000 times each year!**

Can you see why it's so important to give 100% effort and nothing less? Just think how your life (and the world) would work if you were committed 100% to everything you did.

You can create a habit of going the extra mile and exceeding expectations very simply by:

GIVING 100% REALLY PAID OFF...

PERSISTENCE

Champs

* Returning something you borrow in better condition than you found it. (For example, if you borrow a friend's car, give it back with a full tank of gas.)

* Saying "hello" to new students at your school to make them feel welcome. (You'd be surprised how thankful people are when you acknowledge their presence.)

* Washing your dishes when you're done with them.

* Saying "please" and "thank you" *regularly*.

* Calling someone when you said you would call.

* Taking on new responsibilities at work without demanding more pay or begging for acknowledgments . . . or offering to help with tasks that aren't in your job description.

* Doing more than you're asked at school, at home, or at practice without expecting any special treatment or acknowledgement.

* Writing a handwritten thank-you note when someone does something nice for you.

* Focusing on how you can *give* more, instead of focusing on how to *get* more.

19.5 Johnny the Bagger

Don't be **afraid** to **give** your **best** to what seemingly are **small jobs.** Every time you **conquer one**, it makes you that **much stronger**. If you do the **little jobs well**, the **big ones** tend to **take care of themselves**.

—Dale Carnegie
American writer, author, trainer, and speaker

Everything you do will affect other people—and, in most cases, it *will* be noticed. If you're truly dedicated to giving your best, you will always find ways to do your best. What could Johnny, a sixteen-year-old kid with Down syndrome, do to exceed expectations? Apparently, much more than his fellow employees thought was possible.

The grocery store where Johnny worked as a bagger was looking for ways to increase sales, so the company decided to hold an employee training event. They invited a well-known and respected speaker, Barbara Glanz, who explained that each employee created "the customer experience" and that each had the power to make that experience positive or negative.

Johnny was excited after the seminar until he heard some bitter employees say, "Well, I'm just running the checkout . . . as if anything I do really matters." Johnny was crushed. After all, he wasn't even working the counter; he was just a bagger. But unlike the other employees, Johnny was still dedicated to finding a way to make a difference. A couple of days passed, but the thought never left his mind. One morning, Johnny arrived at work with a couple of hundred little pieces of paper. Each piece was titled, "Johnny's thought for the day," and under each heading was a different famous quote. One of the quotes read:

> Johnny's thought for the day . . .
>
> *Never miss a rainbow or a sunset because you're looking down.*
>
> Sarah June Parker

Unfortunately, his fellow employees were not so optimistic about his idea. "Do you seriously think our customers are interested in our thoughts?" exclaimed one coworker. Another person added, "Why bother? This is a lot of work for something that's not even your job." Johnny said, "It does matter because this is my personal signature."

One day, the store manager noticed a massive line of customers in front of one checkout lane. He approached the customers and told them other checkout lanes were open, but no one moved. They all wanted "Johnny's thought of the day"—and were willing to wait in a long line for it! One person waiting in line had a shopping list written by his wife. The last item on the list was "Johnny's thought for the day." Some customers went out of their way, bypassing other stores, just to stop by the supermarket where Johnny worked. Sales at this store increased rapidly. Now the other employees couldn't help but recognize Johnny's impact. He soon inspired his coworkers to look for ways they could do something extra, something that would make "the customer experience" positive.

Not only did Johnny increase sales, but he also boosted the morale of his fellow employees because he showed them that their presence *did* matter and that they could all make a difference.

As Barbara Glanz says, "When we truly focus on other people's needs, show them that we care, and do something a little extra to surprise them, then we are making a difference. It doesn't matter what your job is, how much change is going on around you, or what your boss, teacher, friends or teammates are doing; you can always make a difference. It's your choice."*

It is the **greatest** of all **mistakes to do nothing** because you can do only a little. **Do what you can**.

—*Sydney Smith*
English writer

19.6 NO EXCUSES

There is a **difference** between **interest** and **commitment**. When you're **interested** in doing something, you do it only when it's **convenient**. When you're **committed** to do something, you **accept no excuses, only results**.

—*Ken Blanchard*
Bestselling author on the topic of leadership

 orry, we couldn't come up with an introduction for this section. We're just too tired—and, besides, it's late right now, and our computer isn't working either. It's not our fault!

Could you imagine if we actually thought that way? This book would not exist, that's for sure! Were there times we had to write when we didn't feel like writing? You bet! But we also knew:

It's much **easier** to work **around goals** than it is to **work around challenges**.

In other words, it's easy to come up with thousands of reasons *not* to do something. That's easy . . . anyone can do that. But it takes perseverance, dedication, and a "no excuses" attitude to achieve. In reality, the only thing that stops us from getting what we really want in life are the reasons (or "excuses") we come up with for why we can't do or have something. It's that simple. Excuses instantly limit our potential because we justify why it's okay not to try or not to give our best effort. Very dangerous territory!

We can create excuses for different reasons, but the bottom line is always the same: no results, no rewards, no satisfaction. Most people know every reason why they're not good enough, not strong enough, not smart enough, not pretty enough—they know all their limitations. As a result, they create excuses that stop them from becoming the best person they can be and achieving the many things they can achieve.

In this book, there are a total of twenty principles that can transform your life, but it's up to you to use the information and apply it. As long as there are reasons not to apply the information, it will not be useful to you. The value is there, but so are the excuses. If you are to win, you must not allow excuses to get in your way of success.

The day we met Kyle Maynard was a day we'll never forget. Now twenty-two, Kyle was born with a rare disorder called congenital amputation. This left him with only three major joints: a neck and two shoulders. His arms ended before the elbow, and his legs were only partially developed (they were only six inches long). It would be easy to understand if he were depressed and frustrated with his life—but not Kyle. From an early age, he made the decision to learn how to function in the world on his own. In fact, Kyle never looked at his physical differences as a limitation. He was too busy focusing on what he *could do* as opposed to what he could *not* do.

Before his teen years, Kyle wanted to start playing sports, but people were hesitant to support his dreams because they thought it was physically impossible. Little did they realize the power of Kyle's self-determination.

At age eleven, he tried out for the football team. During that same time, he learned how to swim, play hockey, and wrestle competitively.

Even though he stands only three feet off the ground, he is a giant on the inside. And the reason is because of his unwillingness to settle for anything less than he can be. He demands more from himself than anyone else would expect, and this is also why he accomplished more than anyone else would expect. Kyle is a true example of what is possible when we eliminate excuses from our life and make a commitment to give our best at everything we do—*no excuses*.

As a teenager, Kyle became such an inspiration to everyone who had the opportunity to meet him that he was offered a book deal. His book quickly became a national bestseller. The title? You guessed it, *No Excuses*. He has also appeared on all sorts of TV and radio shows around the country. "But it didn't necessarily come easy," he says.

"I've had to make a lot of sacrifices and push myself to the limits, but if I hadn't done that, I definitely would not be where I am today. There was always a reason not to do something, and there were plenty of people who told me what I could not do, but I chose to eliminate all excuses—even the ones other people gave me. I knew that the only person who was going to hold me back was me—and I wasn't going to let that happen!"

By **confronting** the **impossible**, we discover our **true capabilities** and what is **really possible**.

Even without elbows, hands, and fingers, Kyle has learned to write with impeccable handwriting, holding a pen with the stubs on his arms. And believe it or not, he can also type forty words per minute! Not only is Kyle an incredible student with outstanding grades, but perhaps what is even more impressive is that he became one of the top wrestlers in the state of Georgia during his senior year of high school. Kyle also holds world weight-lifting records for his age group and gets thousands of dollars to travel around the country and speak as a valuable member of Washington Speaker's Bureau. Not a bad way to turn a challenge into multiple opportunities!

It's much **easier** to **give your best** when it's the **only option** you **give yourself**.

Excuses give us an easy way to back out when times get tough. *And the easier we make it for ourselves to quit, the harder we make it to succeed.* However, if we eliminate excuses from the start, we instantly increase our willingness to persevere and achieve what we want.

If Kyle can do all of this with a severe disorder that put him at an immense physical disadvantage, then it's worth asking yourself, "What's stopping me from creating the life I really want?" Remember, you can accomplish great things. The question is, WILL you eliminate your excuses and make it happen? Kyle did. Will you?

Successful people who consistently achieve what they want live by the "No-Exceptions Rule." When it comes time to deliver, they make a 100% commitment to doing something, and they allow no exceptions. It's a done deal. Non-negotiable. Case closed! Over and out.

For example, once we (Kent and Jack) made a commitment to write a book together, that was it—we knew we were going to do it. We were dedicated to doing whatever it took to persevere and live up to our commitment. The best part is, we never even had to think about it again. Once we made the commitment, we knew that we must follow through—no exceptions. We didn't give ourselves the option of backing out. As a result, we never had to fight ourselves about whether or not we should start the project or whether or not we should finish it.

When you commit 100% to something, there are no exceptions, no matter what the circumstances. There is no other possibility. You don't have to wrestle with that decision anymore because it's already been made.

If you make the 100% commitment to do your homework each day, no matter what, then it's settled. You simply just do it. It doesn't matter if your sports practice goes longer than expected, or your friends invite you to a party, or you lose an hour due to daylight savings. You simply find a way to get it done *no matter what*—even if you don't feel like it. Just like brushing your teeth before you go to bed. You always do it, no matter what. If you find yourself in bed and you have forgotten, you get out of bed and brush. It doesn't matter how tired you are or how late it is. You just do it.

It's much **easier to focus** when the **only option** you have is **achieving** the **result you want**.

One of our friends, Sid Simon, is truly an incredible example of a person who lives by the "No-Exceptions Rule." He's our inspiration. Sid is a successful speaker, trainer, bestselling author, poet, and a greatly admired teacher at the University of Massachusetts. Throughout his life, one of Sid's highest priorities has been health and fitness. Now, at age seventy-nine, he still bikes on a regular basis, takes supplements, eats healthy foods, and—oh, yes—allows himself a bowl of ice cream only one day a month—when there's a full moon.

On his seventy-fifth birthday, more than 100 of his family members, close friends, former students, and other admirers traveled across the country to celebrate with him. For dessert, there was birthday cake and ice cream, but there was a problem: It wasn't a full moon. Knowing this, a few of his friends dressed up like moon goddesses, and they entered the room holding a huge full moon made of cardboard and aluminum foil. A virtual full moon for Sid!

But even with all of their creativity and efforts to persuade him, Sid stood firm on his commitment and still declined the ice cream. He knew that if he broke his commitment this time, it would be much easier to break it the next time he was offered ice cream. It would be easier to rationalize, justify, and explain away his commitment. Sid knew that a 100% commitment is actually easier to keep, and he was unwilling to give in and throw away his years of success just for other people's approval. Talk about self-discipline!

19.8 Ditch Mediocrity

Successful people **create habits** out of the things that **unsuccessful** people are **unwilling** to do.

—Unknown

There are many different things you can do to become successful, but we believe it all begins with a simple decision. You must decide that you will not settle for anything less than the best you can do . . . and, therefore, you ditch mediocrity. We mean ditch mediocrity *entirely*—a half-effort is not even an option. We've said it once, and we'll say it again: *Demand more from yourself than anyone else would expect.*

TIP: Raise your standards. It may sound really simple, but the standards you set for yourself have a lot to do with what you're willing to try and what you're willing to endure to get a specific result. Let us explain . . .

What's a "standard"? Good question. A "standard" is a measure of achievement you must attain to allow yourself to feel like you did your best. What you're willing to settle for is often going to be what you achieve. In other words, it's rare to achieve more than you set out to do or get results beyond your expectations or personal standards.

If we lower our standards, then we instantly limit our potential, lower the level of happiness we can experience, and cheat the rest of the world of the many gifts we've been given to share with

Doing the **best** at **this moment** puts you in the **best place** for the **next moment**.
—Oprah Winfrey
Emmy Award-winning host of *The Oprah Winfrey Show,* the highest-rated talk show in television history

everyone else. This is why we need to demand the best from ourselves.

The standards you set for yourself have a lot to do with what you're willing to try and what you're willing to endure to get a specific result. Don't settle for less; *settle for more*. Easier said than done, of course, but the quality of your life lies in *your* hands. If you don't take responsibility for yourself, no one else will.

What's the bottom line? Exceeding expectations helps us stand above the crowd, get more from ourselves, and get more from our life. Successful people simply do more. As a result, they not only rise to the top (and often make more money), but they also experience personal transformation, create more self-confidence, develop more self-esteem, get more done, and accomplish more than they ever thought possible. Not bad side effects, huh?

MY "TO-DO" LIST

☑ **Realize that the way I will get the best, experience the best, and become the best I can be is by consistently giving my best effort.**

☑ **Redefine what "cool" means and understand that the people we look up to and admire often share the trait of giving their best.**

☑ **Understand that exceeding expectations and going the extra mile instantly makes me a more valuable person.**

☑ **Realize that there is a big difference between a 99.9% effort and a 100% commitment to always giving my best—and anything less than my best will not do.**

☑ **Search for ways to give more because there is always some way I can overdeliver and make a difference.**

☑ **Apply the "No-Exceptions Rule" to my life so I will be dedicated to follow through with my commitments, promises, and personal goals.**

☑ **Ditch mediocrity, raise my standards, and demand more from myself than anyone else would expect.**

☑ **Give my best to be my best!**

Start NOW . . . . Just DO It!

Things **may come**
to those **who wait**,
but only the **things left**
by those **who hustle**.

—*Abraham Lincoln*
The sixteenth President of the United States

Three frogs are floating down the river on a log. One of them decides to jump into the river. How many are left on the log?

Most people answer "two," but that's not the right answer. There are actually still three frogs on the log. Why? Because *deciding* to jump and jumping are two completely different things. All over the world, a lot of people decide they're going to get good grades, graduate from college, get their dream job, and make a ton of money, but they do nothing to make it happen.

This means that even the best plans combined with a positive intent are not enough to get the life you want. You must take action and do something to move you closer to your goals. When the rubber hits the road, what matters most is what you do—not what you say you're

The road to failure is paved with good intentions.

going to do. There are so many people with high hopes, big dreams, and good intentions. Why, then, do so few get an extraordinary life? Because hoping and dreaming is not enough. To achieve our goals, live our dreams, and reach our full potential, it all comes down to taking a step forward and putting our plans into action. In other words, we need to leap off the log to get the results we really want.

20.1 Take That Leap Of Faith

If you want to **accomplish** anything in life,
you **can't** just **sit back** and **hope** it will happen.
You've **got** to **make** it **happen**.

—*Chuck Norris*
Actor

It's amazing how many people glue themselves to home plate by overanalyzing, overplanning, and overorganizing when what they really need to do is take action.

Kent: I recently spoke to a group of college students majoring in business. One student approached me for advice. He was about twenty-seven years old. He described how he'd been working on his business plan . . . for eight years! Obviously, he was concerned about perfecting his plan. But before he got lost in all the detail, I politely asked, "You have some great ideas, but where in your plan does it say, 'Take action'?"

He looked at me with a blank face. No answer. Then I asked him, "When would *now* be a good time to get started?" He smiled. He got the message. The problem was that he spent so long overanalyzing the situation that he had become paralyzed. He was so confused and worried about creating a failproof plan that he was afraid to get started.

The truth is, nothing happens until you take action. Do you remember the rocket example from Principle 18, "Use Feedback to Fast-Forward"? It's easy to spend years on the launch pad trying to get the trajectory just right, but sometimes we just need to "take off" and get going so we can adjust our course as we get feedback. We must be moving in order to move forward.

When you get started, you trigger all kinds of helpful things. You'll start getting valuable feedback, you'll learn new skills, you'll gain experience, and you'll show those around you that you're serious about achieving your goals. As a result, people will wake up and start paying attention to you. Things that were once confusing will start to become clear. Things that appeared difficult will become easier. You begin to attract others who will support and encourage you.

20.2 Talk Is Cheap

You **can't build a reputation** on what **you're going** to **do**.

—*Henry Ford*
Entrepreneur and founder of Ford Motor Company

fter working with and studying many people over the years, Jack and I both agree that one thing that seems to separate winners from losers more than anything else is that *winners take action*. They simply get up and do what has to be done. Once the plan is developed, they start. They get in motion. Even if they don't start perfectly, they learn from their mistakes, make corrections, and continue to take action until they finally produce the result they want. Check out this old proverb:

A good plan today is better than a perfect plan tomorrow.

If we expand this, we would add, "And there really is no such thing as a "perfect plan." The world is always changing, and as a result, our techniques will need to change as well. So just get started . . . you can adapt your approach as you move along.

We've covered a lot in this book: how to create a vision, set goals, anticipate

obstacles, believe in yourself, persevere, and visualize and affirm your success. Now it's time to put it all into action. Get a mentor, write down your goals, and read them each day. Then fill out and submit that college application, start that savings plan, ask that special person out on a date, or book that trip to Europe! Life won't get any better until action is taken.

If you **do** the things you **need to do**
when you **need to do** them, then someday
you **can do the things** you want to do
when you **want to do them**.

—*Zig Ziglar*
Motivational speaker and author

20.3 Rewards Are Given to the Action Figures

"Who wants $20?" We ask the audience this question as we hold up a twenty-dollar bill. Not surprisingly, most people raise their hands. Some wave their hands vigorously back and forth; some even shout "I want it!" But we just stand there calmly holding the bill until someone *takes action*. Eventually, someone jumps out of his or her seat, rushes to the front of the room, and takes the bill from us.

After this person sits down—now $20 richer for her efforts—we ask the audience, "What did this person do that no one else in the room did? Yeah, she got off her butt and took action. She did what was necessary to get the money. And that is exactly what you must do if you want to succeed in life. You must take action, and in most cases, the sooner the better."

Our next question is, "How many of you *thought about* getting up and taking the money but stopped yourselves?" Hands go up. Then we ask, "What did you tell yourselves that stopped you from getting up?" The usual answers are:

- ※ **"I didn't want to look like I wanted or needed it that badly."**
- ※ **"I wasn't sure if you would really give it to me."**
- ※ **"I was too far in the back of the room."**
- ※ **"I didn't want to look greedy."**
- ※ **"I was afraid that I might be doing something wrong and that other people would judge me or laugh at me."**
- ※ **"I was waiting for more instructions."**

We then explain that these are usually the same things that stop them in all other parts of their lives. Same answers! A universal truth says, "How you do anything is how you do everything." If you're cautious about getting out of your seat to take the money, then you are probably holding yourself back in other areas of your life as well. In order to get the life you really want, you have to identify those patterns and break through them. It's time to stop holding yourself back. Be an "action figure" and just go for it!

20.4 Get Antsy to Get Going!

xcessive planning and too much talking make most successful people antsy. They are eager to get going, get involved in the action, and get their hands dirty.

One good example is Otis Kriegel. As a freshman in college, Otis came home for the summer with his new girlfriend, and they both began looking for jobs. While Otis just picked up the phone and started calling around to see who might need someone, his girlfriend spent the first week writing and rewriting her résumé. Otis just took action. He figured if someone asked for a résumé, he'd deal with it then. As it turned out, Otis got a job before his girlfriend had finished her résumé! Planning has its place, but we must keep it in perspective.

Planning is important, but if you **don't take action**, you can plan on having **nothing** more than **you started with**.

20.5 Ready, Fire, Aim!

Yes, you read the above heading correctly. You were expecting, "Ready . . . aim . . . fire," right? Well, the problem is that too many people spend their whole life aiming at the target and never firing. Yes, that's a big problem! Remember this old saying: "You miss 100% of the shots you don't take." It doesn't matter how long you aim or how accurate your sights are if you never take the shot.

The quickest way to hit the target is to fire, see where the bullet lands, adjust your aim, and fire again. Keep firing and keep readjusting until you hit your target. Soon you'll be hitting the bull's-eye. This rule also applies *off* the target range.

Kent: Once my brother Kyle and I wrote *"Cool Stuff" They Should Teach in School,* we knew we would be put in situations where we had to speak in front of big audiences—and, frankly, we were terrified! But we faced reality and immediately signed up for Mark Victor Hansen's MEGA Speaking seminar. We made a commitment to learn how to speak in public. Although we were the youngest people at the event, we set out to make new friends. One of them was Matt, who also wanted to learn how to become a public speaker.

At the end of the weekend event, the three of us were enthusiastic to take "the next step." On Monday, Kyle and I called Toastmasters (a nonprofit, open-to-the-public organization where members meet once a week, deliver speeches, and offer valuable feedback to each other) and signed up for a club in our area. On Tuesday, we attended our first meeting and gave our first speech. It was awkward and uncomfortable, but we used the momentum we created over the weekend and *just got started.* Two weeks later, Kyle and I were invited to give our first public speech at a local high school. In spite of our fear and uncertainty, we agreed to give the speech anyway—and it was the best thing we could have done.

Matt, on the other hand, decided to go home, settle in, research the professional speaking industry on the Internet, and ask other people more questions about public speaking. Nearly three months later, we discovered that Matt had given only one speech; then he decided to go back to the "drawing board" to research how he could get better.

Instead, of course, Kyle and I could have sat down and read book after book about how to become a great speaker, but if we had taken that approach, we'd still be reading! We knew *experience is often the best teacher*. So instead of doing more research and planning a speaking career, we simply started building the skills and experience we needed. Today, Matt knows all the best books and resources about speaking, but he lacks the hands-on experience to be booked as a professional speaker. Kyle and I took the opposite approach. For a year and a half, we spoke anywhere at anytime for free, simply so we could learn and improve. Now we get thousands of dollars per speech, and (yes!) we get to travel all over the country—but we first had to create the courage and faith to jump off the log. And this is something we're *all* capable of doing.

20.6 Fail Forward

Never be afraid to do **something new**.
Remember, an **amateur built the Ark**; **professionals**
built the ***Titanic***.

—*Author Anonymous*

Even top performers don't hit their target every time, but they are willing to take action in spite of the possibility of failing.

Successful people, on the other hand, realize that failure is just an important part of the process—it's a way to learn and an opportunity to try something different. Not only should we stop our fear of failure, but we should also be willing to fail—even *eager* to fail. We call this useful type of failure "failing forward." Every experience we have builds up more valuable information we can use "next time."

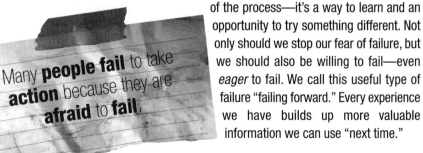

Many **people fail** to take **action** because they are **afraid** to **fail**.

One of our favorite stories is about a famous scientist credited with several very important medical breakthroughs. While being interviewed by a newspaper reporter, he was asked why he thought he was able to achieve so much more than the average person. In other words, what set him apart from others?

Without missing a beat, the man responded by saying that he credits his mom for a lesson she taught him when he was only two years old. He was trying to take a bottle of milk from the fridge when he lost his grip and spilled the milk all over the floor. Instead of scolding him, his mother said, "What a wonderful mess you've made! I've rarely seen such a huge puddle of milk. Well, the damage is already done. Would you like to play in the milk before we clean it up?" She didn't need to ask him twice!

After a few minutes, his mother continued, "You know, whenever you make a mess like this, eventually you have to clean it up. So, how would you like to do that? We could use a towel, sponge, or mop. Which do you prefer?"

After cleaning up the milk, she said, "What we have here is a failed experiment in how to carry a big bottle of milk with two tiny hands. Let's go out in the backyard, fill the bottle with water, and see if you can discover a new way to carry it without dropping it." And they did.

What a fantastic lesson learned! The scientist then explained that from that moment he knew he didn't have to be afraid to make mistakes. He learned that *mistakes are just opportunities for learning something new*—which, after all, is what scientific experiments are all about. That one spilled bottle of milk led to a lifetime of learning—experiences that were the building blocks of a lifetime of world-renowned success.

The only **man** who makes **no mistakes** is the **man** who **never does anything**.

—Theodore Roosevelt
The Twenty-Sixth President of the United States

It's true: We're all going to fail at times, so why not get the most out of the situation and then do what's necessary to learn a better way to do it next time? Failing in itself doesn't have to be a painful disaster. It can be an interesting and amusing experience if you choose it to be—and taking action is the one ingredient that allows us to learn, create, and experience the best life has to offer.

20.7 satisf—action

Have you ever noticed that the last six letters in the word *satisfaction* are a-c-t-i-o-n? In Latin, the word *satis* means "enough." What the ancient Romans clearly understood was that enough action ultimately produces "satisfaction." And if you want to take it a step further, it's also interesting to know that the root word *facere* means "to make"—hence the word *factory* (a place where things are made). So . . . you could also say that satisfaction comes from making change—which can only be done by taking action. Cool, huh?

The **secret** of getting **ahead** is getting **started**.

Even though people seem so different on the surface, underneath it all, everybody wants the same things: happiness, love, respect, and the satisfaction of knowing that they created a life of value and meaning. It's simple psychology—these are needs we all have. The people we've met who are both successful and satisfied with their lives are those who are constantly learning, trying, doing, and improving. Science has proven this. In his book, *100 Secrets of Successful People*, David Niven mentions a study which revealed that "Those who do not feel like they are taking steps toward their goals are five times more likely to give up and three times less likely to feel satisfied with their lives."

We need to feel as though we're always making progress—and progress comes by taking action. To fully experience the amazing results that these Success Principles can create in your life, you must act on them and use the information.

One of the greatest benefits of taking action comes from using the knowledge you have to create your life the way *you* want it—that's extremely rewarding. And, remember, you don't need to do everything in one day, but you do need to do *something* every day that will move you closer to where you really want to be. In the end, all those steps *will* add up.

It's one thing to **know what to do**, but it's completely different to *use* what **you know**.

It's time to quit waiting for . . . perfect circumstances . . . a huge dose of inspiration . . . someone to change . . . permission . . . the right person to come along . . . next week . . . a new teacher . . . a new school . . . this nagging fear to disappear . . . a clear set of instructions . . . more self-confidence . . .

The time is NOW. If you apply these principles to your life and use them every day, you will notice a difference. Want proof? Just look at our lives. Neither of us—neither Jack nor Kent—was born with extraordinary abilities, but by studying these same Success Principles and consistently applying what we learned, we've been able to accomplish things beyond our wildest imagination. And we are certainly *not* "exceptions." We're *all* capable of doing such incredible things. The question is, will *you* believe in yourself, set goals, take action, and be persistent in getting the results you really want? Your potential is waiting, and this is your opportunity to use it. Will you take that leap of faith? The choice is yours.

The best way you can **predict your future** is to **create it**.

—*Stephen Covey*
Bestselling author and speaker

MY "TO-DO" LIST

☑ Understand that even the best plans combined with a positive intent are not enough to get the life I want. I must take action and do *something* to move me closer to my goals.

☑ Realize that *deciding* to do something and *taking action* are two separate things.

☑ Take action immediately because I will start getting valuable feedback, learn new skills, and gain experience that will help me as I continue to move toward my goals.

☑ Realize that when I take that first step and get started, I will begin to attract the people who support and encourage me.

☑ Plan and prepare, but be cautious about perfection because a perfect plan does not exist.

☑ Understand that planning is important, but if I don't take action, then I can plan on getting nothing more than I started with.

☑ Identify the patterns that have stopped me from taking action in the past and break through them.

☑ Always be ready to "fire first" . . . take action because, if needed, I can readjust my aim and fire again.

☑ Never let fear of failure stop me from taking action, because no matter what happens, I will learn something new and valuable.

☑ Understand that the people who are the most satisfied with their lives are those who are constantly learning, trying, doing, and improving.

☑ Start applying the Success Principles to my life *today*!

CONCLUSION

OUR challenge TO YOU

Nobody can **prevent** you from **choosing** to be **exceptional**.

—*Mark Sanborn*

Internationally recognized author, speaker, and entrepreneur

o here we are . . . the very last chapter. You made it! You didn't just skip to the end, did you? If you actually did read every principle, then we congratulate you! This shows that you're not just a "talker" who's interested in getting a better life. No, not you. You're a "doer"—you're the type of person who *does* take action and follows through. That's an extremely valuable skill!

The world is full of people who say they will do amazing things such as get straight A's, run a marathon, learn to play the guitar, climb Mt. Kilimanjaro, write a book, etc., but few people actually set the goals *and* make them happen. Therefore, few people get the results. And it's not because they lack the ability; it's often because they just didn't apply themselves 100%. But that's not the type of person you are, because you made a commitment to finish this book and you stuck with it! Hats off to you! If you've read this far, then you're not the type of person who would be willing to settle for anything less than you could be, correct? (No answer needed . . .) Then you're not going to have any trouble taking on our challenge to you.

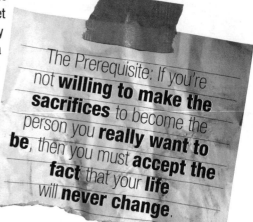

The Prerequisite: If you're not **willing to make the sacrifices** to become the person you **really want to be**, then you must **accept the fact** that your **life** will **never change**.

★start NOW

ike we have already talked about, success is a science—if you follow the principles and experiment with the habits of successful people, you will get positive results. There are universal laws that apply to everyone—no matter who you are, where you came from, where you live, or what you want to accomplish. When it comes to living the life of your dreams, the principles are all the same. And the best part is you now know many of these exact principles! The same information in this book has helped thousands of people create lives beyond their

Knowledge is **not power**; it's **how we use** the **knowledge** that determines our **power**.

wildest dreams, but they all had one thing in common: They acted on what they knew. Knowing is not enough.

If you're a teenager or a young adult, there has never been a better time to be your age. Use your youth to your advantage and get a head start. Too many people put off their dreams to wait for enough education, inspiration, experience, money, blah, blah, blah. The truth is that you have all the resources you need to start creating the life you want today! Instead of looking at youth as a disadvantage or a lack of experience, see it as an opportunity to get ahead, to learn from others, and most importantly, to take risks. This is the best time in history to be a young person because there are so many opportunities available . . . but you have to look for them and then be willing to take the plunge and *lean into it.* But that's how you learn anyway!

Cameron Johnson was nine years old when he started his first business making greeting cards on his home computer. Today, at age twenty-two, he has started twelve super-successful businesses that have earned him the freedom to fully retire (which he refuses to do). He's also the author of two books, including *You Call the Shots!* In an interview, Cameron told us, "I took big risks when I was fifteen and started my next company. I knew it was okay, though, because I didn't have to pay rent, put food on the table, or support a family. I was a teenager with very little to lose. I didn't have a lot of experience, but I was willing to learn as much as I could. Not everything worked out, but when it did, it really paid off. At fifteen years old, my company had sales in excess of $15,000 per day."

The interesting thing is that—and Cameron will be the first person to tell you—he's not any better, smarter, or more talented. "I'm no different than anyone else," he says. "I just wasn't willing to settle for any less than I could be."

Don't wait for things to be perfect before you decide to get started with projects and goals that are important to you. The time will never be "just right." When he started his company at age nine, did Cameron have a degree and tons of business experience? No way! But he took action anyway. If you're feeling something calling you to action, then lean into it and give it a try. Start where you stand. The more often you take action, the easier it will become to get started again the next time.

Just don't keep putting things off, waiting for twelve doves to fly over your house in the shape of a cross! Do you really need a sign to tell you it's time for you to begin? Just start . . . *without* the twelve doves! If you want to be a professional chef, then sign up for classes. If you want to write a book, dust off your computer and start *today.* If you want to be a better public speaker, then schedule a free talk at your school, library, or a local youth group. Or sign up for Toastmasters. But don't just wait! Having a set date will put the pressure on you to do what's necessary to prepare and get started. You don't need to know everything to get started. Just get into the game. You will learn by doing.

Don't get us wrong. *We believe in the importance of education, training, and skill building. If you need more training, then go and get it, but don't wait until you are "perfectly ready."* You never will be. Most of life is on-the-job training. Some of the most important things can be learned and accomplished in the process of *doing* them. When you do something, you will get feedback about what works and what doesn't. But if you don't do anything in fear of doing it wrong, poorly, or badly, then you will never get the feedback you need to improve and ultimately succeed.

There are a million things you can do to get the ball rolling, but no one can force you to chase your dreams. It's up to you—no one else. And, hey, if you don't chase your dreams, who will?

Expect the Unexpected

The information you've read in this book is enough to start creating an extraordinary life. Will it be easy? No, not necessarily, but no one said success comes easy. It's extremely important to see the best and expect the best in life, but we must also be prepared for the inevitable and unexpected challenges that lie ahead. If we're not ready, we could be taken by surprise, thrown off our high horse, and be afraid to get back on. If that happens, we won't be going anywhere near our dreams!

One of the most important keys to achieving your goals is the ability to believe in yourself—even when no one else does! The reality is that not everyone will support you on your quest to achieve your goals and make your life an exciting adventure. Some people will be pessimistic and negative, while others will just try to protect you so you don't get disappointed. But whatever the reason, don't let anybody make you feel like you don't deserve success. There will always be people who will challenge your commitment, but if you study the most successful individuals, you'll find they stuck with their dreams in spite of the naysayers.

This is where feedback is extremely valuable. You'll learn what's working and what isn't, if you should keep going or change your approach, or maybe you'll get a sign (no, not necessarily doves) to try something new entirely. Keep in mind, however, that not every attempt you make to achieve your goals will work. *So what!* We (Kent and Jack) live by this philosophy:

Expect the **best**, **but** be **prepared**
for the **worst**.

There will be friction and bumpy times ahead, but we all go through that—even the highest achievers. The road to success is not always a smooth one, but that's okay.

If you get bumped off the road, just get back on. If you fall nine times, then get up ten times. The key is not to stop when we get shaken up. When a plane takes off, the pilots don't hope that the air gets thinner and friction decreases. Instead, they've prepared for the resistance and the turbulence. Science shows that the faster the plane goes, the more friction it generates. But instead of complaining about it and going slower, the engineers accept it and build engines that work harder. What about you? Will you step it up and break through the barriers? We sure hope so!

★Mastery Takes Time

 nly you can decide to apply these principles and persevere—and the more often you do it, the easier it will become. But understand that mastery takes time. True success does not happen overnight. It always amazes us when people say, "I've been trying all of this stuff for a week, but I haven't achieved all my goals yet!" Well, would you ever go to the gym to work out for one week and expect to be fit, strong, and healthy for the rest of your life? Of course not! Why make the same mistake of expecting immediate results when using these principles?

Don't use these twenty principles a couple of times and expect your whole life to fall into place. It takes time to learn to master something and become good at it. Some people never achieve anything because they're always looking for the "quick-fix" solution (often simply the easiest option at that moment). As a result, they just continue to bounce through life until they receive a wake-up call later on, after they realize they never stuck with anything long enough to fully master it and succeed. Not such a good feeling!

HEY! IT'S BEEN TEN MINUTES WITH NO SUCCESS!

IT DOESN'T WORK LIKE THAT...

THE SUCCESS PRINCIPLES FOR TEENS

Kent: Recently, I was snowboarding at Big Bear Mountain (CA) when I heard two guys about sixteen years old talking about a young professional snowboarder. "I can't believe he's only sixteen years old!" His friend nodded in agreement and then added, "Yeah, he's our age. Why aren't we as good as he is? We suck." I couldn't believe my ears!

What most people don't realize is that many of these super-successful professionals (no matter whether their success is in sports, academics, business, music, etc.) started at a very, very young age. Nobody becomes a professional at anything overnight.

OUR CHALLENGE TO YOU

But those who do follow though and succeed are those who always know why they're doing it. They keep their eyes on the prize and remain motivated. Think of the process of learning to drive a car. It's really frustrating at first because there is so much to think about and learn. But the motivation to master the skill of driving a car is really high because you want that freedom to drive where you want to go when you want to go there.

Well, just like driving a car, there is often an awkward stage to anything new we attempt to do in life. This is why it's important to have goals that inspire us enough to work through those challenging stages. When we're excited about the outcome, we'll be much more willing to work long enough to develop and master the skills and abilities we need to accomplish even more.

What matters most is that we're committed to constantly growing and improving ourselves. And the process starts when we take action initially. It all begins with the courage to take that single step. Here's a quote that has really helped us take action in spite of our fears and doubts.

> ## You **don't have** to be **great to get started**, but **you have to get started** to **be great**.
>
> —*Les Brown*
> Speaker and author

⭐our challenge

Our goal was to provide you with the tools and information you need to live the best life you can. There is a lot of information in this book. If you're not careful, this could be a bit overwhelming. So here's what you should do:

> **The future** is not somewhere we arrive at; it's something we're **constantly creating**.

1. **Go back through each section of the book and work through each principle one at a time.** Reread, highlight, and take notes of what's most important to you.

2. **Begin taking action and applying each principle to your daily life.** It helps to focus on one principle each day. Write down your goals, spend time visualizing, use your affirmations, find a mentor, ask for help and assistance, use feedback to your advantage, make an effort to overdeliver and consistently give your best, and so on. You have what it takes to do that. The question is not can you, but *will* you?

3. Schedule some time every week to review your progress. You may want to to start a success journal and record your experiences each day. (Don't laugh, but you'll have fun looking at your journal in five, ten, twenty years, when you really are living your dreams. You will be able to look back and share your experiences and wisdom with your friends and family.)

Some people are thinking, "Ha! Who's really going to do that?" These steps may sound corny, but we wouldn't include them in this book if they didn't work. You've committed to reading this book; don't you want to get the most out of the time and energy you've already invested? Would you go to a doctor and get a prescription filled and then *not* take the medication? That wouldn't make any sense! This is your chance to go the extra mile and start creating an extraordinary life. Will you step up to the challenge?

Today is the **first day** of the rest of your **life**.

—*Unknown*

Make It Happen!

More **powerful** than the **will to win**
is the **courage to begin**.

—*Unknown*

Remember this line: *The principles always work if you work the principles.* The most important part of reading this book is using what you know. No, the world is not concerned about what you know; it's only concerned about what you do. It's what we do with what we know that will determine our success. Knowing is nothing until the knowledge is put into action. All the so-called "secrets of success" **GREAT** will not work unless you work them into your life. **JOB...**

NOW LET'S
GET TO
WORK!

So this is it . . . we've done the best we could to give you the principles and the tools you need to make all of your dreams come true. They have worked for us and countless other teenagers, and they can work for you as well. But this is where the information, motivation, and inspiration stops, and the hard work and perspiration (provided by you) begins. You and you alone are responsible for creating the life you want. You have the talent and resources you need to start right now. *We* know you can do it. You know you can do it . . . so get out there and do it!

As Henry James once said . . .

It's time to **start living** the
life you've imagined!

⭐ Speaking Information

Don't forget to say hello!

Did you enjoy the book? We certainly hope so. We would love to hear your thoughts and your success stories. Don't be a stranger! Send us an email at kent@coolstuffmedia.com.

Your Guest Speaker Solution!

Would you like to meet Kent in person? Well, now is your opportunity to book him as guest speakers for your next event.

Why Kent Healy?

At age 24, Kent is a successful author, columnist, entrepreneur, and highly requested speaker who inspires and empowers audiences of all ages. Often referred to as "America's coolest young success coach," Kent uses humor and compelling personal experiences to share timeless insight from a fresh, young perspective. His expertise on the psychology of success combined with his contagious enthusiasm has earned him invitations on more than 100 television and radio shows across the nation.

Kent is available as a keynote speaker for:

* ❋ Youth Conventions
* ❋ School Assemblies
* ❋ Faculty/Student Workshops
* ❋ Parenting Conventions
* ❋ Corporate Events

Book Kent today! Contact us at speaking@coolstuffmedia.com or 1.866.928.COOL (2665)

Visit Kent online today at www.coolstuffmedia.com for more free life-tips, updates, and information you can't afford to miss!